The emergence of two recently discovered diaries affords a new way of looking at Catholic chaplain's roles, responsibilities, fears, and dilemmas. Accompanying the fighting soldiers in Picardy, Flanders, and Artois, these diarist chaplains daily recorded their first-hand experiences telling us much about life at the Front, the nature of war, their Church in action, and the post-Armistice civil state of affairs. Their narratives are supported by a plethora of original correspondence between diverse chaplains and their superior at GHQ. Paintings by a Jesuit chaplain also serving at the Front add context and consolidate their experiences.

As if by design, the two diarists occupied opposite ends of the social spectrum. Their personalities were diverse and colourful and together ought to dovetail with their counterparts in the British Army from soldier to officer. Would accommodation between clergy and the military be possible given the prevailing contemporary climate of sectarianism and secularism, not to mention class, snobbery, and racism?

In examining Catholic chaplaincy evidence at large, contexts will be drawn from history, geography, politics, roles, and general conditions. Our diarists will then be assessed on a daily basis as they encounter the Somme in 1916, then Ypres and Arras in 1917, when their physical and mental endurance will be put to the test. Nothing, however, will compare with 1918 and particularly the German Spring Offensive. Each day of the assault will show the fear, desperation, and panic of both the military and civilian populations: even one of our chaplains was arrested twice as a German spy! How would our priests in khaki cope with the prevailing madness?

These genuine accounts written as they happened are punctuated by the deaths of fellow chaplains, sometimes just a short distance away. Unreal, bizarre situations are created in the same time frame and location by simple comparison. The incongruity of war becomes exposed from the unlikely source of clergymen who experienced many of its absurdities including: false allegations of espionage and drunkenness, attendance at a soldier's execution, a cover up of an officer's suicide and more. With the benefits of hindsight and knowledge which they did not have, the lighter and bizarre incidents will also emerge.

Uniquely in the Christian world the Catholic Church with all its rites, was and remains, universal. This meant that soldiers from all countries including Germany were catered for, as were French and Belgian civilians, in fact anybody who sought chaplain's services. These new sources of information also add light to the post-Armistice period in 1919 when the chaplain's deployment diversified. Thus we can experience life in France and Germany in a novel way. Interleaved with duty and routine, one chaplain will enjoy French peasant and religious culture, American exuberance, always empathising with soldiers; the other will content himself with the officer class, Mess duties and high culture. The contrasts are marked, the spiritual offerings the same.

After a successful career in the electronics industry Steve made the change into academia in 1995. A first class honours degree at The Institute of Irish Studies at the University of Liverpool was followed by a Masters. The Institute specialises in multi-disciplinary education with literature, cultural geography, politics, and history among the topics. Dissertations included ethnographic accounts of the River Barrow in Ireland, and Church-State relationships with radicalism in 1930s Ireland. Identity is at the heart of Steve's work, unsurprising as his four grandparents were born in Wales, Ireland, Scotland, and England. He enjoys travelling and honing his interests in cultural geography, luxuries which retirement has allowed, but prefers to call this relaxation simply as 'watching the world go by'. This broad grounding, combined with a long term fascination with the Great War and a specific curiosity with Catholic chaplains, encouraged a further study of both. The disciplines embraced were further shaped by chaplaincy conferences at Amport which fired the imagination and led to the delivery of three papers, with further presentations at Galway and Liverpool universities. Two themes emerged. The first was to refresh and challenge the predictable and laboured existing accounts of Catholic chaplains. These versions were often sentimentalised and invariably concentrated on the well-known, with little new evidence, if any submitted. Chaplains in general have been ignored. The second theme also addressed the need to rebalance historiography. Chaplains of Irish extraction, who followed their missionary calling abroad, became out of sight and out of mind, forgotten men of whom many became chaplains in the Great War. These perceived injustices influenced the doctoral thesis which developed intuitively as 'Catholic Chaplains on the Western Front 1914-1919 – Lancashire's Pivotal Role', being completed in December 2015. The book is an evolution of a long interest in social and military history, with a religious and Irish flavour, underpinned by a desire to add new evidence to the overall history of the Great War and especially chaplains.

Faith of Our Fathers

Catholic Chaplains with the British Army on the Western Front 1916-19

Stephen Bellis

Helion & Company

Helion & Company Limited
Unit 8 Amherst Business Centre
Budbrooke Road
Warwick
CV34 5WE
Tel. 01926 499 619
Fax 0121 711 4075
Email: info@helion.co.uk
Website: www.helion.co.uk
Twitter: @helionbooks
Visit our blog http://blog.helion.co.uk/

Published by Helion & Company 2018
Designed and typeset by Mach 3 Solutions Ltd (www.mach3solutions.co.uk)
Cover designed by Paul Hewitt, Battlefield Design (www.battlefield-design.co.uk)
Printed by Lightning Source Limited, Milton Keynes, Buckinghamshire

Text © Stephen Bellis 2018
Images © as individually credited. If no credit shown Author's Collection

Every reasonable effort has been made to trace copyright holders and to obtain their permission for the use of copyright material. The author and publisher apologize for any errors or omissions in this work, and would be grateful if notified of any corrections that should be incorporated in future reprints or editions of this book.

ISBN 978-1-912390-91-5

British Library Cataloguing-in-Publication Data.
A catalogue record for this book is available from the British Library.

All rights reserved. No part of this publication may be reproduced, stored in a retrieval system, or transmitted, in any form, or by any means, electronic, mechanical, photocopying, recording or otherwise, without the express written consent of Helion & Company Limited.

For details of other military history titles published by Helion & Company Limited contact the above address, or visit our website: http://www.helion.co.uk.

We always welcome receiving book proposals from prospective authors.

Contents

List of Illustrations		vii
List of Abbreviations		x
Acknowledgements		xiii
Introduction		xiv
1	Society, History, Geography, Politics, Attitudes: 'The Irish are Vermin and Scum of the Earth'	21
2	Mission, Education, Landscapes, and Training: 'I am begging you as a mother to look after my son'	33
3	Role, Organisation, Structure, and Deployment: 'Not a Society Entertainer, nor a Vendor of Buns and Cigarettes'	44
4	Conditions at the Front: 'Not the Kind of Life to Select as an Amusement But there will be plenty to do'	60
5	1916: À Partir De La Belle Époque À Folie	90
6	1917: 'Bah! What a game… The world is supposed to be civilised'	113
7	January–June 1918: 'Seesaw Margery Daw – Johnny Shall Have a New Master'	150
8	July–December 1918: 'End of Bloodshed and Strife, Everybody Going Mad With Delight'	175
9	1919: 'Sic Transit Gloria Khaki!' – 'Ave Atque Vale!'	202

Appendices

I	Statistical Dilemmas	237
II	Chaplains KIA and Buried on Western Front	240
III	How CFs with British Army Died on Western Front	241
IV	Catholic Chaplains Died in Other Theatres of War	243
V	Pre-War Missions of CF's KIA	244
VI	Chaplaincy Organisation	245
VII	Burial Directives	246
VIII	Example of Letters to Families of the Deceased	247
IX	A Portrait of Fr Robert Steuart SJ	248

X	A Portrait of Fr Fred Gillett	250
XI	The Hymn Faith of Our Fathers	252
Bibliography and Sources		254
Index		262

List of Illustrations

Stonyhurst College OTC 1916. (SCA, *The Stonyhurst War Record*)	37
Ushaw OTC Cadets November 1918. (Milburn, *A History of Ushaw College*)	37
Corpus Christi Procession 1916. (SCA, *The Stonyhurst War Record*)	38
A Chaplain's Horse. 'E' spends all 'es time between 'oppin up to 'eaven and poppin darn on e's knees, sir'. 'Very well: get another – and give this one – with my compliments – to the Chaplain'. (DAA, Ephemera. *London Opinion,* 12 February 1916)	68
Rawlinson and Staff Car. (DAA, Ephemera)	69
Sketch of Fr M J Galvin. (PRO, WO 374/26288)	79
Map of Frs. Gillett and Steuart on the Somme 1916.	91
The Locon Express. (JAD, Paintings of Fr Leslie Walker)	97
Fr John Gwynn SJ.	100
Headstone at Bethune Cemetery. Age 50. 1 Battalion Irish Guards. KIA 12 October 1915.	100
At Bouzincourt Cemetery.	101
Headstone. Fr Donal V O'Sullivan. Age 26. 1 Irish Rifles. KIA 5 July 1916.	101
Fr Denis Doyle SJ. MC.	102
Headstone at Dive Copse British Cemetery. Age 39. 2 Leinster Regiment. KIA 17 August 1916.	102
Four Stages in the Growth of a French Farm. (JAD, Paintings of Fr Leslie Walker)	104
Headstone. Fr David Guthrie OSB. Age Unknown. 8 East Lancashire Regiment KIA 21 November 1916.	107
At Varennes Cemetery.	108
St Riquier Abbey, 5 May 2012.	111
Map of Frs. Gillett and Steuart on Three Fronts 1917 – Somme, Arras, and Ypres.	114
Headstone. Fr Peter Grobel. Age 52. DAPC Boulogne. Died of Pneumonia 1 January 1917.	115
At Boulogne Eastern Cemetery.	116
Taking the Rations – Givenchy 1916. (JAD, Paintings of Fr Leslie Walker)	119
Guarbecque Church, 17 July 2013.	122
Guarbecque Church. February 1916. (JAD, Paintings of Fr Leslie Walker)	123
At Cabaret-Rouge Souchez Cemetery.	124
Headstone. Fr Herbert Collins. Age 35. 9 Battalion Black Watch. KIA 9 April 1917.	124

Fr Mathew Burdess.	126
Headstone at Villers-Faucon Cemetery. Age 40. 6 Gloucester Regiment. KIA 18 April 1917.	126
Headstone. Fr Jim Leeson. Age 40. 13 Royal Fusiliers. KIA 23 April 1917.	127
Headstone. Fr Simon Knapp ODC. DSO. MC. Age 59. 2 Irish Guards. KIA 1 August 1917.	136
At Dozinghem Cemetery.	136
At Tyne Cot Cemetery Panel 60. Age 44. 8 Royal Dublin Fusiliers. KIA 17 August 1917. (Shared panel with Fr Stephen Clarke bottom left. Aged 29. 9 Lancashire Fusiliers. KIA 4 October 1917.)	137
Fr Willie Doyle. MC.	137
Headstone. Fr Michael Gordon. Age 34. XV Corps ADS. KIA 27 August 1917.	138
At Coxyde Military Cemetery.	139
No 16 Flying Squadron – No 4195 (BE 2c). Leaving the Aerodrome Merville – La Gorgue – April 1916. (JAD, Paintings of Fr Leslie Walker)	140
St Vaast Post – Neuve Chapelle. May 1916. (JAD, Paintings of Fr Leslie Walker)	142
Headstone. Fr Patrick Looby at Poelcapelle Cemetery. Age 28. 5 Northumberland Fusiliers. KIA 26 October 1917.	143
War Memorial Cahir, Co Tipperary. (Also fellow chaplain Fr. Shine.)	143
Headstone. Fr Robert Monteith. Age 40. 70 RFA. KIA 27 November 1917.	146
At Ribecourt Cemetery.	147
Rats on the Somme 1916. (Ramparts Museum at the Ramparts Public House, Lille Gate, Ypres)	148
Map Frs. Gillett and Steuart January – June 1918, (including German Spring Offensive).	153
At Beuvry Cemetery.	163
Headstone. Fr John J McDonnell. Age 41. 55 West Lancashire MGC. KIA 9 April 1918.	163
At Boulogne Eastern Cemetery.	165
Headstone. Fr James Shine. Age 37. 21 Middlesex. KIA 21 April 1918.	165
Contay Church, 24 July 2012.	166
Bavelincourt Church, 10 April 2013.	167
At Bagneux British Cemetery. (Situated on the site of former CCS.)	169
Headstone. Fr Carl B Whitefoord. Age 33. 6 London Regiment. KIA 30 May 1918.	169
Labour Corps at La Gorgue February 1916. (JAD, Paintings of Fr Leslie Walker)	170
Fr Thomas Baines.	171
Headstone at Aine Communal Cemetery. Age 31. 152 Brigade RFA. KIA 31 May 1918.	171
Map of Frs. Gillett and Steuart Late June to the Armistice November 1918.	176
Fr John Fitzgibbon SJ. MC.	183
Headstone at Trefcon Cemetery. Age 36. 6 Div RAMC. KIA 18 September 1918.	184
'The Transit of Our Late GOC' – January 1916. (JAD, Paintings of Fr Leslie Walker)	188

The Advantage of a School for Officers – 29 December 1915. (JAD, Paintings of Fr Leslie Walker)	188
Fr Walter Montagu SJ.	194
Awoingt British Military Cemetery Frs. Watters and Montagu.	194
Headstone at Awoingt. Age 32. 22 Brigade RFA. KIA 30 October 1918.	194
Fr Gillett at Marian Shrine Lourdes 1926. (Lancaster Diocese Lourdes Records in Talbot Library Preston)	208
Bouzincourt Memorial, 8 July 2013.	209
Neuve Chapelle Jan 1916. (JAD, Paintings of Fr Leslie Walker)	210
Neuve Chapelle, 20 July 2013.	211
Richebourg St Vaast, 10 January 1916. (JAD, Paintings of Fr Leslie Walker)	212
Richebourg St Vaast, 19 July 2013.	212
Vielle Chapelle, December 1915. (JAD, Paintings of Fr Leslie Walker)	213
Mailly-Maillet Church – 19 July 2013. (Notice bullets holes remaining from the First World War.)	217
Engelbelmer Church, 2 May 2013.	217
Portable Altar – Interior. (UCA)	218
Portable Altar – Exterior. (UCA)	218
Fr Timothy Carey SJ.	221
At Adruicq Churchyard in a civilian grave. Age 41. Audruicq Catholic Club. Died 27 February 1919 Influenza.	222
Robert H. I. Steuart SJ. (JAL Obituary)	249
Fr Harry Gillett – Identical Twin of Fr Fred Gillett. (Obituary in *Lancaster Diocese Directory* 1959)	250

List of Abbreviations

Research Facilities

BAA	Birmingham Archdiocesan Archives
Dub AA	Dublin Archdiocesan Archives
DAA	Downside Abbey Archive (Stratton-on-the-Fosse, Bath) [Rawlinson Papers]
JAD	Jesuit Archives Dublin
JAL	Jesuit Archives London
LAA	Liverpool Archdiocesan Archives
LDL	Lancashire Diocesan Library (Talbot, Preston – now closed)
NAM	National Army Museum (London)
NDA	Nottingham Diocesan Archives
PRO	Public Record Office (London)
RACD	Royal Army Chaplain Department (Amport)
RCBFA	Roman Catholic Bishop to the Forces Archives (Farnborough)
SDA	Salford Diocesan Archives (Manchester)
SCA	Stonyhurst College Archives (Hurst Green, Clitheroe)
UCA	Ushaw College Archives (Durham)

Other Abbreviations

ADC	Aide de Camp
ADS	Advanced Dressing Station
AG	Adjutant General
APM	Assistant Provost Martial
APC	Assistant Principal Chaplain
ASC	Army Service Corps
BRM	Birmingham Archdiocese
CAP	Order of Capuchins
CF	Chaplain to the Forces
CCS	Casualty Clearing Station
C of E	Church of England

CO	Commanding Officer
CSM	Company Sargeant Major
CSSR	Order of Redemptorists
CWGC	Commonwealth War Graves Commission
DAC	Divisional Artillery Column
DAPC	Deputy Assistant Principal Chaplain
DORA	Defence of the Realm Act
DLI	Durham Light Infantry
DRLS	Despatch Rider Letter Service
DSO	Distinguished Service Order
EFICAS	European Federation of Associations and Centres of Irish Studies
GOC	General Officer Commanding
GHQ	General Headquarters
HEX	Hexham Diocese
HLI	Highland Light Infantry
HMHS	His Majesty's Hospital Ship
KOSB	Kings Own Scottish Borderers
KOYLI	Kings Own Yorkshire Light Infantry
KLR	Kings Liverpool Regiment
KRRC	Kings Royal Rifle Corps
LIV	Liverpool Archdiocese
MC	Military Cross
MID	Mentioned In Despatches
MO	Medical Officer
NDA	Nottingham Diocese
ODC	Order of Carmelites
OFM	Order of Franciscans
OMI	Oblates of Mary Immaculate
OP	Order of Preachers [Dominican Order]
OSB	Order of St Benedict
OTC	Officer Training Corps
PC	Principal Chaplain
RAMC	Royal Army Medical Corps
RAP	Regimental Aid Post
RC	Roman Catholic
RF	Royal Fusiliers
RE	Royal Engineers
RFA	Royal Field Artillery [sometimes RA]
RGA	Royal Garrison Artillery
ROD	Royal operating Division
RSF	Royal Scots Fusiliers
RS	Royal Scots [sometimes reversed]
SAL	Salford Diocese

SBY	Shrewsbury Diocese
SCF	Senior Chaplain to the Forces
SJ	Society of Jesus
STK	Southwark Archdiocese
TMB	Trench Mortar Bombs (bomber)
WO	War Office
WSM	Westminster Archdiocese
YLI	Yorkshire Light Infantry

Acknowledgements

There have been many people who provided invaluable material and psychological support throughout the research and production of my PhD thesis which is the basis of this book, and their gratitude remains as stated. The bibliography lists their institutions.

The impetus to take the thesis a stage further was assisted by the kind encouragement of Dr Maria Power my PhD supervisor at the Institute of Irish Studies, Liverpool University. In addition external PhD examiners, Dr Downham and Professor Richard Grayson provided invaluable constructive criticisms and encouragement.

The diaries came in to my possession as follows. Fr Gillett's through chance conversations with Martin Purdy following his MA on Catholic chaplains, and then recovery from oblivion by Fr David Lannon at the Salford Diocesan Archives. The diary of Fr Steuart and the paintings of Fr Walker were unearthed in the Jesuit Archives London by Anna Edwards and Fr MGoog SJ. Permission for their use was kindly arranged by Rebecca Somerset, Archivist on behalf of the Society of Jesus.

The inspiration for the study of Army chaplains was generated in no small way by the encouragement I received at the Armed Forces Chaplaincy Centre, Amport: David Blake, Michael Snape, Peter Howson, and Edward Madigan among others, whose early support and knowledge were invaluable, as too were the annual conferences with like-minded historians and enthusiasts.

A particular thanks to Peter Howson who introduced me to the publisher and for the staff at Helion with a special mention to Duncan Rogers for a generous welcome.

Introduction

The popular hymn *Faith of Our Fathers* [*We Will Be true To Thee Till Death*] epitomises Catholic unity and defiance in the face of religious suppression, contemporary and historical. As a rallying call for British Catholics it promoted freedom of the Faith from political and religious subjugation at a time when sectarianism was rife and secularism and nationalism challenged the worldwide nature of the Church.[1] Written by a convert, Frederick William Faber, *Faith of Our Fathers*, as Mary Kenny points out is: 'Truly the faith of our [Irish and Irish diaspora] mothers'[2] who underwrote British Catholicism thus many of her chaplains. Troops sang this hymn with gusto but would their chaplains aspire to these lofty aspirations? In a non-ecumenical world characterised by intolerance at home, how would religious men from a worldwide church, whose philosophies eschewed the core of the conflict, namely ardent nationalism and materialism, cope when they were catapulted out of their enclosed and sometimes cloistered world into an inherently indifferent or hostile institution? Moreover, this sector of war essentially between two great Protestant or secular power blocs, was paradoxically conducted in historically and culturally Catholic countries. Was it possible then to be 'True Till Thee to Death'?[3]

This study examines unique and newly discovered diary testimonies acting as buttresses around which a plethora of supporting evidence from all these young, and not so young men, will be constructed. Combining both secondary and primary sources it draws on the style of Emmanuel Le Roi Ladurie who scrutinises history through two different but eventually converging processes and sources, which he names 'parachutists' and 'truffle hunters'. His parachutists are: 'those who survey the broad historical landscape from a great Olympian height', and his truffle hunters:

---

1   It still held resonance in 1958: 'Screaming women and children attacked the Archbishop (Heenan), some wielding brooms, some throwing stones and tomatoes at him and his car. The large Catholic crowd began to sing "Faith of Our Fathers" [with more venom then religious fervour, according to the Archbishop's own account], and the Protestants feared an invasion of "their streets". Peter Doyle, *Mitres and Missions in Lancashire: The Roman Catholic Diocese of Liverpool 1850-2000* (Liverpool: Bluecoat Publishing, 2005) p358.
2   Mary Kenny, *Goodbye To Catholic Ireland* (London: Sinclair Stevenson, 1997), p. xlv.
3   For the words see Appendix XI.

'those grubbing around in dense thickets of local detail'.[4] By deploying both parachutists and truffle hunters their mutuality encourages a deeper understanding of Catholic chaplains, with a deliberate emphasis on discovering truffles. Diaries and correspondence comprise the greater part of researching truffles, whilst literature satisfies the context delivered by the parachutists. What was their mission, for whom, how did they do, and what did their endeavours tell us about their Church? These men were not on a theological exercise, they had already prepared themselves at seminary, but they were on a divine mission. Answering these questions establishes their spiritual direction, moreover, their experiences as men and priests at war helps define the overall Catholic project.

This is a new way of looking at the chaplaincy role. All the essential evidence is primary, authenticated, and does not suffer from post-war sentimentalism or triumphalism. Early accounts were influenced by post-war euphoria which when dissipated over time led to studies which have tended to concentrate on organisations or the famous, rendering 'ordinary' chaplains anonymous. To counter this trend this account examines the day-to-day pressures of all the men who left evidence and have been subsequently marginalised or forgotten. Ability or otherwise to fulfil their tasks, training, anti-Catholic bias, class prejudice both within and outside their own members, and many other considerations will see the light of day, many for the first time. Bravery, resolution, and commitment will be balanced by those whose human frailties found their tasks too much. The mundane also needs air. Conditions including transport, health, deployment, danger, leave, injury, death, boredom, loneliness, and humour abound. Copious but fragmentary quantities of evidence have been painstakingly gathered then pruned, enabling a meaningful cross-section to be analysed and compared with the diarists own daily and complete witness. To add value and context their testimonies are located within the actual historic and geographic framework of where they were written. The dates 1916-19 have been chosen because they coincide with the arrivals and departures of Fr Gillett and Steuart who both left remarkable accounts of their time in khaki. It also conveniently coincides with Principal Chaplain Bernard Rawlinson's tenure who fortunately retained much of the chaplaincy correspondence. All chaplains shared commonalities but also irregularities. Fr Gill SJ MC set the tone for a chaplain's life: 'Not the kind of life to select as an amusement – but there will be plenty to do'.

For those not familiar with the Catholic project the scale of the enterprise and commitment might be revealing. Not only were British soldiers accommodated but also those of the Empire and all countries in combat including German PoW's and occasionally German soldiers on the battlefield: as were civilians in the beleaguered battle zones and those individuals seeking an introduction into this faith. Examples and testimonials will demonstrate that a supplicants spiritual needs transcended their

---

4   Emmanuel Le Ladurie quoted in David Cannadine, *Making History Now and Then: Discoveries, Controversies and Explorations* (Basingstoke: Palgrave Macmillan, 2008), p. 30.

nationality or status. American soldiers, black or white, were treated the same as were French civilians, Chinese labourers, and converts: all followers or would-be followers alike. Primarily this book aims to offer the reader an insight into these men without embroidery.

Many people have witnessed the newsreels capturing forever the images of khaki soldiers clambering awkwardly over tangled barbed-wire as they venture into no-man's-land in the Great War. They are on a military mission. Soon many fell to their deaths or were torn and mutilated. Their sacrifice in Christian terms of a justifiable war, *jus ad bellum*, now becomes sacred and the Western Front by extension becomes holy ground.[5] A hundred years later multitudes of immaculately manicured cemeteries stand testimony to their sacrifices. Nonetheless, comprehension of the gravity and scale of their labours remains elusive, almost beyond adequate intellectual and emotional grasp. Fortunately Fr Fred Gillett and Fr Robert Steuart's diaries afford first class windows into the efforts of Catholic chaplains as a whole; whose own albeit haphazard evidence supports the diary testimonies. How close would they and their colleagues be *true to thee till death*?[6] What would real-life experiences reveal about these brothers *not in arms*?

In the current and sometimes hectic scramble for 'big event or big personality' history, men and women who volunteered for humanitarian or sacred missions are continually ignored or forgotten. Among those who provided spiritual, compassionate, and practical assistance in support of the military were: nurses, doctors, stretcher-bearers, veterinarians, labourers, and clergy. Civilians too, complete innocents in the enormity of the Great War, should also be remembered. This study concentrates on Catholic chaplains and their own particular mission to deliver spiritual comfort to co-religionists in this theatre of war, thereby bridging gaps in historiography which Michael Snape, a leading advocate of general chaplaincy history has recognised: 'The history of British Catholic involvement in the First World War is a curiously neglected

---

5   For an explanation of the Catholic Church's long-standing and contemporary attitude to a just war, or more accurately a justifiable war, read Frederick William Keating, Bishop of Northampton's Pastoral Letters throughout the war. Keating's Lenten Pastoral Letter 1916, on "The Priest and Military Service" developed this theme and is a concise, historical, legal, and unambiguous statement that Catholic priests are not immune to fighting in their own way, but that does not include bearing arms, and extends the simple idea of a just war to chaplains in the field. Other bishops expressed similar views. Whiteside of Liverpool wrote in the 'Report of the Liverpool Diocesan Mission Fund 1915 LAA': 'The teaching of Christianity on the lawfulness of war is clear and unmistakable […] not only is it lawful for a nation to enter into a defensive war and resist the unjust aggression of another nation, but it may also with a clear conscience undertake an offensive war, provided certain conditions are met'.

6   The hymn states categorically 'We Will Be True To Thee Till Death', acting as a yardstick for chaplaincy success. Appendix XI.

subject'.⁷ Other denominations may share many of the attributes, fears and triumphs, but their histories are accommodated elsewhere by the bulk of researchers in the fields of military and religious history.

It should be emphasised at the outset that the crucible of a Catholic chaplain's mission was to promote and maintain spiritual sustenance. The study of their devotion to sacred duty has been recorded elsewhere,⁸ but it is now time to observe these men in the whole, that is both their spiritual and real-world experiences. To engage in the killing fields of France and Belgium armed with a set of Rosary Beads, a captain's uniform, a portable altar and little else, raises questions beyond the courage of the military. The motivations of these men and how they went about their duties is hindered through the fragmentary and incomplete nature of the evidence.⁹ Despite these frustrations sufficient individual accounts survive in a variety of archives in Britain and Ireland, when referenced to the substantial personal diaries of Frs. Gillett and Steuart they offer a reliable account of their fears, activities, failures, and achievements. The privilege of interpretation belongs to the reader.

Who were these diarists? Fr Fred Gillett, a Liverpool Archdiocese priest, was born in 1882 and ordained with his identical twin brother Harry in St Peter's church, Lytham in 1908.¹⁰ Hailing from a small coastal village on the Fylde coast in Lancashire, they swapped a lower-middle class background to work as parish priests in inner-city Liverpool, a city ravaged by sectarian strife.¹¹ Fr Robert Steuart born 1874, belonged to the English Province of the Society of Jesus. His early priesthood was spent in Mount Street, Mayfair, London. Born in Reigate, Surrey, his roots were, however, firmly Scottish with a traceable lineage to the Stewart's of Ballechin, Perthshire, direct descendants of the natural son of King James I of Scotland. Each of these highly educated men largely represents the range of Catholic social and religious composition. How they tackled their chaplaincy functions is representative of their consistency of spiritual delivery despite possessing strikingly distinctive personalities. Spiritual matters were the overriding concern of all chaplains but these were also men whose daily secular concerns straddled their true mission. We will follow their journey throughout the Western Front during the war in France and Belgium, and also the post-armistice scenarios in France and Germany respectively.

---

7 Michael Snape, 'British Catholicism and the British Army in the First World War', *Recusant History*, 26, (2002), pp. 314-58.
8 S. Bellis, 'Catholic Chaplains on the Western Front, 1915-1919: Lancashire's Pivotal Role' (Unpublished Doctoral Thesis, University of Liverpool 2016).
9 See Appendix I: Statistical Dilemmas.
10 Harry enlisted as chaplain at the war's end.
11 Frank Neal, *Sectarian Violence: The Liverpool Experience 1819-1914: An Aspect of Anglo-Irish History* (Manchester: University of Manchester, 1988).

The Catholic Church defines itself as the Universal, Apostolic, Catholic, and Pilgrim Church.[12] By extension the Church's credibility came under scrutiny by the actions of its clergy at war. It expected much from its missionary priests, whether chaplains in khaki or missionaries in China or anywhere else in the world. As a rule Catholic chaplains will be shown to have celebrated their responsibilities with aplomb, the maxim of St Thomas Aquinas: '*Quantum potes aude*',[13] or: 'Dare to do all that you are able to' prevailed in the Great War. Further, any failure to deliver sacramental or pastoral care for all Catholics on the Western Front might impinge on the wider political ambition at home.[14] All well and good, but at war chaplains were practically detached from the world at home, many for the first time.[15] Rapid adaptation was necessary. If they encroached into the secular world of the British Army they had to ensure that their behaviour was not only impeccable as priest practitioners, but also within the bounds of officer social and behavioural expectations. This potential conflict between military and spiritual imperatives caused a dilemma for some chaplains, as did the mechanisms that were employed to deal with any real or imagined indiscretions, whether social, military, religious, or political in character. Contemporary scrutiny of chaplains within the larger Catholic project was sometimes subtle, undefined, and operated intuitively. At other times it was rudimentary and transparent. In order to protect her good name at home and at war, the uncompromising management and execution of discipline was delivered by Principal Chaplain Rawlinson and senior chaplains on the ground.

Chaplain's backgrounds and that of the attendant external influences will be probed to help understand how they negotiated a completely new world where violence knew no bounds and conditions stretched even the most patient to breaking point. How did they adapt, live, and flourish in these times? Did extreme environments impinge on their missions or their personalities? What did they think, and did these thoughts represent their organisation? In the final analysis, how does the personal deconstruction of these men contradict or correspond with Fr Bernard Rawlinson's overall post-war assessment of the chaplaincy effort:

---

12 Catholic Truth Society, *The Penny Catechism of the Catholic Church* (London: Catholic Truth Society, 1912).
13 Timothy Radcliffe, *Why Go To Church?* (London: Continuum, 2008), p. 199. Thomas Aquinas circa 1260, origins from the Sequence Lauda Sion Salvatorem, for the New Mass for the Feast of Corpus Christi, (Body of Christ). <http://www.hymnary.org/text/lauda_sion_salvatorem_lauda_ducem_et_pas> (Accessed 31 August 2012).
14 There were no instances of religious or spiritual lapses discovered. Disciplinary lapses will be examined.
15 This is true of most priests from both Diocesan and Religious orders, with the notable exception of the Society of Jesus who fostered and maintained active bidirectional communications. Their data was cared for in archives in Dublin and London. Any distortion towards the Jesuits resulting from their availability of resource material is balanced to a degree in the Rawlinson Papers and diaries, one of which was unearthed during research and another rarely if ever accessed.

The cessation of hostilities after four and a half years of ghastly war must be indeed to you a most happy relief. For during that time you have frequently had to minister to the living, and to the injured and dying, under shell fire or bombing or gas attacks, and in daily companionship with death; and you are worthy of very sincere congratulations for the noble and self-sacrificing way in which you have carried out your sacred trust. It has been shown by the discharge of your spiritual duties, and the remarkable response from the men, that in these days of stress, there has been 'No failure of the Church'. During the war, no Catholic man has been allowed to die without the sacraments when there was any possibility of him being reached ... Whilst the work of the Catholic chaplain has been most faithfully performed, it has been seriously hampered by the shortages of priests in the Field.[16]

The great majority will be shown to have acted in accordance with this assessment, but their journeys were not easy ones and caused much heartache and pain. Still, our diarists were among the lucky ones escaping with their lives and in Gillett's case without physical injury. In spite of this, Gillett was on the receiving end of an anonymous allegation which caused him great angst even though he was totally exonerated after investigation.[17] Rawlinson concluded: *'It is of course easier to make a report of this sort than disprove it'* lending perspective to accusations against his men in general.[18] Rawlinson was a diplomatic, fair, and intelligent manager, conversely, his was the iron fist in the velvet glove and you crossed him and his strategic objective to promote the good name of Catholicism through the deeds of his chaplains, at your peril.

The experiences of those less fortunate will be interleaved with our chaplain's diaries, revealing a continual and at times surreal juxtaposition between same day-to-day incidents. Contrasts are frequent even routine, for example: Gillett might be idle in one village whilst only six miles away Fr Steuart was struggling in a life-threatening situation, and vice versa, or Fr Steuart might be lunching at Poperinge whilst a fellow Jesuit chaplain was being annihilated a short distance away at Passchendaele. As these men were Divisional chaplains with fighting units, the real world of the soldier is revealed in parallel with their own exposing the disingenuous and commonly repeated assumption that this was a stationary war. True the trenches were virtually static but troops were constantly on the move and chaplains went with them as they rotated

16 DAA, Ephemera, Rawlinson to 'Reverend Father', 3 December 1918. This was a round-robin letter to chaplains as a post-war thank you. It was repeated in short in The Tablet 14 December 1918. It is a positive message and reflects Rawlinson's genuine thanks and appreciation of chaplaincy endeavour. However, his assertion that; '[...] no Catholic man has been allowed to die without the sacraments when there was any possibility of him being reached', cannot be authenticated. Rawlinson was still wooing priests, as the war's finale was still some time away in 1919.
17 DAA, 3231, Rawlinson to Keatinge, (20 April 1918). Author's italics.
18 Ibid.

between Picardy, Artois, and Flanders, representing the main battle arenas of the Somme, Arras, and Ypres respectively.

Despite the Armistice of 11 November the army did not melt away. There were many clearing up operations to be completed and potential military dangers to be negated until the conclusion of war on 28 June 1919. Gillett and Steuart provide a unique insight of this period. The former in France witnessed the civil efforts of reconstruction and the British Army's own role, whilst the latter in Germany prepared for military intervention in the eventuality of non-compliance with the Armistice terms. The cooling of guns allowed both men to explore their own interests and presents an interesting insight into their personalities, their social observations and priorities. These are balanced against a fundamental question, namely was it possible to balance the responsibilities and duties of a priest in khaki with an officer in the British Army, and if so to what degree? Both men represented the opposite ends of the chaplaincy experience and by default a further insight into British Catholicism, and occasionally the Irish equivalent.

Chapter 1 introduces social, historical, geographical and political perspectives thereby exploring contemporary mores. Chapter 2 examines priestly education at home and training as chaplains at war and describes the landscapes in which they were formed and in which they operated. Chaplains' roles within the organisation, sense of mission, and management are explained in chapter 3. In chapter 4 conditions at the Front are exposed, this is the last of the preparatory chapters. The remaining 5 chapters represent a period of time and place. These are prefaced with the context of the war in overall terms. 1916 and 1917 each occupy a chapter whilst the year 1918 has been divided in two to allow the German Spring Offensive to be covered in detail; it also allows the subsequent response from the Allies and victory to be chronicled. It is unusual if not unique to have this chaplaincy evidence alongside the military, written as it was at the time, thereby safeguarded from alteration. Finally chapter 9 deals with the period in 1919 between the cessation of violence and demobilisation, allowing Gillett and Steuart to be observed in an altogether different and calmer climate. It is here that their hugely different personalities are given oxygen, whilst maintaining their customary spiritual obligations. Germany's high culture found an avid participant in Fr Steuart, whilst the French *joie de vivre* and American exuberance were heartily embraced by Fr Gillett.

1

Society, History, Geography, Politics, Attitudes: 'The Irish are Vermin and Scum of the Earth'

The majority of Catholic chaplains with the British Army were English. Some were subjected to snobbish attitudes but unlike their Irish brothers never had to contend with racism.[1] The Irish background, therefore, needs to be briefly explored to establish the Irish contribution to the overall chaplaincy experience, and to tease out their specific struggles. The Irish were significant players in the Catholic chaplaincy story.

The Irish Episcopacy and External Challenges to its Religious Independence

The Act of Union between Great Britain and Ireland in 1801 determined that the British Army recruited its chaplains from the four countries of the United Kingdom in the Great War. Prior to union the Irish had a long tradition of supplying manpower to the British Crown. By the outbreak of hostilities in 1914 Catholicism in England and Wales had been a combined ecclesiastical entity since the Restoration of the Hierarchy in 1850, [if as we shall see attaining a somewhat probationary status]. Scotland gained its own ecclesiastical territory in 1878, both episcopacies re-establishing themselves after centuries of persecution and exclusion. Ireland had always retained a close relationship with Rome and resisted dis-establishment, despite repeated attempts at subjugation and the harshest of Penal Laws. The Irish Prelates pragmatically retained a degree of religious independence within British political reality, aided by geography which helped maintain distance and differences between those on either side of the Irish Sea. Distance with Rome was nonetheless overcome and Irish Catholicism was able to maintain a continued presence with, and within, the Papal See.

The Irish episcopacy, therefore, cherished its independence from other British prelates, valuing its close ties with Rome. This relationship had been maintained for centuries contrary to the rest of Britain whose ability to remain connected to Rome had been

---

1   Bellis, 'Catholic Chaplains', Chapters 5 and 6.

severed or strained since the Reformation, and only achieved 'missionary status' [and then with controls] in 1918. The Vatican both understood and were reconciled to the political reality that had existed since 1800, when Ireland was politically subsumed into Britain. On the other hand, on all religious matters Ireland remained independent from the rest of Britain. Why was there Papal reluctance to grant full status to England, despite the Restoration of the Hierarchy in 1850? This stemmed from the fact that the Vatican had not yet been convinced of the new episcopacies' ability to succeed. Rome did not deem England strong enough in talent [bishops], or Roman enough, to be left to their own devices, or as one historian has noted: 'They [priests and former Vicars Apostolic] had been cut off from Rome for so long that they had become too English in outlook and had developed an unhealthy spirit of independence from Rome'.[2]

In Ireland, therefore, juxtaposition existed between politics and religion. The Irish bishops were aware that in this war the possibility of blurring these politico-religious boundaries existed. Many in Ireland were working towards some form of national self-determination but on the whole had recognised the political status quo. The Irish episcopacy were largely in line with this position, but conversely wished to maintain absolute religious independence from Westminster. Consequently it was no surprise that tensions arose when at the start of war, the senior English primate Cardinal Bourne, Archbishop of Westminster, assumed *de facto* control of all British chaplains, including Irish and religious of all nationalities with the British Army.[3] To the Irish hierarchy Bourne was stepping on their toes and threatening their authority, thereby, confirming the Vatican's astute analysis and concern that the English bishops were 'too English in outlook'. Self-appointed as *Episcopus Castrensis* or Army Bishop he answered to no one, and even if it were argued that the situation demanded such action, his past track record would dispute this. Bourne's autocratic and Anglocentric assumptions and attitudes had not gone unnoticed in Ireland, the rest of Britain, or Rome.[4] His overbearing opinions caused friction even within his own English and Welsh episcopacy. In 1918, Bishop Frederick Keating of Northampton described Bourne as: 'an autocrat of the most Prussian type, who consults no one but himself and wishes to stifle all opinion opposed to his own'.[5] Bishop Amigo agreed adding: 'that whenever Bourne wanted something, he discovered it was the will of God!'[6] Distrust of Bourne continued, frequently annoying the Irish episcopacy: 'It is quite clear that the Irish hierarchy resented the interference of Cardinal Francis Bourne. The Irish received support from Pope Benedict XV'.[7] This was an issue of providing Irish

---

2   Doyle, *Mitres and Missions*, p. 95.
3   Appointed Cardinal in 1911.
4   Rome pushed for Keatinge to replace Bourne which occurred in 1918, but by then the damage had been done.
5   Doyle, *Mitres and Missions*, pp. 104-5.
6   Op.cit.
7   Aan de Weil, *The Catholic Church in Ireland 1914-1918: War and Politics* (Dublin: Irish Academic Press, 2003), p. 51.

chaplains for Irish regiments, a promise made to Irish prelates but sometimes ignored. The Pope intervened supporting the legitimate Irish cause. Rawlinson decided it was politic to reiterate this position assuring Fr M. O'Connell of the 16th Irish Division [Fr Willie Doyle's SCF]: '... As I have always told you, I would on no account let the 16th Division go short'.[8]

Francis Bourne's thoughts and intentions had previously emerged in 1903. In a meeting with the War Office after the South African campaigns, he promoted the idea of a Catholic Army Bishop defining the role as: 'Ecclesiastical Superior of all Catholic Commissioned Chaplains, and delegate of the Holy See in all that regards the spiritual care of the Catholic soldiers in the British Army'. Characteristically he assumed that he would be that person without any negotiation with his peers, the British Army and crucially Rome.[9] It may have been a legitimate effort to secure the Catholic position in future conflicts, but his complete lack of awareness of Irish sensitivities or respect for their opinions, not to mention his English peers, or Roman superiors, left him vulnerable to Irish criticism at a time when Home Rule was in active ferment and tensions ran high. He: '... never made any attempt to assimilate or accommodate an Irish sense of aspirational political difference, culture, or identity'.[10]

Did these differences between Bourne and the Irish prelates cause problems at war? The underlying tensions owed everything to differing national aspirations and personality clashes and not religion. Suitably confined within the establishment, there is no evidence that chaplains were aware of these difficulties in the field. Within Irish episcopacy circles it is not known precisely how Bourne's interference in Irish matters affected chaplaincy recruitment, but it certainly was not welcome or advantageous. Despite their reluctance to defer to Bourne and resentment at his autocratic comportment, Irish prelates on the whole remained supportive of their soldiers and provided a large number of Irish priests for that cause.[11] Bourne was a nuisance for Irish bishops, but in spite of everything a working reconciliation prevailed through homogeneity within its shared religion, education, mission, and sometimes ancestries.[12] The spiritual provision for Irish troops, and by extension Irish chaplains, transcended unwelcome English megalomaniacal interference.

---

8   DAA, 3235, Rawlinson to O'Connell from the Hexham Diocese, date illegible.
9   DAA, Bishops Correspondence, #28.1.31, 4 May 1903, p. 1.
10 Bellis, 'Catholic Chaplains', p. 65.
11 There were two exceptions. Bishop O'Dwyer of Limerick was staunchly anti-Redmond and opposed him throughout the war, particularly his recruitment campaigns for the British Army. O'Dwyer was in tune with the Pope's insistence on peace which made him a natural opponent to Redmond's support for the war as a way of achieving Home Rule. The second was Bishop Walsh of Dublin who had taken the decision to withdraw from the political limelight before the war started and was not at this time in good health. He maintained a publicly apolitical stance towards war.
12 Francis Bourne, for example was London born with an Irish mother and English father.

The Irish in England, Scotland, and Wales

The concept of a singularly British Catholicism is too simple despite *realpolitik*. Cultural, organisational, and historical differences existed between countries in the British Isles despite a large degree of religious homogeneity across all Catholic nations. Copious immigration from Ireland had a significant influence on Catholicism in the rest of Britain. The Catholic population in England, Wales, and Scotland had swollen by the mid-nineteenth century, for example, in 1841 Irish Catholics in Lancashire numbered 106,000 and by 1851 the figure reached 191,506, representing an increase of 81%.[13] Irish priests and nuns accompanied their flock in great numbers. Chaplains drawn directly from Ireland, or those Irish priests working in the rest of Britain, shared similar yet distinctively different worlds from other Catholic clergy.[14] Bishop Ward of Brentford Diocese summed up the effect of the Irish dimension:

> Irish immigration after the Great Famine, affected the future of Catholicism in this country more than even the Oxford Movement, for it was the influx of the Irish in 1846 and the following years which made our congregations what they are and led to the multiplication of missions ... for example, go to East Anglia, whither the Irish hardly penetrated, and see the desolate state of those counties so far as Catholic religion is concerned.[15]

Religious demography affected chaplains at the Front. Those with higher percentages of Catholic soldiers in their units would enjoy camaraderie and religious fortitude, imitating their pre-war communities and parishes at home. Fr Looby for example, was responsible for units from East Anglia with few Catholics in its ranks. Increasingly frustrated he implored a move to a unit with more, but his devotion had fatal results. Fr Looby was killed serving his new unit, 'The Fighting Fifth' – 5 Northumberland Fusiliers at Passchendaele.

Catholic Expansion in England, Scotland, and Wales

There were massive social problems for late Victorian society and none more so than for Catholics in England, Scotland, and Wales. In part fuelled by demographic shifts due to industrialisation, and in part by Irish and continental immigration, they were resolved in the main within their own communities. Church expansion and social and educational welfare developed to meet the needs of their society defining and strengthening

---

13 Doyle, *Mitres and Missions*, p. 36.
14 Bellis, 'Catholic Chaplains', Chapter 1.
15 Denis Gwynn, 'The Irish Immigration', in George Beck (eds.), *The English Catholic, 1850-1950* (Glasgow: Burns and Oates, 1950) pp. 270-1.

the unity of that group.¹⁶ Emerging from centuries of obligatory, institutional isolation, the fostering of religious independence remained a priority which could best be achieved by a large degree of self-sufficiency. This pragmatic approach was advanced by the hierarchy encouraging a policy of confirming secular fealty to the state and King, whilst jealously defending the Pope as the unrivalled head of the Faith. Consistent with Matthew's Gospel [22:21]: 'Jesus said "Render to Caesar the things that are Caesar›s; and to God the things that are God›s»,' and is based on the principle that all authority has been ultimately established by God. The policy was working before the war as the Protestant establishment slowly, if begrudgingly, accepted the need for greater emancipation. In line with episcopal ambition it was important that all her chaplains attached to the British Army complied with this project. Any misdemeanours might endanger the post-war development of social policy, especially education.¹⁷

Ireland's Priests

Catholic Ireland's traditional missionary role, or 'Spiritual Empire',¹⁸ meant that many of her priests intuitively volunteered as chaplains at war. The Society of Jesus contributed 32 men from the Irish Province alone and these were supported by clergy from other religious orders and dioceses throughout the island.¹⁹ In addition the Irish contribution has been somewhat overlooked in the case of those priests who were born in Ireland and served in overseas territories such as England, Scotland, India, Australia, South Africa and elsewhere. Those Irish born émigrés were frequently lost in the gap between two identities, being no longer Irish but not always accepted as English or Scottish.²⁰ The part that both the Irish and their missionary priests played needs to be recognised.²¹

Political Ireland

In the decades before the Great War, Ireland underwent a long chapter of political, cultural, and national realignment, comprising both violent and peaceful components.

---

16   Bellis, 'Catholic Chaplains', Chapter 1.
17   This ambition was not singularly that of political pragmatism; the Church was also very concerned morally in the growth of materialism and the power of the State over personal and human affairs, see Leo X111, *The Workers Charter: Rerum Novarum*, (London: Catholic Truth Society 1958, 1891 original).
18   Kenny, *Goodbye to Catholic Ireland*, Chapter 5, Ireland's Spiritual Empire.
19   Exact statistics should be treated with care, see Appendix I Statistical Dilemmas.
20   S. Bellis, 'Re-Assessing Irish and British Historiography Approaching 1916. What can a Study of Lancashire Catholic Chaplains in WW1 Add?' EFICAS Conference Galway June 2013.
21   See Appendix V.

By 1850 the devastating famine in Ireland was petering out.[22] The date 1850 also had great import ushering in Ultramontanism.[23] The Irish Church shared this shift towards Roman devotions and organisation with the rest of Britain. Ultramontanism stimulated all aspects of Irish church expansion and pushed Celtic strains of the Faith to the margins. Meanwhile, social and economic development in Ireland remained at the behest of Westminster whilst the rest of Britain fought its own direct political battles.[24] Changes in Ireland were slow and motivated in the main by British political expediency and self-interest. Many Irishmen attributed her woes to the coloniser and saw political self-determination as the antidote. Some were convinced of the need for armed struggle, others including the majority clerical opinion preferred Redmond's Home Rule option, thus remaining as active members in the Empire. These debates had been long fermenting but were reaching a climax in mid-1914, only international war prevented the civil alternative. Unrest continued throughout the Great War, not by those fighting Irishmen on the Western Front, but by those at home. Conversely men volunteering to fight for the British cause and who were dying in their droves were callously subjected to anguish and suspicion. The majority of the clergy and hence its chaplains, reflected Irish society at large and as such were not exempt from the unfolding drama. These men were by and large from farming, commercial, or business communities and by nature conservative. As noted, most were initially allied to Redmond's Irish Party, whose constitutional approach supported a pro-British Empire which precariously relied on Westminster support for Home Rule. By demonstrating their loyalty at war Irishmen would be rewarded politically by a grateful parliament. Belief in the success of this strategy declined as the British Government's failure to implement promises of Home Rule tested Irish patience to the limit. In its wake disillusionment and mistrust towards the government's intentions gained momentum. 1916 witnessed the simmering eruption of frustration and desperation through the Easter Rising, which although conducted with bravery and chivalry, was on its own an almost suicidal affair and doomed to inevitable military defeat whilst generating a new generation of martyrs, as the leaders had recognised. Many Irishmen, and particularly those engaged in fighting at the Front, initially abhorred the insurrection, reviving as it did distrust of the Irish, as this letter to *The Liverpool Catholic Herald,* [A Captain's Letter] demonstrates:

> In the trenches the men regard Sinn Fein with a bitterness they cannot express. When hundreds of thousands of Irishmen were fighting for their lives against superior odds, they begin an insurrection, the effect of which was to keep at

---

22 Kinealy convincingly argues that 1852 was the final famine year. Christine Kinealy, *This Great Calamity: The Irish Famine 1845-1852* (Dublin: Gill and Macmillan, 1994).
23 'Over the Alps', a move towards the Roman Catholic model regularising discipline, organisation and devotional practices.
24 Irish parliamentarians did, however, provide troublesome and tactical difficulties for the law and policy makers in Westminster.

home reinforcements sorely needed in France, and in doing so consigned to death thousands of Irish soldiers.[25]

The punishment meted out to the insurrectionists was markedly counter-productive. The protracted and systematic executions of ring leaders, with the speculative and random rounding up of suspects to be sent to camps in Frongoch, Wales, created sympathy for their cause, and anger at the heavy-handed approach of the British authorities. It also founded a furtive training facility for Irish republicanism injecting energy and commitment for the cause of militant Irish radicalism. The clergy at home were slowly inclining towards the emerging political sea change, but radical militancy which threatened social homogeneity within Ireland was frowned upon, any use of violence was strictly prohibited.[26] In spite of this, British military fears of subversion involving the clergy demonstrate a complete lack of cultural awareness and commonsense. Police reports gathered by informants and the British intelligence services, show that following the 1916 Dublin Rising Ireland remained a placid country. For example King's County [now Offaly] in the Irish midlands reported that: 'some of the younger RC clergy, with a few exceptions, gave expression to the Sinn Fein views, but the older Parish Priests were loyal and quite opposed to Sinn Fein'.[27] These reports were typical across all counties with the exception of Ulster which were not published.

At the Front – Racial Prejudice and Snobbery

The Dublin Rising soured the air between Irish and other British relationships and in spite of the contradictory evidence, fear and distrust within the military of Irish troop disloyalty, and by implication some chaplains, fuelled suspicion and posed a threat to English Ecclesiastical ambition. Fr Gill a divisional CF asserted his view of the situation:

> We can't think of anything else but the terrible things that have been going on in Dublin. Please God it is over now and that the authorities will use as much tact as possible in dealing with it. Nothing has affected Irishmen out here more than this ... I pity the poor young fools who got entangled into so horrible an affair.[28]

As has been noted, tact from the British authorities was conspicuous by its absence. But there were Irish chaplains who were clearly having serious concerns about the

---

25 The *Liverpool Catholic Herald*, (20 October 1917).
26 Bellis, 'Catholic Chaplains', Chapters 1 and 5.
27 Choille, B, MacGiolla, *Intelligence Notes 1913-1916* (Dublin: Oifig an tSoláthair, 1966).
28 DAA, Gill to Rawlinson, 3 May 1916 with the 2nd Royal Irish Rifles. Gill was later to alter his diaries twice in the 20s and 30s. His original entry as above as written at the time, has more import.

Irish political situation. The case of Fr Tom Duggan is straightforward to understand, and given Rawlinson's desire to appease the authorities, his removal from service was a foregone conclusion. He had imported strong Sinn Fein views with him when he signed up, and was not shy in expressing them: 'When in 1917 Cardinal Logue issued a special appeal for Irish Chaplains, I volunteered. And I went off to France with the blessing and encouragement of every friend I had in advanced Sinn Fein circles in Dublin'.[29]

Other cases were less clear. The politics of Fr Cotter, attached to the 6th Royal Dublin Fusiliers, were reported by General W. Hickie of the 16th Division. He wrote to Rawlinson:

> I have been a little uneasy about the influence that Fr Cotter, now with the Munsters, has been exerting on the men. He has very pronounced political views and although I knew of them, I had hoped that he was keeping them more or less to himself and doing no harm. *It must not be thought that I was asking for his transfer on account of his politics*.[30] [Author's italics]

Next Fr Moran, a Salford Diocesan priest informed Rawlinson that:

> I have just heard with regret that Fr McGrath has been forced to leave our Division. My senior chaplain [United Board] was very sorry and acted very nicely to Fr McGrath. I understand things would have been far more serious except for the intervention of Major Martins on his behalf. I do sincerely hope that no Irish priest will have recourse to "The Green Flag" argument in the future. It does an immense amount of harm to the rest of us who have to remain on in the Division.[31]

It seems reasonable that some Irish priests opted for a more radical progression towards national independence, more so as events unfolded over time. Of course having strong Sinn Fein or other radical views does not necessarily equate to disloyalty, and although these examples were in the small minority, the real vulnerability was that such allegations would be exaggerated and do irreparable harm to the overall English Catholic cause. Despite provocation the line held and any potential disloyalty among its chaplains was dealt with by the Catholic authorities at the Front with firmness.

An Irish chaplain Fr Phelan demonstrated how this worked. When confronted in his own Officers Mess with shouts of: 'The Irish are vermin and scum of the earth',[32] the protagonists were not censured. Fr Hegarty, his SCF, explained this to Principal

---

29 Diarmaid Ferriter, *The Transformation of Ireland 1900-2000* (London: Profile, 2004), p. 151.
30 DAA, 3235, Hickie to Rawlinson, 21st December 1917.
31 DAA, 3235, Moran to Rawlinson, 16th June 1917.
32 DAA, 3234, Hegarty to Rawlinson, 20 November 1916.

Chaplain Rawlinson as: '[this occurred] when feeling against the Irish was running pretty high because of the recent Rebellion'.[33] Fr Phelan an Irishman working in the Salford Diocese, was moved on when he reacted by saying: 'damn and blast'.[34] His choice of language had crossed the line of officer conduct despite outrageous provocation. This was merely a disingenuous albeit convenient ploy to remove a chaplain, his dismissal subsumed within the niceties of social etiquette. This despite that SCF Fr Hegarty, himself an Irishman, had recorded: 'He [Phelan] has been of the greatest assistance and has done excellent work. However, in the circumstances, I am prepared to make a sacrifice of him'.[35] Catholic imagery abounds but this example demonstrates how the blueprint of protecting the good name of Catholicism was intuitive for a SCF, irrespective of nationality. It is unlikely that Hegarty was responding to, or had comprehension of the English hierarchy's ambition, his actions were instinctive. Despite the duplicitous method chosen, in this instance by some device that remains veiled, Phelan continued in uniform and appears in the Army lists until 1918 when, as we shall see, he was proposed by his bishop to join the forces in Russia. Did Bishop Casartelli of the Salford Diocese intervene? It is decidedly improbable that a bishop would enter the military arena and more plausible that on reflecting on the whole affair Colonel Rawlinson [for he could always rely on his rank when dealing with the Army] and his army counterparts simply let the matter drop. In the final analysis pragmatism was preferred to protracted bitterness: both sides were appeased by degrees.

Anti-Irish racism did not stand alone, often being socially entwined with class snobbishness and sectarianism. Fr Charles Plater SJ remarked that: 'We are riddled with snobbishness and split into cliques and coteries. Yet we ought to be taking the lead in healing the breaches of society in dissipating the fumes of class hatred which threatens to poison the nation'.[36] An Oratorian priest, Fr Philip Oddie, demonstrated the whole time a range of prejudices, mostly against the Irish and Protestants [to follow]:

> If you are sending a priest, would it be possible to send someone who is not a wild, rabid and rough Irishman? Fr Kenneddy of the 26th Highland Brigade is very holy and very good but frightfully Irish. He disapproves of me strongly (I think) liaison is difficult as a consequence. Fr Walshe is easier to get on with but he also disapproves of me and is also very Irish. I am at present in a rather forlorn minority. Fr Doherty [another Irishman] is a splendid little chap, but he seems to avoid the society of us, and we hardly ever see him. I beg you not to send another rough Irishman to this Division, [9 Scottish].[37]

---

33 Ibid.
34 Ibid.
35 Ibid.
36 JAL, *Month* 135, January-July 1920, p. 256.
37 DAA, 3235, Oddie to Rawlinson, 29 August 1918.

Sectarianism was a serious regional problem at home, but war seemed to amplify and embellish religious bigotry with class-snobbishness, and racism. Lord Derby, one time Under-Secretary of State for War, and a smugly vituperative anti-Catholic missed little opportunity:

> The Liverpool-Irish Battalion was an unsatisfactory lot. Very subordinate and slack in peacetime and not too satisfactory during the war. We were never able to get a good CO for it, and never will as long as it is known as the Irish battalion. The Irish in Liverpool are synonymous with all the lower classes.[38]

Colonel Hussey-Walsh, himself a Catholic with the Northumberland's, launched an attack on Fr John Clarke of the Liverpool Archdiocese accusing him thus:

> I am writing you a private note about one of your Padres. His name is Father Clarke from the Liverpool Diocese [sic]. I am told that he comes from that very charming and delectable manufacturing town in Lancashire called St. Helens. The first thing we noticed was how very *common* and generally *bad-mannered* he was. Nothing whatsoever of the '*Sahib*' about him: however, in this war we have all got to get accustomed to that sort of thing, so there was no protesting: he has somewhat of the '*Maynooth*' *type* about him I used to encounter in Ireland so I saw at once that I will probably not have very much to say to him.[39] [Author's italics].

What is mystifying is that Hussey-Walsh had nothing to gain except to mistakenly think that he was ingratiating himself with Rawlinson whom he had known from the South African wars. He was a poor judge of character.

The snobbish motif was not restricted to the English. Fr Edward Keane, an Irish Redemptorist chaplain had a sideswipe at Irish diocesan priests, again Maynooth was the recipient of the insult. Maynooth, a seminary funded by the British Government, was reduced to 'Maynoot' to emphasise his disdain towards its priests: 'It is difficult to get a man for the Munsters but for the sake of all the virtues don't send Maynoot'.[40] Gwynn places Maynooth in its rightful context:

> In its long tradition, [Maynooth] had aimed always at producing zealous missioners, rather than men of spectacular gifts and individual distinction like Wiseman, with his vastly different Roman training. They were not trained to be either diplomats or administrators, or scholars intended for Catholic universities.

---

38 Helen McCartney, *Citizen Soldiers: The Liverpool Territorials in the First World War*, (Cambridge: Cambridge University Press, 2011). pp. 184-5.
39 DAA, Ephemera, Hussey-Walsh to Rawlinson, 16 December 1917.
40 DAA, 3238, Keane to Rawlinson, 16 May 1916.

Their whole training ... and mission, whether in the congested cities or as pioneer missionaries in remote places, had been for directly personal work among their growing and precarious congregations, As such, they lived and laboured until death took them. Their monuments are to be seen in the flourishing churches and schools and institutions which have arisen from their personal labours, each man performing all that lay within his power while he lived, and relying on his successor to continue and to develop further what he had begun.[41]

Ironically Keane was himself from a simple rural upbringing in county Cork, and offered to resign from the Redemptorists to support his family who had descended into penury.[42]

Snobbishness and lack of respect, not to mention the lack of Christian principles, was not endemic within chaplaincy circles, but it did exist. Rawlinson wrote to Fr Chapman OSB: 'Fr Green [a working class, Liverpool born diocesan priest] has been two years out here and has done very good work in the line, being twice Mentioned-in-Dispatches. He is an excellent worker, but not a very taking (sic) man either in appearance or manner'.[43] Chapman a fellow Benedictine of Rawlinson, based at the main hospital in Calais replied: 'Fr Green is a *common* little man. This is written as man-to-man, for your information, and is no means intended as a formal complaint'.[44] It took Chapman less than a week to form this opinion which he delivered in spineless fashion and hardly man to man. His egotistical and innately snobbish motive was to protect the social status of his type. If that meant deriding a fellow chaplain's social standing, rather than the positive promotion of Green's acknowledged bravery and hard work, notwithstanding mutuality of religion and mission, it is a disappointing indictment of both perceived Army susceptibilities and institutional snobbishness of which Fr Plater had recognised. English working class chaplains, as well their Irish colleagues were to be sacrificed when deemed necessary by the English Catholic élite: excuses based on contemporary norms are simply unsustainable from a group who set themselves above the ordinary and professed to be Christ's emissaries on earth.

Is there another reason? Can we trace Fr Chapman's attitude to historic differences between religious and diocesan priests? In general Morgan Sweeney's assertion that this divide had been largely overcome since the bishops assumed the reins of authority after the Restoration of the Hierarchy, almost 70 years before, holds true. He argues that: 'It cannot be claimed that all the problems were solved completely, but if they were not solved, a *modus vivendi* was established that has stood the test of time'.[45] Superior attitudes developed over the centuries endure, but there was no substantial evidence

---

41   Gwynn, 'The Irish Immigration', Beck the *English Catholic* p.290.
42   DAA, 3238, Keane to Rawlinson, 8 August 1915.
43   DAA, 3234, Rawlinson to Chapman, 25 May 1917.
44   DAA, 3234, Chapman to Rawlinson, 3 June 1917.
45   Morgan Sweeney, 'Diocesan Organisation and Administration', in Beck, *The English Catholics*, pp. 123-4.

to suggest that they were anything but individual and isolated quirks as might be expected from a large organisation comprising strong, individualistic, historic traditions. A study of chaplains concluded that: '… evidence demonstrated that occasional personal lapses by a minority of Catholic chaplains reveal unresolved historical prejudices of race, class, petty jealousies, and snobbery, although to attribute these idiosyncracies simply to intra-religious historical competition is problematic. Instead, as will be shown that social and personal traits were the significant contributory factors'.[46]

Fortunately, Rawlinson rose above such superficial character defects; his relationships with all priests were demonstrably impartial and genuine.

---

46   Bellis, 'Catholic Chaplains', pp. 57-58

2

Mission, Education, Landscapes, and Training: 'I am begging you as a mother to look after my son'

This chapter provides background information to offer the reader the relevant contexts that will assist in the comprehension of subsequent chapters. Alternatively, it can be used as a reference document against later action.

The Catholic Mission at War

The Catholic Church recognised that it was morally and practically proper to support the Allied armed struggle, not as avid warmongers but rather as loyal citizens. Many bishops produced and delivered Pastoral Letters emphasising the church's position, the Pope's pleas for non-violence being subsumed within national imperatives. As a consequence it hoped to secure and develop its domestic expansion in both secular and religious spheres at home. But the Church had a much more profound and longer-term mission to achieve and that was to bring the Faith to as many as it could reach. War provided further opportunities to evangelise and this mission allowed its chaplains to accomplish universal, catholic, and apostolic objectives by providing religious support for all those of any nationality, gender, or colour. Those interested in converting were also welcome but not actively pursued.[1] This was another pilgrimage conducted with missionary endeavour whose depth and scope differentiated Catholic chaplains from their counterparts. Sacramental and devotional services including Confession, Absolution, and Extreme Unction, further emphasised distinctions.

This study aims to add the human experience to their spiritual story, thereby developing a fuller picture of their total endeavour.[2] Spiritual services for troops were urgent and vital necessities. Chaplains were generally viewed with great respect by Catholic

---

1 Conversions here do not necessarily mean changing one's religion they also include those without religion.
2 Bellis, 'Catholic Chaplains', Chapters 3 and 4.

soldiers at the Front. They were also valued highly at home by desperate parents and family anxious to have their sons spiritually prepared, as the risk of death was perpetually before them. To be equipped and in a state of spiritual well-being, before, during and after battle, was a vital spiritual necessity. Mrs Katharine Leslie illustrated this as she pleaded with Monsignor Keatinge, Rawlinson's predecessor: 'I am begging you as a mother to look after my son. He has always had religion and I have never heard a Leslie with all their faults say a word against religion, or listen to a word. Begging you kindest officer, my son Captain Alan Leslie is in the 8th Gordon Highlanders'.[3]

The spiritual centrality of chaplaincy missions aimed to deliver the services and support expected of priests back home, but war frustrated their ability to consistently achieve these goals. The frequency of services always depended on circumstances, as a result some chaplains were dissatisfied and upset when they were denied access to troops. These were in a minority, by comparison most improvised and worked quietly away at their task. Naturally they were subject to many of the same terrors and deprivations as others at the Front, but traditions of mission and pilgrimage added nourishment to their motivation.

Chaplains will be defined by their own beliefs and judged on how successful they were through practice at the Front. The standard for Catholic chaplains in the First World War was high, matching both ecclesiastical and lay expectations. Stephen Louden stated: 'Catholic chaplains went to war for a greater victory than a military victory'.[4]

Seminary Education

The Catholic Church's monastic roots demonstrate its historical influence in the education of society. A good education was at the centre of the successful implementation of Catholic ambition, consequently it followed that a priest's education at seminary was both intense and extensive. It required at least six years seminary study preceded by seven years classical introductory education at pre-seminary college. Education could be supplemented by training in a continental college adding cultural and linguistic skills. The curricula represented both ancient and modern subject matter and although these varied between colleges, were broadly consistent. Fr Gillett's curriculum at Ushaw is insightful:

> Natural Sciences, Philosophy [at least 3 years Christian Philosophy], Ecclesiastical History, Sacred Scripture. Later: Greek Philosophy and Criticism, Cosmology, Ontology, Psychology, Natural Theology, and Ethics. The Structure

---

3   DAA, Bishops' correspondence, Mrs Leslie to Keatinge, 12 May 1915.
4   Fr Stephen Louden, ex Principal Catholic Chaplain to the Forces, RACD Conference, July 2009.

of Materials was followed by: Physiology, Pathology and the Ethics of Biology. Natural Sciences were accompanied by the advanced Scripture Study of the New Testament and further Ecclesiastical History. Theology was next studied including: Morals, Sacred Scripture, Dogmatism and Canon Law.[5]

By any standards this was an extensive educational programme. The rubrics and liturgy of the Church, not to forget elocution lessons and an emphasis on character and physical development through sport, added to the learning process. Discipline was also inculcated in the work and through the general routine of communal living. Discipline was vital for any mission, none more that at war.

Language Education for War

The war in France and Belgium was truly international. Ulusoga describes it as: '... the most diverse and dangerous place on earth ... [and] the greatest gathering of peoples and races of the world'.[6] Knowledge of languages enabled chaplains to minister to participants from all nations including, German PoW's, Chinese labourers, French and Belgian civilians and more. Latin added to the pot pourri of linguistic talent. Language skills were essential communication tools in a widespread Church, extending within and beyond continental Europe. All Catholic chaplains on the Western Front had at least some knowledge of French and possibly German, others Italian, Portuguese, Russian and more, including Walloon. Fr Gillett, a competent French and partial German speaker liaised between the French clergy and British soldiers: 'In the evening Bishop addresses my soldiers and I interpret for him.'[7] Similarly, Fr Steuart used his considerable knowledge of the German language to tackle German prisoners: 'Hardie & Sutherland, severe shell-shock. Miserable time. Casualties coming in. Acted as interpreter for 4 prisoners'.[8] The language skills acquired depended on: the projected area of mission post-ordination, availability, and preference. On occasions family coincidence became a factor. Bishop Casartelli in the post-armistice period provides an example: 'I have two priests who have volunteered for Russia, Fathers Phelan and Day. Fr Phelan [Salford Diocese but born in Waterford discussed earlier] has lived in Russia for some years and speaks Russian'.[9] Further abroad the talents of Frs. Hartigan and Bergin in Arabia show the breadth of knowledge and mission. These two Jesuits who sacrificed their lives as chaplains, were

5   Bellis, 'Catholic Chaplains', p. 105.
6   David Olusoga, *The World's History*, (Head of Zeus, 2014), p. 272.
7   SDA, Gillett Diaries, 26 June 1917.
8   JAL, Steuart Diaries, 1 August 1917.
9   DAA, 3231, Rawlinson to Monk, 18 April 1919.

more than capable in Arabic: '[Michael Bergin[10]] His thorough knowledge of French and Arabic means that he will be a great loss to our Syrian Mission'[11] and: '[Austin Hartigan[12]] He had an unusually brilliant career at the University of Beirut where he obtained a Doctorate of oriental letters as he was proficient in Arabic'.[13] A lesser known originally French order, the Oblates of Mary Immaculate [OMI], offered their support through Fr Scannell's linguistic innovation, which although well-meaning now seems anachronistic. He informed Rawlinson that: 'I have succeeded in getting a number of phrases translated into Chinese. [To assist with Confessions] I have been rather interested in the 'Chinks'[14] for some time and found a fair number of Catholics among them'.[15] On occasion linguistic skills were not mandatory. Fr Page a Preston Jesuit who worked in both the Irish and English Provinces, set foot in Archangel, Russia with the 'North Russian Relief Force' in 1919: 'I think I can claim to be the first Jesuit to set foot in Russia since the restoration of the Society'.[16] With no prior reason or intelligence of this move it is unlikely that he was able to speak the native tongue.

Pre-War Catholic Landscape – Military

Chaplains were priests but they were also men with all the diversity of character and behaviour that is the human condition. Frs Gillett and Steuart were decent and hard-working chaplains but they also represented the range of clergy whose backgrounds, expectations and idiosyncracies were often poles apart. One question that was asked at the Front and will be repeated throughout is: 'Is he more an officer than a priest?' Most fell into the latter camp but some the former, including Fr Steuart SJ. The reasons are two-fold. First the Jesuit tradition was based on the soldier-priest founder St Ignatius of Loyola and Stonyhurst Jesuit College signifies his military influence. It was a firm promoter of the OTC system for its pupils as the military influence in the college photograph makes clear:[17]

---

10   Fr Bergin MC, an Irish Jesuit from Tipperary, incurred wounds received from a shell at Passchendaele whilst attached to the Australian Army and died on 12 October 1917 aged 38.
11   JAD, *Obituary in Our Past*, 1919.
12   Born in Foynes, Co Limerick he died in Iraq aged 33 of cholera and not the jaundice sometimes reported. JAD CHP 1/53 (17) Fr Roche to Provincial 2 October 1916.
13   JAD, *Obituary in Our Past*, 1919.
14   This is an unfortunate term today but was in common usage. Daryl Klein, *With The Chinks: The Chinese Labour Corps*. (Uckfield: Naval and Military Press and the IWM, reprinted in 2009. Original was undated, but almost certainly in the 1920s), is a case in point.
15   DAA, 3235, Scannell to Rawlinson, 12 June 1918.
16   JAL, *Letters and Notices, XXXV*, (Manressa Press, Roehampton 1919-20).
17   Trained by 8 East Lancashire Regiment.

Mission, Education, Landscapes, and Training 37

Stonyhurst College OTC 1916. (SCA, *The Stonyhurst War Record*)

Conceding that it was openly supportive of its students defending King and country, the northern diocesan college at Ushaw had no pre-existing military culture. Nevertheless, many students joined the hastily formed OTC and feature in the Ushaw College roll-call. Ushaw's OTC displayed a more relaxed disposition than that of Stonyhurst. Father Gillett emerged from Ushaw without the same leanings towards the military as his diarist colleague and was not a member of the OTC. In the OTC photograph below the uniforms in the picture arrived after the end of the war. This lax attitude to the military implies that in the Ushaw worldview the priesthood had a higher priority than the military.

Ushaw OTC Cadets November 1918. (Milburn, *A History of Ushaw College*)

Stonyhurst may have had militarist leaning but it was first and foremost a Catholic college as the next photograph demonstrates. Note the relative positions of clergy and OTC:

Corpus Christi Procession 1916. (SCA, *The Stonyhurst War Record*)

Pre-War Catholic Landscape – Social

In deciding whether a chaplain was more or less a priest than a soldier, the second and more important factor goes to the heart of understanding the Catholic project. Narrowly portrayed as the Church of the poor it certainly had its fair share of the dispossessed, the sick, and the uneducated with whom to deal. But it also had an emerging middle class and a solid base of wealthy co-religionists on whom to rely. The immigrant and indigenous poor had created an immense challenge, but by the end of the 19th century and beyond, they were benefitting mainly through their own devices. Material benefits were accompanied by a rapid rise in trained religious, both men and women, providing greater opportunities for spiritual guidance and support. These were paid for across the classes. The 'penny poor', emerging middle-classes, and wealthy benefactors all contributed. Many families across the social strata were keen to have a son or daughter follow the religious life. In addition, partly as a result of discrimination and partly as a need to protect their interests from renewed outside intervention, the Church needed to develop talent and promote from within. Administrators, educationalists, ambassadors and many more went hand-in-hand with those working in the slums, in rural backwaters, parish priests painstakingly building worthy parishes, or those abroad on foreign missions.

Consequently the situation at home might be expected to be replicated at war with the parish priest being well equipped for the average Tommy, and those from a diplomatic or administrative background being placed in senior roles at war. Two types of role did emerge: a few were assigned to management and administration being selected from those who could best associate with the upper-echelons of the British Army, but employment opportunities at senior level were rare with specialist talents being restricted by the requirements and limitations of chaplaincy in the Army. The second role of accompanying the troops in action or sickness, was performed by the majority of all chaplains at war who were designated Captain Class 4. Some priests were casualties of a mismatch. Fr Gillett fitted well with troops, alas Fr Steuart's background did not lend itself to a sense of cohesion with ordinary people and he had to satisfy himself with lower ranking officers rather than the higher echelons to which he, not without precedent, aspired. Nevertheless, even Fr Steuart concealed any personal ambition [except for military recognition] and provided the spiritual and pastoral services required of him.

It seems that career ambition was by no means an overt problem, any potential rivalries for the key jobs were mitigated by collective seminary experiences which fashioned mind-sets and expectations, fostering homogeneity. Furthermore, collective and standard responsibilities ironed out most of the remaining individual differences; after all, priests were spiritual leaders and not men with singular military intent. Hence, when Benedictines occupied the most senior positions at war the only hint of resentment that could be found among either diocesan chaplains or from those of other orders was Fr Gill SJ whose dismissive comment that: 'The only Catholic representative we have is Fr Rawlinson, who is simply a kind of head clerk'.[18] This iniquitous remark owes more to Fr Gill's own personality than reality.[19] Generally there was an intrinsic acceptance of each other's position within the common bond of Catholic priesthood. This comfortable state of affairs has already been challenged in chapter 1, but historic schisms failed to re-emerge in relation to GHQ and seem to have been restricted to the occasional individual outburst of a personal nature.

Geographical and Religious Landscapes at War

In the Western European context, the political jurisdiction in the Great War was firmly in the hands of Protestant or secular governments. By 1914 many Churches

---

18 JAD, CHP1/25 (38) Gill to Irish Jesuit Provincial, 27 January 1917.
19 DAA, 3234, Grobel to Rawlinson, 23 November 1914. Fr Grobel DAPC assessed Fr Gill as 'dissatisfied and awkward to deal with'.

were under threat from anti-religious sentiment expressed as: materialism, increasing governmental control, Darwinism, atheism, or apathy. Attendances at services in the Church of England were on the decline. Even so the Established Church retained legitimacy as the official Church which overarched a number of other Protestant religions and remained the significant religious figurehead for the great majority of Britain's, practicing or not. The Catholic Church continued to expand in Britain but it retreated in France under determined anti-Catholic legislation,[20] which was not always well-received or successful as Fr Gillett observed: 'French attempted to collar it [L'Abeele church] when their cruel laws were passed but the civilians all turned out and drove the wretched officials back – after they were left in peace'.[21]

In this war zone, the battle grounds were undeniably culturally and spiritually Catholic. Churches, crucifixes and roadside shrines were stumbled upon by most British troops for the first time. Non-Catholics may have been puzzled at their proliferation but to believers they were a constant reminder of the connection between Christ and his sacrifice on Golgotha, which was also manifest in the sacrifices of soldiers and civilians. Other Christians will have embraced the Christ-Calvary connection but others misinterpreted the devotional significance at the heart of Catholicism as mere superstition. This argument is mediated by Snape who claimed: 'Protestant Britons encountered a Catholic landscape ... But there was little or no animosity towards a symbol [crucifix] that was historically alien to the landscape of Protestant tradition.'[22] Another historian argues that: 'For combatants residing within the Catholic countries of the Western Front, the material culture of Catholic rituals that surrounded them soon infiltrated their Anglican practices [...] eliminating some of the foreign character of the Catholic religion for Anglican Soldiers'.[23] For Catholics they were essential parts of their Faith and practice. They were also a reminder and connection with home with wayside shrines having a special resonance with Irish and French troops.

In this geographical and religious paradox, it was Catholic chaplains to whom we can look to provide their unique spiritual and pastoral interpretation of events. Fathers Gillett and Steuart, together with a range of chaplains when appropriate, facilitate that insight. Familiarity with religious principles, services, devotions, traditions, and artefacts are common denominators for all practising Catholics, but it was chaplains who provided the spiritual development, guidance, and sustenance of their men. With death a daily companion, Extreme Unction was a duty which sometimes

---

20   Bellis, 'Catholic Chaplains', p. 63. It was also under internal pressure from Modernism, a European movement which sought to lessen Rome's authority in favour of local decision making. It never took root in Britain.
21   SDA, Gillett Diaries, 5 July 1917.
22   Michael Snape, *God and the British Soldier: Religion and the British Soldier in the First and Second World Wars* (Oxford: Routledge, 2005).
23   Amport Armed Forces Chaplaincy Conference 2011, Ashleigh Melvin, Birbeck College, University of London, produced an insightful paper: 'Fluid Faith: Religious Rituals and Their Emotional Effect'.

demanded the chaplain's supreme sacrifice. Of course chaplains from other denominations or other non-combatant participants such as: nurses, doctors, veterinarians, and more, exhibited similar courage and professional dedication. Variations also existed between Catholic chaplains as might be expected. Nonetheless, the uniquely Catholic Sacrament of the Last Rites reveals the desire and duty by both soldier and chaplain to prepare the soul for its last journey. A non-Catholic officer observed the calm bestowed by the Sacrament on a soldier immediately before execution, after which he remarked: "Good God, yours is the religion to die in".[24] In the popular imagination this Sacrament was delivered in no-man's land but in reality hospitals, dressing stations and the wayside were more common place. Time was of the essence. Not all chaplains 'went over the top', but if they chose not to there was a reason. Nevertheless, the majority of chaplaincy deaths occurred where they could reach most men, not in the no-man's land but at medical facilities close to the line.

Chaplaincy Training

Catholic chaplains were fortunate that their antecedents had invested time and resources on their early development as formal chaplaincy training of priests as raw chaplains in the First World War was a non-event. It simply did not happen: 'There are no Schools for padres',[25] claimed Fr W J Brown SCF precisely describing the state of affairs for all chaplains regardless of creed.[26] In theory formal chaplaincy training for priests was a luxury insofar as they had sufficient priestly training. Importantly their missionary and pilgrim ethos, tempered over the centuries, should have allowed them to adapt to any situation. But this was not any situation; the Great War was not a mission in China, Venezuela, or indeed Liverpool or Cork. Chaplains, ministering to troops in a war where the scale, intensity, and violence were completely new experiences, would undoubtedly have benefited not from spiritual guidance but from knowledge of Army ways. Best practice, military etiquette, and the religious limitations which this war had uniquely imposed, were eventually negotiated by most of these men but they had to learn lessons the hard way.

On rare occasions, newly commissioned chaplains were fortunate to accompany their intended army unit at the outset as new formations were created from an assemblage of new recruits and officers. This should have yielded benefits for new chaplains to familiarise themselves with army life and provide an opportunity to create chaplaincy-army bonds. In reality this was not the case. Fr Gillett's correspondence

---

24 Charles Plater, *Catholic Soldiers*, (London: Longman Green, 1919).
25 DAA, 3234, Brown to Rawlinson, 12 August 1918. Brown 38 Welsh Division was writing to Rawlinson ref Richmond as a means of mitigating bad chaplaincy behaviour.
26 Bellis, 'Catholic Chaplains', p. 119. Church of England chaplains did have a 'school' founded in 1917 known as the 'bombing school for padres', although it functioned mainly as a respite facility.

illuminates the situation. He was to accompany his newly formed unit, the 2/8 Irish Battalion of the Kings Liverpool Regiment. In reality, after a period in Ipswich, he was attached to Rugeley Camp with responsibilities for three reserve Brigades. Meanwhile his men trained on Salisbury Plain. His function in the midlands was conventional priestly work in camp with no specific army or chaplaincy training or familiarisation and crucially no contact with his men.[27] Ironically this separation from Fr Gillett's intended troops turned into a fortunate intervention which potentially saved his life. A stomach ulcer delayed his embarkation thereby protecting him from being among the hideous casualties of the early Somme fighting, including many in the Liverpool Irish Regiment, men he would ordinarily have seen at Sunday Mass at home. Nevertheless, disconnection from men he knew would have adverse consequences for his mission at the Front. He continued his priestly function at camp until fit again, almost as if the camp was simply another parish in Liverpool. He was as naïve about war chaplaincy after eight months of work at base, as if he had gone directly to the Somme, Arras, or Ypres, his eventual destinations: a training illusion.

This was a missed opportunity but there was nothing in place and no apparent impetus to deliver any benefits of chaplaincy training. Inexperienced chaplains, in common with most actors in the Great War simply had to make the best of the situation. Chaplains were simply treading water until they were ushered to the continent and if that meant subsuming their own personal pre-war missionary agendas for the war effort, then so be it. Their wartime sacred mission would have to rely on their priestly preparation. Incredibly, and against all odds, this melange actually worked, and worked well.

Nothing changed in training terms when newly commissioned chaplains disembarked on continental soil. They were met at the port or at a local headquarters and directed either to a Base Hospital, or increasingly as the war continued, directly to a fighting unit. The exigencies of war informed that deployment decision. Reporting to Base Hospitals theoretically allowed a period of acclimatisation, perhaps a degree of training and chaplain assessment, but it mainly satisfied shortages at these hospitals. In reality the level of acclimatisation was debatable and formal training non-existent. Later, Gillett will eloquently describe the significant differences between a Base Hospital in Boulogne and the active war zone in Albert, Somme. Early induction directly to a fighting unit became more common from late 1917 as Base Hospitals became the province of recovering or ailing chaplains. Severe chaplaincy shortages increasingly demanded immediate front line occupancy for new recruits. By 1918 they were over 100 short of establishment, a purely Catholic problem.

To bridge the training gap chaplains' exercised self-help between each other at: meetings, casual discussions and by example. Belatedly a 'Red Book' or formally:

27   RCBFA, Gillett wrote to Keatinge from Rugeley Camp, (17 March 1916), suggesting that chaplains should be deployed 1 per Brigade in these large permanent camps rather than migrating to local towns.

Roman Catholic Chaplains: Information and Hints was published in 1917. Some advice was remarkably undiplomatic: 'Remember to be always courteous. You are probably a Captain in rank, and as such you are only 'small fry' in the Army'.[28] Yet despite these disadvantages the great majority of chaplains negotiated a path through army officialdom. There were exceptions. Even Fr Steuart with the advantage of high social status was occasionally obstructed by army indifference or incompetence, but Fr Gillett's military life was plagued by both. Social differences played a part but the main reason was the former had a fair contingent of Catholics in his Scottish regiments, whilst Fr Gillett had few in his eastern English units. By contrast, Fr Gillett did exceptionally well with troops passing through with whom he enjoyed great affinity, especially Lancashire, Irish, and American soldiers. Fr Steuart had little or no comprehension of the common man and rarely mentioned anyone other than officers.

A word of caution, judgement about either of these men should be reserved as each operated consistently within contemporary Catholic zeitgeist which balanced requirements to resources. Each man had a relevant role to play reflecting his own position and background. Consequently differences may be viewed as distinctions rather than shortcomings and will be explored as such.

---

28   DAA, Ephemera, *Roman Catholic Chaplains: Information and Hints*. Author unnamed (Army Printing and Stationery Office, January 1917) p. 18.

3

Role, Organisation, Structure, and Deployment: 'Not a Society Entertainer, nor a Vendor of Buns and Cigarettes'

Catholic chaplains had four distinct types of duties. The Sacraments and Devotions were their priority obligations, pastoral care came next whilst secular support was a distant fourth. Celebrating the Sacraments and Devotions were obligatory for chaplains. Soldiers were compelled to celebrate some of the Sacraments whilst other services including the Devotions were voluntary. Pastoral care was solely the responsibility of the chaplain. A secular function was a different experience altogether, where alien to their world at home and in conditions outside all previous experiences, engagement between chaplains and the authorities occasionally led to differences of opinion.

The perception of a non-Catholic chaplain being an entertainer or vendor of buns was proffered by a Catholic soldier to the Plater report *Catholic Soldiers* of late 1918.[1] His observations contain a grain of truth but were unfair. Other religious traditions promoted this type of social provision at home and many non-Catholic soldiers expected their own chaplain to continue this approach. For Catholics, the converse was true. Central to soldiers' expectations, the spiritual priorities of a Catholic chaplain were merely the extension of the priest's responsibilities from home *writ large*. The Plater enquiry of 1918 was conducted to evaluate perception of Catholic chaplains and their performance in the war. Social provision at the expense of delivering spiritual sustenance was not an option for these chaplains or soldiers, illustrating the fundamental differences between religious philosophies and their implementation.

What were Catholic chaplain's roles? First, it is beneficial to first ascertain what the roles were not: 'I went to Barles trenches with Grieve at night to be at the gas carrying,[2] a silly, dangerous, and useless business'.[3] Fr Drinkwater was conducting an occupation with which he did not approve. His remarks after his sojourn with the military

---

1 C. Plater, *Catholic Soldiers*, p. 140.
2 Gas carrying referred to gas shells. It was a dangerous job blurring the lines between what constitutes combat and what does not.
3 BAA, Drinkwater Diaries, 6 July 1916.

anticipate a misunderstanding of Catholic chaplains' responsibilities. It should be appreciated that they were not in the business of conducting: 'silly, dangerous, and useless business', neither was his concern the distribution of Woodbine or Carroll's cigarettes,[4] nor of delivering morale boosting sermons. They were not social secretaries, nor involved in the plethora of peripheral comings and goings, but they were priests in khaki. Chaplains regularly experienced danger but that should be restricted to conducting their priestly duties and obligations.[5] If an auxiliary task was required, it was only possible when circumstances allowed and by personal choice as apparently with Drinkwater.

This was the Catholic position. Bishop William Frederick Keating of Northampton wrote many pertinent Pastoral Letters during the war.[6] In his 1916 Lenten Pastoral he concluded that the priest's responsibility at war was as a non-belligerent and crucially to do God's business:

> On the lowest ground of mere expediency, it would be folly to deplete the thin ranks of our Clergy for other deployment. But we take our stand on the higher ground of principle, deprecating with all the force at our command any departure from the traditional Christian attitude, that in war as in peace, in the army as in civil life, the most useful and only fitting occupation for priests is God's business; and that, although a priest might expose his own life, and will cheerfully do so at the call of duty, to call him to take the life of another is an outrage on the sanctity of his profession.[7]

For Catholics there was no room for prevarication. Chaplains knew their principal responsibility was to deliver all aspects of Catholicism to Catholics as a continuation of their priestly domestic endeavours. They shared this duality of expectation with soldiers and this relationship immediately extended to civilians in the war zones, substituting Curés with chaplains. Soldiers demonstrated this special relationship by addressing chaplains as Father, thus confirming the linkage between civilian and military spiritual life. Religious accountability was sacrosanct and merely reflected the pre-war *modus operandi* in an era where ecumenism was a rare commodity amid widespread sectarianism. Hence a remarkable lack of ambiguity existed within Catholic circles as to their professional deportment. Nevertheless, this outlook should not be misunderstood as spiteful isolationism or superciliousness, owing more to self-reliance

---

4   JAL, '*Our Army Chaplains Experiences*' p. 441. This did happen as Fr Denis Doyle noted: 'The men like to see me around, especially if I am carrying cigarettes'. This was the only occasion discovered.
5   Encountering danger was a common experience, but they were not expected to run the risk of danger lightly – chaplains were too few on the ground.
6   Ironically representing a diocese with few Catholics but became the Archbishop of Liverpool after Whiteside's death in 1921.
7   SDA, Lenten Pastoral Letter of Bishop Keating 1916, pp. 360-61.

and self-defence, plausible responses given the treatment handed out to Catholics over the centuries. Of course good will and cooperation were essential in daily routine but they existed within clearly expressed boundaries. Despite these demarcations, it was possible to achieve a positive ambience with other denominations. Fr Keane CSSR demonstrated what could be achieved, albeit with his usual sarcasm: 'Everything here [36 CCS, Ulster Division] goes well, no one fights anyone else and the spirit that prevails is conducive to the mutual understanding of each other's religious differences, so the C of E padre says!'[8] Unfortunately, on occasion defence of their Catholic ethos could land chaplains in trouble with the authorities, to whom their traditions were sometimes a mystery. This faded in time as both the army and clergy absorbed each other's idiosyncrasies and developed mutual regard.

If Catholicism's desire for religious sovereignty was fashioned in response to a history of persecution and exclusion, how did that translate at the Front? This will be explored, at this stage the example of the homily or sermon will give an insight. The difference between a sermon and a homily is small, yet it is indicative of an approach which is less Biblical and more behavioural. Catholic priests often used homilies derived from texts in the Bible but tailored the messages to the current situation with less emphasis on literal interpretations and more on promoting the messages and philosophy of Christianity which lay within the Gospels.[9] Selecting a text, particularly from the Old Testament to fit military expediency, was an anathema for Catholic chaplains who ignored attempts to use a spiritual occasion to rouse the men for military purposes. The Established Church had no such room to manoeuvre: 'The GOC told the C. of E. chaplains to preach fighting sermons and to take them from the Old Testament'.[10] These instructions owe more to the perilous military situation following the German Spring Offensive than any desire to exercise undue authority over the Church of England. Nonetheless, they highlight the military belief and trust in the morale boosting powers of the clergy.[11] If Catholic chaplains were expected to follow suit then this misconception was quickly dispelled, naturally they wanted to encourage the troops but not through the pulpit. The separation of Christ's message from secular necessity sits at the very core of the Catholic pilgrimage.

---

8   DAA, 3238, Keane to Rawlinson, 7 November 1916.
9   That is not to suggest that the same does not apply, to varying degrees, within other denominations particularly at home. To interpret the Bible for military purposes went against the grain for Catholic chaplains, although those homilies which emphasised good behaviour would deliver secondary military benefits.
10 BAA, Drinkwater Diaries, (30th April 1918).
11 For an Anglican perspective, Reverend Middleton-Brumwell's, *The Army Chaplain: The Duties of Chaplains and Morale* (London: Black 1943).

Sacraments and Devotions[12]

Chaplains supplied services to support not only the soldiers at rest and in battle, but the local Catholic civilian population and soldiers from the entire combatant and support nations without exception. French and Belgian civilians offered up their churches and chaplains reciprocated by donating both time and effort to replace French Curés who were compelled by French civil law to fight. These were not negotiated arrangements being purely symbiotic and intuitive.[13] This needed to be achieved without aggravating military operational requirements. The British Army funded chaplains and took a remarkably tolerant view of chaplains conducting civilian services. It is questionable whether or not those in society harbouring extreme anti-Catholic sentiment would have been so conciliatory or pragmatic. Nevertheless, common sense on both sides prevailed, there were far more pressing matters with which to contend.

Services for troops were celebrated in public behind the line in French or Belgian villages, where churches provided the natural environment, although makeshift ceremonies in the war-zone were organised almost anywhere that circumstances allowed. Responses from civilians appeared constant but for soldiers it was patchy and dependent on the tradition and co-operation of the unit concerned. Service attendance was mediated by the legitimate demands of the army, weather conditions, sickness or injury, and occasional administrative lapses. Understandably pulses of increased response were noticeable before and after a major battle, being amplified in those units from strong Catholic communities at home.

When chaplains were thrust into an entirely new environment, some like Fr Gillett found succour by comparing religious services between French and British Catholic traditions displaying a penchant for exploring both social and religious cultural distinctions. He enthused that: 'The day closes with solemn Benediction in the Cathedral. Quite a day of piety and an eye-opener to the British soldiers. What a blessing must come to France through the piety of its many devout women'.[14] Two months later in a chapel at Albert he observed: 'What a comfort the peace and quiet of Mass and Benediction seems to be to the lads after the dangers of the trenches. They enter their Devotions with great spirit. They appreciate the chance of using a priest'.[15] Personal dedication to Benediction also applied to other Devotions, Sacraments, and particularly Holy Mass. Their importance to chaplains and their congregations created not only spiritual enrichment, but also an opportunity to unite and be at peace which together with the recognition of priestly efforts by the soldiers and civilians signified the unifying power of the Church.

---

12   Bellis, 'Catholic Chaplains', Chapters 3 and 4 for a detailed description.
13   Local bishops provided the requisite faculties to cater for civilians in their diocese, the Bishop of Arras the most prominent.
14   SDA, Gillett Diaries, 20 August 1916. He conducted Benediction 38 times as a chaplain.
15   Ibid., 29 October 1916.

It was not always so smooth. Fr Steuart's *entente cordiale* was tested when he remarked: 'Mass at 9:30. Curé frightfully late as usual, so the Mass didn't begin till nearly 10. Benediction in the evening: which was rather terrible as it was all French singing and far too long".[16] Meanwhile, Fr Francis Drinkwater described a tragedy: 'Back at Bethune and found that a bomb got a direct hit on the sacristy last night: sacristy disappeared, all church windows smashed etc. The organist and chanter killed, also a boy named Ducanne who used to serve my Mass. Archpriest wounded. They were just starting Benediction'.[17] This misfortune exemplified the sacrifices which civilians and local clergy made that often go unnoticed. Both Sacramental and Devotional care, in a variety of circumstances and to a range of supplicants, justified the Catholic chaplaincy effort. That being so what else did they achieve?

Pastoral

Catholic chaplains shepherded a range of pastoral amenities and services including: funerals, burials, attendance at and in preparation for execution, letters of condolence to relatives, and the collection of statistics usually of conversions. This latter chore was erratic and not always popular with chaplains, the underlying conundrum between officer and priest re-emerging. Fr O'Connor MC and SCF, a Salford Diocesan priest with 14 Brigade including 2 Battalion Manchester's and 2 Battalion Inniskillings, grumbled with some justification, at the effort required in compiling statistics: 'Are we priests or officials first? Or does GHQ know anything of present conditions. Are weekly returns the most important things in a fighting advancing Division containing four Catholic Battalions with two priests to do the work?'[18] He might have added what are they used for? The reasons were for Rawlinson to compile data which might help his organisation at the Front, but equally to sate the appetite for Catholic propaganda in the shape of *The Tablet* publication at home. It was hoped that the war would provide an opportunity to create many new converts. On the contrary, reality was very different to the over-optimistic and utterly asinine exaggeration of 40,000 conversions at war claimed by *The Tablet* in 1918.[19] Sparse and erratic statistics in the archives, plus the minimalistic entries both in quantity and apparent relevance from the control group diaries, provides ample proof that conversions were conducted in a piecemeal fashion and could not have reached the levels claimed by propagandists. The dreams of newspaper or journal proprietors, no matter how well-intentioned, were

---

16 JAL, Steuart Diaries, 5 May 1918.
17 BAA, Drinkwater Diaries, 19 December 1917.
18 DAA, 3235, O'Connor 50 Division to Smith his Army DAPC, 14 October 1918.
19 The Tablet, 30 November 1918, claimed 40,000 conversions, a figure taken as correct in O'Rahilly, Alfred, *Father William Doyle SJ*, 2nd edition (London: Longmans-Green, 1920), p. 255. The inference was 'at war' and not by conversions at home.

grossly exaggerated.[20] The whole nature of war with constant change, danger, and movement, did not facilitate the instruction or assessment of significant numbers of converts, notwithstanding the mandatory prerequisite and time-consuming preparatory instruction. Some did take place, but even Fr Peale SJ's evangelising skills led to a mere ten conversions throughout the war.[21] Such high estimates would require mass ceremonies which in biblical times were feasible but which were simply outside contemporary Catholic custom, apart from the small matter of operational reality. Based on the evidence an estimate of around 4,000 would seem at the optimistic end of realism. Those impressed by their chaplains may have sought to convert after the war but any figures would be conjecture. The reality of war made conversions problematic and even if desirable, hardly a top priority. For every soul gained hundreds might be lost through sacramental deprivation, leakage, or disillusionment. It is ultimately futile to speculate on conversion numbers inside or outside the cauldron of the battlefields, or those lost to the Faith in the confusion of war.

Secular

The distancing of secular activities from spiritual requires clarification. Chaplains did provide non-religious facilities to assist the authorities when they considered that it was the right thing to do, within the guidelines already established above. Chaplains realised that they were not immune from the war and its consequences and helped whenever appropriate, but a wholly material activity without any direct religious interpretation, such as organising social events, bore little significance to the spiritual obligations of Catholic chaplains. In any case they were sorely under-resourced even to fulfil their spiritual duties.

The following demand for Catholic chaplaincy participation in censorship signifies the crossing of the line from spiritual to secular. The case of Fr Staniforth acts as an exemplar for other secular demands made on chaplains in other areas:

> The CO here insists on the chaplains taking it in turns to act as Chief Censor and it is put in Orders. The Chief Censor is supposed to apportion a number of letters to certain Officers deputed to act as censors. Now I am willing to take a share in censoring, when it is necessary, & when it does not conflict with my proper duties: but I do not quite see why a chaplain should be appointed in a kind of official manner which lie outside his own proper sphere: especially when it involves a kind of supervision over other officers.[22]

20 These claims were muted in the *Catholic Universe* whose editor Mr Harding was in close contact with Rawlinson through Catholic Club and Lourdes Pilgrimage schemes. He visited France regularly and had a realistic view of the activities of Catholics at the Front.
21 Fr John Peale SJ, *War Jottings* (Calcutta: Catholic Orphan Press, 1916), vols 1-3.
22 DAA, 3231, Staniforth to Rawlinson, 1 November 1916.

Staniforth perfectly crystallised the Catholic position. Wishing to act in accordance with the Commanding Officers mandate, he could not in conscience accept that this was a proper function for a Catholic chaplain, yet he wanted to comply. He pointed to the dangers of upsetting other officers whilst prepared to do his share, but his main concern was the disruption to his 'proper duties' which were spiritual. This was a situation where the CO did not understand the Catholic position. On the other hand criticism of the CO is harsh, from his perspective surely he was treating all officers equally? The problem was lack of officer training and knowledge of relationships with the various and different religious bodies. From a secular perception it may seem absurd that a senior military man had to consider the sensitivities of a Catholic priest in the bloodiest of wars. Nonetheless, the great majority of the Army Commanders, including Haig, realised the benefit accruing from the work of chaplains: even when they were engaged in a spiritual war which clerics considered of greater significance than that of the military. Conversely it was also prudent for chaplains to appreciate military tenets. Both parties were loyal to their respective objectives and masters, and both wanted victory. Censorship was an isolated event, yet the principles hold true for all the secular incursions into a Catholic chaplain's unwavering function. Wanting to assist was a natural thing to do for one's comrades and the victory was desperately desired by all, but spiritual affairs could not be compromised.

Determined protection of independence from denominational interference was a reasonable position, but when expressed in hostility was dangerous, unhealthy, and unnecessary. On occasions, Fr Oddie 26 from the Brompton Oratory showed his inexperience, over-zealousness, and bigotry, deservedly triggering a reprimand from his supremo. Oddie's underlying concern was an inability to accept a non-Catholic as senior, a normal state of affairs in the Army, but he lamentably failed to separate officer from chaplain. One issue was the withdrawal of chaplaincy horses in 1917 due to chronic shortages which applied to all denominations. Rawlinson informed Oddie that: 'The withdrawal of your horse has filled up your cup with bitterness. Of course I can't say I agree with everything you say, especially your diatribes against His Majesty's Army!'[23] Oddie continued his vitriolic outpourings, albeit in a pusillanimous way and only privately to Rawlinson. If he thought he was impressing Rawlinson he was way off the mark. When Rawlinson retorted and called him a 'grouser' the aggrieved young chaplain responded with:

> I am very sorry that you called me a grouser, because a grouser is, in my opinion, the most horrible type of man in the world. It is my strong faith that makes me grouse sometimes but I will not bow the knee to a heretic because I am fifty million times better than any heretical chaplain and I know that all heretical ministers are bad men and children of Satan.[24]

---

23 DAA, 3235, Rawlinson to Oddie, 4 April 1917.
24 DAA, 3235, Oddie to Rawlinson, 20 November 1917.

His professors of doctrine and scripture, not to mention his peers, would be alarmed and dismayed at the young man's intemperance; moreover if he had made such remarks publicly in Liverpool, Belfast, or Glasgow he would without doubt have caused a sectarian riot. Oddie's scornful and immature remarks raise doubts about his suitability as chaplain, if not his mental state, and do not in any way reflect the views of the vast majority of rational chaplains. Fr Oddie was inclined to grandiloquence rather than rational thought or action and censure was appropriate, but Rawlinson managed Oddie like a tolerant father might treat his naughty and petulant child. This was the most sensible way of keeping the lid on a potentially volatile storm that would justifiably follow if this hot-blooded rhetoric became public.

The defence of Catholicism had evolved through justifiable fears of proselytism and materialism which occupied the thoughts of many before the war,[25] but Fr Oddie's lack of control was unbalanced, misplaced, and unrepresentative. The great majority of chaplains simply got on with the job and adopted a positive stance towards their relationships with non-Catholics. They recognised the possibility of creating a good impression from their actions. Rawlinson would have approved. Priests in khaki were human beings and as part of a unified fighting force they were more than willing to do their bit when appropriate. Bertrand Pike, a Dominican chaplain with 55 West Lancashire Division attached to the 166 South Lancashire Royal Field Artillery, saw an opportunity to further the Catholic cause writing:

> I find myself surrounded by men, the majority of whom are not Catholics. [Despite this being the most Catholic English Division]. This being so, I must remember that for the present, at any rate, I stand in their eyes as a representative of the Catholic Church. They may or may not know what are my duties. At any rate I can show them that I know them and am ready to stand by them. I must remember that the honour of the Church is vested in me. *It is just possible that they may judge the whole Catholic Church by my individual behaviour.*[26]

Fr Pike's attitude defines the classic Catholic position, stated throughout, of the need to demonstrate the Faith through good deeds and behaviour. He appeared to have succeeded in his objective when Major Hornby of 55 Division wrote to his General Hugh Jeudwine on 21 February 1915:

> I am writing a few lines, a liberty I trust you will forgive, in a semi-official way to ask your help. Fr Pike is doing simply splendid work. We could not have a better man and he hits it off simply splendidly with everybody. Everybody likes him, Catholics and non-Catholics alike … we do not want to lose Fr Pike … [could you] arrange for Fr Pike to stay with the artillery as it really would be a great pity

---

25 Concerns over materialism expressed in Leo XIII, *Rerum Novarum: The Workers Charter*.
26 *On Active Service* (Catholic Truth Society, undated), p. 7.

to lose him in view of all the good work he is doing and the way he gets on with all the artillery officers, none of whom are Catholics.[27]

Chaplains did encounter constraints in the area of military protocol and some Catholic bureaucracy, but they were not too tightly harnessed. When the Army requested secular duties of Catholic chaplains wily clergy deferred whilst calculating the consequences of non-compliance. Chaplains could not disobey legitimate orders from an Army authority, but they could and did challenge any order which contradicted agreed procedures over-arched by Kings Regulations, usually through Rawlinson. This included non-interference in Catholic services. For both parties the distance between Army orders and chaplaincy acquiescence was jealously protected by Rawlinson who succeeded in remaining diplomatically neutral throughout, quite an impressive balancing feat at times.

On occasions chaplains acted as stretcher bearers or prisoner escorts interpreting their responsibilities in accordance with their training and conscience. Fr Gillett reported that: 'German prisoners were made to do the heavy stretcher bearing and very keen to work, they work. Evidently they were glad to be out of the firing line. Took a prisoner down to a cage myself, to the amusement of overlookers'.[28] Gillett now with the stretcher bearers: 'Accompanied the MO's stretcher bearers to pick up the wounded, treatment and first aid'.[29] Similarly, assisting in the carrying of rations will follow demonstrating that these supportive manual activities, although of little practical help, were nonetheless meaningful gestures. They did not impinge on spiritual protocol and furthermore might create opportunities to supply spiritual comfort.

Intellectual assistance allowed Catholic chaplains' special talents, encouraged and developed in seminary, to be offered to good effect in assisting the Army. Linguistic skills were readily volunteered. Fr Prevost: 'I say Mass for the German prisoners and preach in German. I thought I could never do it but German has come back to me'.[30] Sometimes being an expert was not a requirement: 'Your knowledge of German will be useful in almost any sphere, even if it is only to point out to the enemy the way to the cages'.[31] Others seeking to volunteer were not needed: 'We have already quite a good supply of chaplains that have a really good knowledge of Italian'.[32] The benefit of a geographically extensive linguistic education has been mentioned but there were other areas where a priest's talents could help. Fr Gill, an eminent Cambridge

27 DAA, Ephemera. Major Newby to General Jeudewine. This is a unique document in the sense that it is the only army to army letter [not facsimile], in Rawlinson's files. How it got there and Rawlinson's response is not known.
28 SDA, Gillett Diaries, 17 February 1917.
29 Ibid., 12 September 1916.
30 DAA, 3235, Prevost to Rawlinson, 9 May 1917. Prevost, born in Switzerland, could speak both French and German.
31 DAA, 3235, Rawlinson to Scully, 2 February 1919.
32 DAA, 3234, Rawlinson to Darvell, 7 January 1918.

qualified scientist who had worked with Cavendish before the war in the field of physics, invented a signalling machine. This probably came too late: 'I enclose copy of GRO 5131 with regards to inventions, which may interest you. I do not know if anything further has taken place with regard to your suggestion for signals'.[33] The study of the sciences had been advancing rapidly in seminary education.

The Catholic chaplaincy group was also rich with men from educational backgrounds. Frs Baines, Gordon and O'Herlihy, for example, had been professors in either Diocesan or Religious order colleges.[34] In 1918 a radical plan was introduced by the Army called: 'The Educational Training Scheme' with two stated purposes. First was the moderately patronising aspiration: 'To give the men a wider view of their duties as citizens of the British Empire', the second a more practical purpose: 'To help men in their work after the war'.[35] These two ambitions encapsulate the contemporary mentality being at the same time pompous yet paternal. The clergy were quick to reciprocate with Fr Plater SJ promoting the scheme. He wrote to Rawlinson enlisting support. A few teacher's volunteered such as: Fr T Molloy, 7 years in English Literature, European History: Fr J Byrne-O'Connell, with 3 years' experience in Moral and Mental Science and Philosophy: Fr O Claeys, 10 years in Social Science: Fr A Johnston, a teacher and lecturer of 24 years specialising in 'Talks to Working Men, Labour Questions and Temperance': Fr W J Brown, 6 years teaching the 'Value of Education, Historical Geography, Citizenship, French, Labour Questions', who is a specialist in Catholic Social Guild subjects.[36]

It was anticipated that this part of the scheme would be an enterprise to support Fr Rawlinson's team of trusted men who would be influential in the implementation of English strategy. These tutors were instilled with Catholic social teaching and their co-operation with the authorities was welcomed. In return the authorities generally recognised that their chaplaincy mandate, based on tradition, morality, and effectiveness, required the distinction between the secular and spiritual to be respected.

Organisation and Structure

The Catholic chaplaincy organisation on the Western Front was dominated by Fr Bernard Stephen Rawlinson OSB. Moreover, he has left a substantial legacy in his papers allowing close inspection of his organisation, his chaplains, and of himself.

By the middle of 1915 when a dual structure of Army chaplaincy was created, with the established Church of England as one strand and the other denominations as

---

33   DAA, 3234, Rawlinson to Gill, 8 October 1918.
34   Baines from Liverpool Archdiocese was a Professor at Ushaw Seminary College, Gordon for the Glasgow Diocese, O'Herlihy a Professor and Cistercian monk at St. Joseph's College, Roscrea Abbey, Tipperary.
35   DAA, Ephemera. Published by British Army GHQ in France, 8 March 1918.
36   DAA, Ephemera, Plater to Rawlinson, 19 April 1918.

the other, the administration of Catholic chaplaincy became simpler. Each Division established 17 chaplains including one Senior Chaplain [SCF] with the rank of Major [CF3], the remainder with the rank of Captain [CF4] to be allotted proportionally by their religious composition. This meant that in Irish Divisions nine of the chaplains were Catholic, eight reserved for other denominations. In the rest of the British Army the reverse was true with the Catholic establishment securing four chaplains per Division out of the non-C of E allotment of 8.[37] The senior chaplain [SCF] was appointed by Dr Simms an Irish Presbyterian who had overall responsibility for all chaplains on non-religious matters, he prudently deferred to Rawlinson on Catholic matters and in effect rubber stamped Rawlinson's opinions and advice. Dr Simms also acted as liaison between the denominations and the War Office.

The arrangement for Corps troops differed slightly but appears to have met with the approval of Fr Gill SJ whose diary records:[38]

> Those chaplains with overall responsibilities for Corps troops became Deputy Assistant Principal Chaplains or DAPC's with the rank of Lieutenant Colonel [CF2] and were usually located in Corps Headquarters. They were required to liaise with SCF's for pastoral care when units of a Corps, for example labour or artillery, became attached to, or operated near, a Division(s). Assistant Principal Chaplains, APC's, were ranked Colonel [CF1] and allotted to each army. In the Catholic situation APC's were grounded at Base Hospitals and took on other duties such as assisting in the evaluation of newly arrived priests.

The head of the organisation in the field was the Principal Catholic Chaplain. In late 1915 the responsibility was transferred to Fr Bernard Rawlinson OSB, CMG, and OBE. He had served as a chaplain in the South African War being twice mentioned in dispatches. Arriving in France in September 1914 he joined 2 Battalion Royal Irish Regiment. Experiencing first-hand fighting at Le Cateau, Mons, the Marne, and the Aisne, he assisted the initial Principal Chaplain, Monsignor William Keatinge. When Keatinge sought to leave HQ to visit chaplains in the line it was Rawlinson who was entrusted with chaplaincy administration. Keatinge writing to Cardinal Bourne on 21 September confirmed his confidence in Rawlinson, comments which paved the way for Rawlinson to step up, simultaneously created opportunities for himself:

> I think everything in our department is satisfactory. The one thing we want is more chaplains, we are I believe about 27 short of our establishment. Rawlinson has written to Msgr Bidwell about this. He [Rawlinson] is excellent as assistant Principal Chaplain. He gets on perfectly well with Dr Simms, in fact the latter leaves practically everything to him. He works very hard, and even goes back

---

37 Appendix VI.
38 JAD, Fr H V Gill Diary 'Chaplains' 1917, p. 98.

to the office after dinner till about 10:30 or 11 … We have now a well organised office with trained clerks, telephone, short-hand writers etc. which is all controlled by Rawlinson.[39]

Rawlinson was promoted in Keatinge's place when the Monsignor was himself promoted to Brigadier-General and Principal Chaplain in Macedonia. Later, in 1918, Keatinge became the first official *Episcopus Castrensis* operating from London. Rawlinson was supported at GHQ by a brother Benedictine Father Stanislaus Young. Young was a quiet and understated deputy, an able administrator but unwilling or unable to make decisions whilst Rawlinson was absent, but overall a safe pair of hands and a man of amiable disposition.[40] He was supported by Fr Michael King SJ whose job was also quietly administrative. All three men had joined early in the war and demonstrated the calm assurance consistent with their earlier monastic/religious training, an essential component within the anger of war. At General Headquarters, Rawlinson as Colonel in the British Army skilfully applied social, religious, and military experiences to advantage in negotiations with various hierarchies. These talents assisted his missions broadly entailing the management and administration of a team of Catholic chaplains and through their endeavours the delivery of the celebration of the Sacraments and Mass to as many as possible; and the protection of Ecclesiastical ambition. Rawlinson understood how the British Army operated and used this knowledge to benefit both chaplains and bishops, repeatedly advising the best way to reach a resolution by the correct process, a 'tactful and tactical operator supreme'.[41]

Calculating the number of operational chaplains in the fluid and confused state that prevailed is beset with complications, but readers should not confuse estimation with sloth. Official figures can be proven to be erroneous and these 'facts' are unfortunately repeated and errors perpetuated.[42] Constant military movement, leave, illness, injury, or contract expiry, plus the volatility and confusion of redeployment on return, makes it impossible to establish with certainty accurate numbers, these were constantly shifting sands. As the war continued even Rawlinson only gave estimates. The best approximation is that there were about 700 priests overall who worked on the Western Front, with approximately 300-400 at any one time from 1916. They put their lives at risk and 22 died directly trying to satisfy this basic Catholic need and are buried in France or Belgium, with three dying as a result of injuries and sickness at home or on the way home.[43] One unfortunate chaplain Fr John McIlvaine from

---

39 DAA, Box 28 File 1, ref 28-2-14, Keatinge to Bourne, 21 September 1915.
40 Impressions gathered through his correspondence scattered throughout the Rawlinson Papers at DAA.
41 S. Bellis, 'The Rawlinson Papers', *The Downside Review*, Downside Abbey, vol. 459, (April 2012) pp. 1-25.
42 See Appendix I: Statistical Dilemmas.
43 34 died or were killed in the First World War but 22 are buried on the Western Front and five died on the way home or at home.

Glasgow drowned on 26 February 1918. He had been injured and gassed at Polygon Wood in early October 1917 with the Sherwood Foresters; he was returning to St Malo from Cardiff on the hospital ship *Glenart Castle* when it was torpedoed off the Cornish coast, aged 39. 155 of 186 crew, doctors, nurses and troops were killed. He is buried in Southampton. Meanwhile Fr McAuliffe, a Franciscan, died on the HMT *Viper* on 6 October 1916, aged 29 and is buried in Limerick.[44] It is sometimes reported that he died of sea sickness on the sea journey home to visit his sick mother, or died of the strain of the trenches, but it is more likely that his long-standing heart condition, which caused his heart to stop temporarily, had been triggered by sea sickness or anxiety. Fr Bergin MC, an Irish Jesuit from Tipperary, incurred wounds received from a shell at Passchendaele whilst attached to the Australian Army and died on 12 October 1917 aged 38. Other deaths will be reported retrospectively or as they happened from mid-1916 when our first diarist arrived in France.

Fr Rawlinson, building on the blueprint laid down by his predecessor Monsignor Keatinge, was tasked with managing the overall mission. Management included discipline. It will be shown that if a chaplain was reported by an officer or fellow chaplain for not maintaining the high, if at times hypocritical standards demanded, for example language or drinking outside the accepted levels of officer behaviour, he would be dealt with without compunction. Chaplains were sent home if they threatened to bring the name of their Church into disrepute. This complex issue will be enlarged later. It is sufficient at this juncture to recall that the hierarchy needed protection if post-war ambitions, dependent on demonstrating support for the war and good citizenship within it, were not to be jeopardised by bad behaviour from its priests. This reasoning especially applied to those priests exhibiting, or accused of exhibiting, political motivations or opinions. Irish priests were in the firing line in more than one sense as war dragged on. Rawlinson's unwavering, albeit sometimes heavy-handed enforcement is evident, but his judgement was remarkably adroit. Behind the bland façade of administration lay a resolve to deliver sacramental and pastoral care through his chaplains, but also a determination to manage the higher ecclesiastical expectations of his seniors, a position he had not been specifically groomed for pre-war but to which he intuitively and seamlessly adapted. Nonetheless, he was not without compassion and when feasible he acted in a benevolent but always prudent manner. Not a risk taker but neither a prevaricator, undoubtedly the right man for the job.

General Deployment

The broad-spectrum deployment of new and returning chaplains was framed by the exigencies of war. Suffice it to say that in the period 1916-1918 not only were there

---

44   HMT, Hired Military Transport, in this case troopship.

insufficient chaplains, Rawlinson claimed 100 chaplains short in 1918,[45] but existing chaplains were not always in the best condition. Rawlinson initially blooded chaplains in Base Hospitals as in Fr Gillett's situation. Others like Fr Steuart were shipped directly to the Front. Base hospitals had initially allowed the DAPC working there to provide an assessment as to the capabilities or otherwise of the new chaplain, information absorbed but not always acted upon by a shrewd and observant Rawlinson. Increasingly ailing health, injuries, resignations, and death took their toll, compelling him to deploy the fittest and most able to work with fighting troops, thereby, resting the aged, fatigued, and more nervous in Base Hospitals.

Once detailed to a unit Rawlinson relied on SCF's and his own observations gleamed from chaplaincy meetings and feedback, to fine-tune future deployments. On the whole he acted in an advisory and supervisory capacity, only intervening when the chaplain himself requested advice or if he had received an adverse external criticism. At that point he would take on an executive role, we will see how that operated later in the case of Fr Gillett in 1918.

When a chaplain served his men at war he did so in the manner determined by his vocation, priestly training and above all his *Discreta Caritas*.[46] Bishops, religious superiors and seminarians had laid the foundations but it was now the responsibility of Rawlinson and his chaplains to develop a successful organisation, their Sacred Duty. If Catholic men dying and being maimed in their thousands at the Front were denied the opportunity to reach a state of grace before death, or fear of death, for lack of Sacramental succour then such a lapse for any Catholic chaplain would be unthinkable, a denunciation of their *raison d'être*. Chaplains were now in place to do the best they could in the spiritual sense. How they coped will be discussed later but where did they function?

Chaplains Deployment in Battle

The pattern of a chaplain's physical involvement in open battle was a chequered one defined by pragmatism and commitment. An attempt to substitute reality with ephemeral or romantic human qualities is fraught with danger, largely irrelevant, and should be resisted. Measuring bravery is speculative, subjective, and precarious; heroes and villains belong to other genres which too often impinge on chaplaincy history. With the exception of the French, chaplains were unarmed volunteers. Undoubtedly some were more physically and mentally able than others, some more reckless or determined depending on opinion, others had greater expectations to satisfy, notwithstanding

---

45   A purely Catholic problem caused by shortages of volunteers. The Army had allocated and honoured the establishment generously.
46   *Discreta Caritas*, Falling in Love with God – a Jesuit tradition ideally applicable to all Catholics.

differences, all chaplains were in danger of one sort or another and could only be classed as courageous, even those who subsequently wilted under pressure.[47]

Idealised visions of chaplains ministering to the dying in no-man's land rightly draws on our compassion and empathy, but if we are to study all chaplains and not the few, we need to understand that the majority of chaplains were deployed and died at medical facilities on or close to the action. These provided the potential to minister to one's own returning injured troops, stray Catholics, Corps troops, and others. Resources were always stretched, it was prudent, therefore, to deploy scarce resources for those units with few Catholics in the most effective way. The rules of engagement for Catholic chaplains were not formerly issued; it was up to the chaplain concerned, his SCF, and his common sense to act in the most effective manner. Having being allocated his military unit by GHQ, he was to a large extent left to his own devices.

How best to satisfy the troops demands? Over and above organisational formalities, the decision making influences which defined a chaplain's final location and *modus operandi* consisted of two components. First, there was a direct correlation between where chaplains ministered in the field during action, and the strength of Catholic numbers in their military unit. At the start of the war, for example, with the exception of a minority in the 36 Ulster Division, Irish regiments were comprised almost exclusively of Catholics.[48] Some English and Scottish units contained a reasonable amount, particularly Lancashire regiments, but others very few. Chaplains wanted to support as many souls as possible. Failure to have sufficient Catholics with which to minister pushed many for a move to units with Irish or Lancashire troops. Fr Philip Devas, a young Franciscan priest aged 29, is typical.[49] Attached to the 1/6 Gloucester Regiment with a moderate amount of Catholics he pleaded: 'I should like if possible – I suppose we are all wanting the same thing – to be transferred to some Lancashire or Irish unit where I should find some Catholics and so have more directly religious work'.[50]

The second component was defined by the troops own beliefs, hopes, and degree of religious immersion developed in their own domestic communities. Large Catholic communities at home exported through their sons a high degree of religious practice and respect for their priest, and in return had high expectations and a sense of obligation from the clergy. Put simply: soldiers, families, and congregations anticipated that their chaplain would fulfil the same role as parish priest at home, especially if in mortal danger. They also expected their sons to actively continue with their Faith. As a consequence this commonality of desire resulted in a higher proportion of front

---

47 Chaplains were not alone. Many other non-combatants such as nurses, doctors, veterinarians, civilians, and others included.
48 Deaths meant that replacements were eventually filled at random, irrespective of religion or geography in all regiments. The notion of the 36 Ulster as Protestant, and 16 Irish as Catholic Divisions became in reality irrelevant demarcations, if not in memory.
49 His two other CF brothers were Francis SJ and Raymond OP.
50 DAA, 3234, Devas to Rawlinson, 16th November 1916.

line casualties among chaplains whilst accompanying Irish or Lancashire regiments. Chaplains repeatedly praised Lancashire or Irish units. Fr Page SJ observed: 'The men, as a rule responded, especially those from Lancashire. They were easily the most satisfactory of all I had to deal with'.[51] Further, Plater quotes an anonymous chaplain:

> 99 out of a 100 Irish would explain correctly Immaculate Conception, difference between Resurrection and Ascension, who was Pontius Pilate, how do you baptize – in fact anything. The English often don't know these things, or say they don't, not being sure. I except Lancashire men, who equal Irish in all aspects, and exceed them in Apostolic zeal. Lancashire's are always bringing up lapsed Catholics or try to convert Protestants. Lancashire men have no shame.[52]

The association of soldier with chaplain derived from both above components helped to overcome a major deployment decision: which is the best place to be so that I can identify my men? It was not feasible to enquire as to the soldier's religion in combat, neither soldiers nor chaplains were allowed visible external identification by denomination, although if conditions allowed religious identification might be established within their tunics in pay books or correspondence. Common sense prevailed. With a high Catholic troop count it would make sense to accompany the advancing fighting men. It follows that in a unit with a strong Catholic presence he would know most of the soldiers and officers by sight having seen them at Mass, Communion, and the other Sacraments and Devotions. In the heat of battle, amid the confusion and danger, he would be more able to identify and tend to a Catholic that he recognised through familiarity. Conversely, in units with few Catholic soldiers, a chaplain would be unable to make effective use of his time and would revert to an aid station during battle. From there the chaplain might temporarily divert from the fighting to minister to men identified by a fellow soldier, often a non-Catholic.

The roles of chaplain's in Base Hospitals, Casualty Clearing Stations, and Advanced Dressing Posts will be briefly explored when individual deaths are reported or when our diarists participate in these deployments. The great majority of chaplain's engagement, inside and behind the battle zone, was to attach themselves to medical units. As Gillett and Steuart were attached to fighting units it is their experiences as Divisional chaplains which will be considered. Whether in close support or in the line, danger was a regular and unwelcome visitor whose indiscriminate behaviour defies any attempt to apportion courage by location.

---

51 DAA, Ephemera – War History Material 103-1085, Page to Rawlinson. This is a post-war report in the archive. Page had an interesting chaplaincy career, ending up as he says: 'the first Jesuit to set foot in Russia since the banishment of Jesuits'.
52 Plater, *Catholic Soldiers*, p. 36.

4

Conditions at the Front: 'Not the Kind of Life to Select as an Amusement But there will be plenty to do'

Fr Gill campaigned for Front Line work shortly after arriving in France, beginning his tasks in late November. The above wry comment to his religious superior in Ireland proved to be remarkably perceptive.[1] Was he aware of the dangers ahead or would the reality be far worse? Gill was an early arrival in November 1914 at a time when many rushed to join imagining the war to be over by Christmas. It is probable that he had little real conception of what lay ahead, in spite of this he caught on quickly as his comment to his religious superior in early December of that year testifies. Other chaplains also appear to have been relatively naive when they first arrived as Fr Gillett in particular will demonstrate. The Front, whether in Picardy, Artois, or Flanders had a penchant for delivering rude awakenings and this is clearly Gill's experience [and later our diarists, Gillett and Steuart's too]. Suitably deployed and ready for action, what would chaplains face at the Front? This chapter will give an overview of the conditions which impinged on their ability to remain safe, sane, and able to fulfil their missions. Pay, billeting, food, routine, transport, and leave will be explored as a whole, and in later chapters re-introduced when appropriate to individual experience. When things went wrong health suffered, both physical and mental. It was far from being an amusement as fitness and suitability became stretched to the limit as the war dragged on, successive years adding further layers of violence and stress for the fighting men, and their chaplains. The effects on chaplaincy numbers is examined as the vice became ever and ever tighter; the demands of the job tested even the hale and hearty to the limit.

Contracts and Pay

Chaplains volunteered to be attached to, and not part of the British Army. Contracts were usually renewed annually, sometimes bi-annually and for the earlier and more

---

1   JAD, Gill Papers, Gill to Provincial, 5 December 1914.

optimistic intake 'for the duration'. Some, such as Fr Gleeson of the Munsters after resigning their commissions were enticed back from retirement because the mutual bond created with their men had remained resilient. A few chaplains did not complete their commissions due to ill health or for disciplinary reasons. Those that did fulfil the original term occasionally attempted to bargain their re-signatures, stipulating conditions such as a transfer to another unit or special leave. Rawlinson responded to them politely but without submission or much sympathy. His hands were tied since the best endeavours of his prelates failed to produce sufficient volunteer chaplains. The Army were generous in its establishment and yet by 1918, Rawlinson campaigning for more men claimed a shortfall of over 100 Catholic chaplains. The great seminaries had their work cut out meeting the demands of the rapidly expanding domestic congregations alone, and such was the extent of the long education process for priesthood the system could not be rapidly adapted, nor indeed were there any such suggestions.[2] They did, whenever practicable assist by allowing seminary novices to replace priests. In theory this created more chaplaincy volunteers but had little practical impact.

The rank of a chaplain was Captain Class 4 [CF4]. Pay was 10 shillings a day [later rising to 10/6d] compared to a veterinarian Captain's 15/6d. Promotion to a Major was possible for a Divisional Senior Chaplain, usually an honoury appointment without the other trappings of office [CF3]. They also received allowances to be drawn against the Mess of the military unit with which they were serving. Fr Steuart made a note of his monthly allowances: 'Field allowance 3/6d, lodging 3/-, fuel and light 8d June to September, 1/5d October to May'. Fr Rawlinson as Principal Catholic Chaplain was ranked Colonel. Each chaplain was allotted a servant and it was customary for chaplains to supplement their servants pay by a small daily gratuity of a shilling a day. Not all followed suit, Fr Mulhall SJ was accused by fellow officers as being tight-fisted with money, not sharing in Mess expenses and not tipping his servant. His retort that Jesuits do not have their own money was factual but misleading – other Jesuits paid their way and gave the balance to their Order.[3] Financial rewards with the Army compared favourably to the stipend a priest received back home. This caused some anxiety when the war was over as Fr O'Herlihy's case demonstrates. He had been retained as a temporary CF but by 1921 became anxious to become a permanent chaplain. He received support by Rev G Standing DSO, MC, CF, also from the Colonel of the Dublin's. Standing wrote to Monk at the War Office:

> I am writing in a friendly, unofficial way re my old friend Fr O'Herlihy. He tells me he is to be demobilised. I am wondering whether you can influence the powers that be in any way. O'Herlihy is a first rate chaplain. If he leaves it means

---

2   Irish seminaries for example had closed their books on new recruits they were oversubscribed ref Kenny, Goodbye to Catholic Ireland, Chapter 5 Ireland's Spiritual Empire.
3   Bellis, 'Catholic Chaplains', p. 163.

getting a parish and a very small salary [£30 pa]. The Colonel of the Dublin's is writing to Bishop Keatinge ... I know this is all irregular but you will regard it as a friendly confidential letter.[4]

O'Herlihy, a pre-war professor at St Joseph's College Roscrea, Tipperary, certainly had friends in high places. Yet it was to no avail and Monk politely but firmly declined the offer.[5]

Composition – Types, Ages, Vigour, Motives

Chaplains arriving on France's shores were a reflection of priests in Britain. Those from inner-city and rural parishes worked alongside priests returning from overseas missions. Those from religious orders rubbed shoulders with diocesan in the common mission of chaplaincy.[6] The range of former occupations from evangelical, educational, monastic, scientific, social, day-to-day parish work and more, was a direct reflection of the work of the Church. In over-simplified terms the bulk of parish work was completed by diocesan priests supplemented by the religious orders, and in reverse the bulk of missionary work by the religious orders with the help of their diocesan colleagues. These assignments were determined by the bishops with due deference given to the different charisma associated with each religious order. At the Front all had the same mission, and despite their differences in earlier life, shared the same conditions in which to practice their chaplaincy.

Chaplain's starting ages at war varied from 26 to 61. Fr Donal Vincent O'Sullivan was the youngest to die aged 26. A typical chaplain was 35-40 years of age, between five foot five and five foot seven inches tall [1.65 – 1.7 metres] and weighing around 150-170 pounds [68-77 kg].[7] They began in sound health as their army medical certificates testify, but how much the pressures of war recruitment dictated certification will never be known, there is evidence of pre-war illness re-emerging on the job. Many suffered from the rigours of war. Violence, death, injury, and fear, combined with the extremes of outdoor weather bringing mud, filth, and insanitary conditions, created an alien environment for chaplains, many of whom had enjoyed a simple and relatively commonplace former life. Rats, lice, and unreliable food aggravated the periods between intense danger and boringly repetitive routine. Some died, those who fell sick or were injured were further discomforted by ad hoc billeting arrangements. Their states of health, whether mental or physical, usually went unrecorded unless they corresponded with Rawlinson or became under official military medical

---

4 PRO WO, 374/51233.
5 Op.cit.
6 Diocesan or Secular priests.
7 These are computed average figures from individual records available at PRO and are representative only. Fr Whiteford for example was 6 feet 1 inch (1.85 metres) tall.

care. The life was hard and physically demanding, especially for chaplains attached to fighting units. Marches were frequent and exasperated many a good-hearted cleric. Fr Arthur Allchin SJ, the oldest chaplain at the Front, attached to 8 East Lancashire's wrote from Hazebrouck for help to overcome his dilemma. Determined to attend a chaplain's meeting with Rawlinson he implored: 'Will you send a car for me? I have no means of transport and I have marched with the regiment (my age is 61) for two days. If I walk to St. Omer [GHQ at this time, some 15 miles distant] and back I shall hardly be fit for the next advance.'[8] Note these are not complaints nor are they defeatist: he simply needed some physical support which in due course was supplied.

In spite of difficulties, it was for many the best period of their lives. Fr Steuart wrote in his diary 15 November 1919 after being demobbed: 'I feel terribly out of it and dull. It has been a good time, the like of which I shall never see again! *Ave atque vale!*' Some priests thrived on the physical aspects of army life, a SCF commented that: 'Fr Galvin will come back from leave like a giant refreshed and continue his excellent work with 90th Brigade'.[9] Spiritual duty and a sense of mission were their overriding motivation, but they were also human. Some enjoyed the pay of £182 per annum far in excess of their minimal stipendiaries at home, although many of the religious orders forfeited their pay to their order in line with tradition. Some liked the uniform, others the medals, some the change of scene, others adventure. Travel and cultural awareness appealed to some as did the relative freedom from constant supervision of religious seniors or the constant gaze of inquisitive domestic congregations. Although personal motivations reflect the range of personality in the field, they all gave the impression of gratification through fulfilling their spiritual mission. In other words what they lived through were unique experiences for each and every chaplain whilst maintaining a remarkable spiritual consistency. As ever the exception proves the rule: but even those shown to have failed in the corporal sense invariably upheld their spiritual commitments.

Billeting and Sustenance

The exigencies of war meant billeting arrangements were inevitably ad hoc. Chaplains sought a billet near their attachment, thereby establishing a physical presence and connectivity with men and officers. As officers they billeted with those of similar rank, usually the Medical Officer, but often alone. They tried to live in proximity with the troops, appreciating the benefits that acquaintance would bring especially with identification. Billets ranged from chateau, convent, or hotel when fortunate: to bivouacs, wayside transport trucks, and ruined houses or dirty farm buildings, with the ever presence of rats, as the norm. Fr Steuart used to a more gentlemanly

---

8   DAA, 3234 V11 A 3f 7611-8418 Friday 6 August (no year given but probably 1917).
9   DAA, 3824 O'Shaughnessy to Rawlinson, (undated but likely to be January 1918).

existence sought comfort whenever the possibility arose, improving his accommodation wherever possible, generously so on leave. This applied to food too, but who could deny him some creature comforts which in any event were few and far between? Fr Steuart as a Jesuit voluntarily agreed to submit any wealth to the Society of Jesus and he testified regularly in his diary to redirecting his pay Mount Street, HQ of the English Province. Letters from home suggest he funded any personal expenditure from friends and family. He realised that accepting Mess duties would give him certain social advantages but the joy he expressed when he managed to obtain favoured private accommodation or refreshment knew no bounds: 'Dined with MO, Cox & Campbell, at the Hotel du Commerce. Had two bottles of Veuve Chequot (at 24 francs apiece).'[10] His continental hotel list was matched by his inventory of English hotels on leave: Charing Cross, Euston, Brown's, Belgravia Mansions, Grand, and Rubens in Buckingham Palace road. We should remember that Belgravia was his home base in peace. His dining provided lavish and important respites, restoring his spirits and confirming his pre-war privileged status within higher officer circles. There is nothing inherently wrong with his conduct but does make for interesting comparison with many other chaplains. He also had discomfort to endure to varying degrees: '9 Jan 1919 – Our first meal since 8:30 am, except for a tin of tripe, which we picked up near Becourt but which I couldn't touch', and: '12th April 1917 – Walked over old Boche lines and arrived at Arras about 7. Muddle about billets, MO and I went to the Hotel de Commerce but could only get biscuits and wine. Found HQ Ingoyghem, arriving about 3 p.m. Wretched billets. Houston, Nelson, Callan, the Doc and I slept on the floor of the Mess. Very cold.' Earlier in the war on 5 November 1916 he noted: 'Moved out to Henencourt. Camped in a wood with Mr Gardiner in a tent. Rats running all over us all night'. This was not an isolated incident.

Fr Gillett also enjoyed the odd stay in a hotel or fine meal, but these were circumspect and uncommon events. Usually his demands were humble confirming in his down-to-earth Lancastrian heritage including a 'gradely meal' in Lourdes and: '… had to put up in Paris – in station subway specially arranged for our British soldiers under the YMCA. Had all my kit pinched there'.[11] Fr Gillett mostly ate on his own or with fellow chaplains whenever he could, sometimes a Curé or an interpreter, entirely consistent with his preferred social circle. There was one exception: 'Mass – dined with Captain Bourgeois, a French officer. Some dinner in best French style.'[12] He too could handle the rough conditions: '7:40 a.m. left Boulogne for the line. 8:45 arrived at Étaples in company of Fr Prescott. Secured some grub and drink at the station. We were roommates in a very filthy farm house – phaw!'[13]

10   JAL, Steuart Diaries, 16 December 1917.
11   SDA, Gillett Diaries, 8 February 1919.
12   SDA, Gillett Diaries, 4 September 1916.
13   SDA, Gillett Diaries, 6 September 1916.

Gillett was not alone in his suffering and showed great compassion for the troops who were having a tougher time:

> Mass at 8 a.m. Troops being relieved today – battle deferred owing to the wet. What a place Albert is and what holes the poor men have to billet in – no windows of course in any houses and you can imagine then how snug it will be – and no fires – well you must do the best you can. Walls are tumbling down and it is as much as one can do to find a place with shelter. The floor has to be our beds and what with the rats and dirt it is not conducive to a good night and to add to all this misery the rain coming down in torrents. Albert too was in easy range of German guns and we knew it. He was constantly firing into the station to smash up the line.'[14]

Inevitably, inexperienced chaplains were disadvantaged but they soon learnt to fend for themselves. On arriving in France, Fr Jim Leeson no stranger to a hard life from a working class background in Liverpool dockland, wrote to Keatinge for clarification:

> I have marched with the Battalion from England [13 Royal Fusiliers] and have been left by the roadside until everyone has been fixed up. On another occasion I was left to find whatever dinner I could on the march and that consisted of some bread (for which I begged) and some water. I do not mind roughing it but I feel I must keep up my position as Catholic chaplain. I simply ask for a clear statement of facts.[15]

Fr Leeson, attached to a regular battalion had to earn his spurs the hard way.[16] As we will discover, he admirably rose to the occasion winning everyone over by his courage in action.

Transport

Transport was the bane of a chaplain's life. Both Gillett and Steuart in common with the majority of chaplains could ride a horse and a bicycle: but these two diarists could also ride a motorbike and drive a car. It mattered little. Such mechanical aides were not available until late 1919 and then of a dubious nature. It was horses, or rather their removal that drove chaplains to despair. Setting aside enemy action, much of the pain of war at the Front was simply moving about, traversing shell-pocked roads was often

---

14   SDA, Gillett Diaries, 25 October 1916.
15   DAA, Leeson to Keatinge, 20 August 1915.
16   Fr Jim Leeson's father was a labourer. They lived in dockland Litherland. 1911 Census and Phillips 1911 Street Maps of Liverpool.

nigh impossible. Bombing, shelling, mud, and mass movements of men and materiel had damaged or destroyed France's fragile pre-war infrastructure. Characterised by small lanes and railways following tortuous routes through a jumble of intercessions, it had evolved to transport agriculture between towns and villages. True there were long Romanesque type poplar tree-lined road but those within the Western Front were soon reduced to wilderness, as was the main railway system between towns if it became within range of the guns. Original transport systems had a very limited lifespan. Consequently, much of Britain's resources were spent repairing existing roads and railways or else laying new, the advent of smaller scale railways became vital to the movement of troops, stores, and ammunition. Chinese labourers became an invaluable support system, not only in labour but skilled repairs and maintenance of locomotives, tanks and other military apparatus.

In this wilderness, interspersed by stretches of open landscape, the preferred or necessary tool for chaplains' to do their job effectively was the horse. Regrettably, horses were also dying in their thousands and replacements took time to train and transport. Chaplains were not amongst those considered neediest by the authorities. 1917 witnessed a chronic horse shortage. The French resorted to employing elephants at Verdun from its colonies in Africa and Indochina. In England the Thomas Ward steelworks in Sheffield built elephant houses to accommodate Indian elephants whose purpose was to haul steel through the Sheffield streets, camels were employed too freeing desperately needed horses for the Front. The Empire may not have been world-wide but it certainly was large enough and convenient.

How would chaplains be able to meet their men for services? Many chaplains fearing an inability to do their job grumbled or threatened not to re-sign their commissions. The correspondence on this subject is extensive.[17] Nevertheless, most chaplains worked their way around it by borrowing another officer's horse and even on occasions persuading Commanding Officers to have their chauffeurs drive them to and from services. Favours could be cashed in: unsurprisingly Fr Oddie had not accumulated sufficient credit in this regard! Horses allowed chaplains the manoeuvrability demanded by the job. SCF's were begging for horses for their chaplains: 'Fr Fitzpatrick has about 340 Catholics scattered around to look after, he seems very willing but having no horse finds it difficult to get around.'[18] The list of enquiry was sometimes polite and mildly humorous: 'I suppose there is little likelihood of our horses being returned as the shortages will increase now that the cavalry is going into action, the army bicycle is a wicked invention, they are terrible things to ride.'[19] Rawlinson replied that: 'The chaplains were by no means the only ones that have lost their horses, many more will lose them yet, no doubt to their surprise and annoyance.'[20] This was the

---

17   116 letters in Rawlinson's Papers mentioned this problem.
18   DAA, Steuart to Rawlinson, 20 January 1916.
19   DAA, McCliment to Rawlinson, 28 April 1917.
20   DAA, Rawlinson to McCliment, 1 May 1917.

understatement of the war as far as chaplaincy was concerned. Frustration replaced politeness. Fr Kelly protested that Fr Cooney has not extended his contract and is returning home and implied that this was due to his horse being taken, he continued: 'My contract with the War Office guarantees me the use of a horse if necessary; there is no doubt of such a necessity to do even a portion of my work in the Brigade and other units.'[21] It is worth noting that these comments are made by SCF's and will almost certainly be a dilution of the ordinary chaplain's comments. Fr Rawlinson placated, used humour, and explained that the chronic shortages were legitimate, but I expect his own transport of Daimler-Benz limousine hardly assuaged annoyance. Fr Oddie employed his usual style of rhetoric to the Principal Chaplain: 'At the present moment I am in a state of furious white heat about the horse question. It is really a most scandalous breach of faith on the part of the army, and the absurd excuse of a shortage of horses is ridiculous on the face of it in view of the number of *unnecessary people* who have *unnecessary horses*'.[22] [Author's italics]

We might imagine to whom he was referring to as unnecessary people. Others sought more positive outcomes. Fr Prevost tried to circumvent the horse shortage by enquiring if he could bring his own horse to France any response was not recorded.[23] On the same day that Fr Oddie was whingeing, Fr Steuart borrowed his Adjutant's horse, Fr Drinkwater for an extended period borrowed his CO's horse, whilst Fr Gillett preferred to provide his own alternative transport: 'Bicycled all over the place to arrange Masses some job, considering how scattered we all are'.[24] The strength of feeling was high but goodwill and humour lightened the load. When all else failed, Fr Brookfield employed his own brand of sardonic humour:

> I have just returned from leave. I am sick of life. I am sick of this old bloody war. My grumpiness is aggravated by the loss of my horse. And moreover to pile on the agony I have spent much money on 1) spurs 2) a snaffle and curb and 3) a riding stick; I have been presented with a bicycle, mind you a "push-bike" weighing some 100 tons. Would it be possible to exchange it for a sewing machine, which would be more useful.[25]

This was not a singularly Catholic issue. Fr Brookfield's humour can be seen in similar vein by an anonymous chaplain who sent this clipping from the *London Opinion* 12 February 1916, before the shortage. A sense of injustice already existed within the entire Chaplains Department even though humour placated army excesses.

Both diarists mentioned riding for both social and professional purposes, but proffered no details of their horses suggesting that they were predominantly tools for the

21 DAA, Fr J M Kelly to Rawlinson, 29 March 1917.
22 DAA, Oddie to Rawlinson, 18 May 1917. Author's italics.
23 DAA, Prevost to Young, 1 May 1917.
24 SDA, Gillett Diaries, 17 July 1917.
25 DAA, Brookfield to Rawlinson, 30 September 1917.

A Chaplain's Horse. 'E' spends all 'es time between 'oppin up to 'eaven and poppin darn on e's knees, sir'. 'Very well: get another – and give this one – with my compliments – to the Chaplain'. (DAA, Ephemera. *London Opinion*, 12 February 1916)

job. Like others they reverted to walking and begging lifts on all manner of vehicles. Some respite came later on 26 August 1917 when the Army issued PC 94/15 easing the horse shortage, allowing 2 horses for HQ Corps and Divisional HQ chaplains.

The Army substituted the ubiquitous bicycle. They were used by chaplains in much the same fashion as their horses, but without the same effectiveness. Motorcycles were rarely utilised being scarce and utterly unreliable. Steuart borrowed a motorbike as late as 1919 but it was continually breaking down. Fr Gillett fared worse, he was: 'rolled over by a motorcycle in all the mud and dirt' on 30 October 1916, and on: 'Mon 25th August 1919. Mass – went to Amiens to secure (at last) the long promised transport for chaplains – a broken down motor byke [sic].' Fr Gill did have a motor 'byke' but it was captured by the Germans whilst under repair on 29 May 1918.[26] Even Colonel Rawlinson would have his transport issues: 'Herewith Private Caruthers with Vauxhall no 59292 is sent in exchange for Daimler 1739.'[27] Here Rawlinson poses with his car despite the numbers not tallying.

26   JAD, CHP1/25 (70).
27   DAA, Transport to Rawlinson, 28 May 1919.

Rawlinson and Staff Car. (DAA, Ephemera)

Leave – Rail and Sea Transport

Leave was critical for morale and recuperation, yet getting away and back could easily occupy two days each way out of the usual 14 day entitlement. Chaplain's needed to organise a lift to the railhead, find room in a dilapidated carriage and then encounter a sea journey with sickness, mines, and torpedoes as unwelcome companions. The interlude between entraining in France and sailing for England usually necessitated an overnight stay in Boulogne or Calais Fr Steuart: 'Mon 14 January 1918. Left Arras at 3:45 by civilian train. Arrived at Étaples at 8, dinner at club: left at 9:45 arrived at Boulogne about 11. Slept at Louvre Hotel: a bed on the floor of a bathroom.' Dangers in sea travel between France and England abounded and the next day Steuart's boat was escorted by three destroyers: 'Left Boulogne by 9:30 boat. Very rough passage, took over three hours. Heard afterwards that we missed a floating mine by a few yards. Arrived in London about 4 p.m.'. It has been noted that Fr McIlvaine returning from sick leave was killed when his hospital ship was torpedoed and sunk off Cornwall. The onward train journey home was invariably via London. In Fr Steuart's case he travelled north to Perthshire often breaking the journey with visits to family and friends in Ryde or London.

The distance between Boulogne and Amiens is 78 miles and today would take one hour and twenty minutes, then it could take the best part of 2 days.[28] Amiens railhead was the southernmost British point on this sector and many troops and chaplains would entrain there on leave and return to resume their responsibilities. Chronic train shortages and unreliability extended the journey time for many hours. Conditions were miserable for middle-aged men returning after a short-lived leave. 17 May 1917: '[Steuart] Left Boulogne at 7:30. Changed at Étaples and St Pol. Arrived Frevent about 2 p.m. Train halted for indefinite time on account of breakdown in front.

---

28 <www.distance-calculator.co.uk/distances-for-folkestone-to-albert-amiens> (Accessed 12 April 2014).

Caught motor lorry just into Arras. Heard that Brigade at Barly. Had to spend the night at Hotel du Commerce. Shelling through the night.' Steuart again: 'Fri 10th August 1917. Left Calais at 10 arrived 11 [Boulogne]. Train so full that I had to travel in guards van'.

The same frustrations applied when chaplains attempted to accompany their military units. Fr Gillett described the lack of direct connection going north from Albert by a circuitous route on his way to Guarbecque, Pas de Calais: 'Tues 27th March 1917. 6 a.m. moving off for rail head when there – hung up for hours. Get going about 10:30 a.m. – all day and all night in train – some travelling I guess. Pass through Amiens, Abbeville, Boulogne, Calais, St Omer and Hazebrouck. Get stranded at Hazebrouck but picked them up again by the next train through which happened to be the RAMC train.' Sometimes the train was used as a temporary dormitory coming to the aid of an exhausted Gillett but not without its dangers: 'Tues 16th October 1917. Tramping, tramping, tramping, so weary at last jumped into a goods train and snatched a little sleep, and woke up just to find the train about to clear off, so jumped out and cleared off to Ypres.'

Health – 'Crocks' and Recruitment

Chaplaincy recruitment had been a continual headache for Rawlinson since 1915 and the shortage of fit chaplains accelerated without abatement. Health issues increased anxieties at HQ, including returnees who had been evacuated for one reason or another and were now willing but not up to the task. Rawlinson expressed these doubts in no uncertain manner to the War Office: 'In the circumstances I do not want the Reverend J Coghlan back on the front. I have had enough of "crocks" lately to put me off any more, and he evidently would not be fit for front-line work.' Overriding the shortage of chaplains, Rawlinson's concern was the nature of the work which would quickly test their physical and mental capabilities. With lessons learned he re-evaluated their competency and stamina to deliver. On leave in Dublin Fr Coghlan contracted a severe bout of flu which took him longer to overcome than anticipated, which Rawlinson noted. On his return, in early 1917 he was injured in the left arm by shrapnel which necessitated his removal to Rouen before being repatriated to Ireland. He slowly recovered and was passed fit for general service. Not as far as Rawlinson's was concerned. His frustration spilled over: 'his wounds had left his arm in a very weak and deformed condition. I answered in the negative ... The machinery is always clogged up with men who are either too old or unfit for one reason or another for Divisional work, and it is of course from this quarter that the casualties come.'[29]

'Crocks' might include those of an anxious disposition. Fr Crisp a Salford priest born in Leicester, displayed a nervous unsuitability and in doing so revealed the

---

29   DAA, Rawlinson to Fr Dey DSO (assisting administration in London) 20 June 1918.

inadequacy of chaplaincy vetting. As soon as he arrived at his unit he bemoaned his physical ailments and revealed his mental anxieties: 'Since leaving Boulogne I have suffered from lumbago very much. I shall soon be unfit for anything shortly. On my arrival here I finished up under canvas which suddenly brought back my lumbago. I am also labouring under a severe cold. Besides I am feeling most depressed having no priests about.'[30] Fr Rawlinson was also working under great stress and his reply was classic Rawlinson. On the one hand he left the door open for an edgy or self-contained priest to find his feet and on the other left Fr Crisp under no illusion as to his responsibilities as a Catholic chaplain: 'My advice would be to throw yourself into your work, with the knowledge that you are badly needed out here, and many are dependent on you for the spiritual and physical betterment, in this way we can forget self and only think of others.'[31] Rawlinson needed to make a stand but his advice did not bear fruit. In January 1918 he conceded defeat in Crisp's case, informing Monk at the War Office: 'I have just received contract forms signed by him [Crisp]. He is of little or no use to me. I do not consider him to be an efficient chaplain.'[32]

Fr Crisp lasted only a year and even the affable Fr Gillett was to remark: 'Caught in hospital in a bombardment. Sweat all over and glad to get away. Poor Crisp didn't quite relish it.'[33] Fr Crisp, like others, was not cut out to be a chaplain at the Front, the omission of a thorough chaplaincy screening process at home had failed him. His work at 17 CCS was satisfactory but chaplains had to be prepared to work with the fighting men in action. Despite Rawlinson's equanimity towards all chaplains the pressure to recruit had to be balanced by too many failures in selection resulting in too many 'crocks'. Within two months Fr Crisp was at home as a priest in the Salford Diocese. He died in 1957, clearly not a physical crock for normal priestly duties, and more likely from Gillett's witness, to have been of a nervous disposition. Curiously in the Census of 1911 Fr Crisp's father was listed as an Army Sergeant Instructor of Volunteers.

Rawlinson adopted an uncompromising line on 'crocks' who were unable to continue effectively, but he had a war to manage and needed to suppress any personal empathy. His arguments were both quantitative and qualitative. First he felt he was being given unfit chaplains purely to satisfy quota, [which in any case never happened], thereby exposing the underlying ineffectiveness of the recruitment system. Secondly, the evolving mobile nature of war intensified and casualty rates increased as a result, this in turn demanded fitter and more robust chaplains. He was concerned both for the returning damaged chaplain's well-being and the plight of the troops. He was caught in the jaws of a vice receiving a shortfall in new recruit numbers whilst being pressurised to accept damaged and therefore less operationally effective personnel. Consistent

30 DAA, A100 Crisp to Rawlinson, 26 January 1917.
31 DAA, Rawlinson to Crisp, 29 January 1917.
32 DAA, Rawlinson to Monk, 17 January 1918.
33 SDA, Gillett Diaries, 14 July 1917.

campaigning for more chaplains failed to overcome the inadequate response from the Catholic community at large, exacerbated by the political situation in Ireland, and the failure of conscription for priests which he supported. These factors all impacted chaplaincy numbers and increased his frustration. Meanwhile, the German Spring Offensive in 1918 further depleted his team through captures and death. He knew that with more resource so much more could be achieved and battled hard with his own authorities for more men. His correspondence reveals his inner feelings of weariness and torment, but he concealed his angst from public view and particularly fellow chaplains. Despite the dark days of 1918, as a consummate politician he managed to maintain the good name of Catholic chaplaincy in its wider sense, failures to do so might unsettle that perception. If chaplains experienced the officer and priest dilemma, then Rawlinson had the added burden of politician.

Whilst Bernard Rawlinson protested to the War Office of 'crocks' he did not extend that epithet to himself. Even so he was hospitalised on at least four occasions between 1917 and 1919. His correspondence reveals he continued his appetite for work even from his hospital bed defusing any criticism of being a crock himself. In October 1917: 'Laid up with bronchitis and in hospital for a week.'[34] Fr Sandiford suggests it was longer, he wrote to Rawlinson in January 1918 that: 'I am very sorry to hear that you have been in hospital and for such a lengthy spell'.[35] 1918 was evidently not a good year for Rawlinson's health but his spirit remained indomitable, writing on 18 May to Fr Stack:

> I am, unfortunately, in hospital, where I have been for a week having being poisoned.[36] I most fully understand you're not being fully satisfied with the conditions as they are ... As far as I can read between the lines, you have not asserted yourself sufficiently. I would just like to see the gentleman who woke you up to pull off his boots. I would certainly let him have my boots somewhere.[37]

His spirits were high but his sense of irony was soon to be tested when five days later he was getting a taste of his own medicine. Mr Monk at the War office refused to take Fr Sproule, one of Rawlinson's 'crocks' for home duty: 'There is no vacancy at the moment in which we can absorb him and I fear we are likely for some time to have more than enough "crocks", for our needs here.'[38] This was a rare but subtle slap on the wrists from a man with whom he had shared a cordial and professional relationship. Finally, in September 1919 he was again hospitalised 'for some days with this

---

34 DAA, Rawlinson to Harding, *Universe Newspaper*, 12 October 1917.
35 DAA, Sandiford to Rawlinson, 14 January 1918.
36 Blood poisoning could be contracted through barbed wire and battlefield detritus. One priest claimed he was poisoned by an aluminium chalice.
37 DAA, Stack to Rawlinson, 18 May 1918.
38 DAA, Monk to Rawlinson, 23 May 1918. It is not clear whether this is light banter, factual or part of a rift between the two men

wretched foot'.[39] Bishop Keatinge responded: 'I am sorry indeed to hear that you are still laid up, you must find it very trying. Still you "stuck it" admirably during the war and you are not exactly robust! It would have been deplorable for the cause, if you had broken down in health.' The same might be said about Keatinge who reported from the Grand Pump Room Hotel on 13 September 1924: 'I have been here for the past fortnight and have been rather unwell.' It appears that there were crocks aplenty whilst the mainstream chaplains carried the flag not to say the monstrance.[40]

General Ill-Health

Battle areas were full of dead and rotting humans and animals, their detritus an enduring health hazard. Infections from all sources were taken seriously by the surgical and hygiene teams, including latrine maintenance, but despite their efforts non-battle casualties for France and Flanders were extensive: 18,220 cases and 16 deaths from Rubella, 26,432 and 155 deaths from Dysentery, 359,808 cases and 25 deaths from Influenza, 7,878 and 975 deaths from Pneumonia, 22,703 and 31 deaths from frostbite and by contrast 9,022 cases and 14 deaths from Malaria. Venereal diseases took their toll with a total of 93,432 hospitalised.[41] No official figures have been collated or analysed for Catholic chaplains with regard to disease or injury, even death statistics produced odd results.[42]

Research has partly filled the void by uncovering examples of general ill-health: Fr Scully contracted trench fever, Fr Morris SJ clinical dysentery which required movement to an isolation ward, and Fr Lowerey enteric fever. Frs Fichter and Ratcliffe both yielded to bronchial pneumonia, Frs. Longstaffe and Bradley acute influenza, and Fr Fitzmaurice SJ to Spanish influenza necessitating his repatriation from a prisoner of war camp in Germany. The usual abscesses bothered fellow Jesuits Fr Page and Fr Paul, the latter being complicated by catarrh causing deafness in his middle ear and hospitalisation. Haemorrhoids inflicted the elderly Bickerstaffe-Drew but his chagrin was diplomatically or sarcastically handled by the hospital doctor: 'What fearful pain you must have been enduring for a long time. Heaps and heaps of those who come

---

39 DAA, Rawlinson to Keatinge, 11 September 1919.
40 An ornate receptacle for holding and displaying the Blessed Sacrament for devotional purposes particulalry Benediction.
41 Iain Gordon, *Lifeline: A British Casualty Clearing Station on the Western Front 1918* (Stroud: History Press, 2013). 15.5% of injuries from whatever source treated at this CCS were facial, head, or neck. Illnesses included cerebrospinal fever, chicken pox, diphtheria, measles, mumps, scarlet fever, smallpox, pulmonary tuberculosis, enteric fever, nephritis, jaundice and trench foot.
42 A few have had a stab at it, including Rawlinson whose 'running totals' were completely out-of-date. Even scholars have had difficulty, Johnston and Hagarty list Padre Bedale as a dead Catholic chaplain when he was in fact a Wesleyan and married. Accurate death details can be found in Appendices 2-6 with each grave being visited and photographed.

down wounded from the front have not suffered a tithe like you have.'[43] Bickerstaffe-Drew exposed his personal fear: 'What I am dreading is that I am not strong enough for the anaesthetic.' Fr Gillett did not suffer from his pre-war gastric problems at the Front but acquiesced to 'spotted fever' or 'tick fever'. This penalised him with the boredom of isolation in his billet and made him feel 'groggy' for four days, ironically from 1 April. Isolation was ordered for two weeks but in ten days he had bought himself 'breakfast in a pub' and the next days 'glorious weather, strolled around' only to be brought down to earth by his APC who ordered him to 'buy a new hat as mine was so disreputable. Thought twice about it but he was insistent.'[44] Fr Steuart complaining of a cold and sore throat was 'evacuated' to 46 CCS and remained there for two weeks which he described as 'lonely'.[45]

Some priests viewed their incapacities with humour. The aforementioned Fr Fitzmaurice SJ, convalescing in North Wales wrote to Rawlinson to explain the treatments he had undertaken to get well. After feeling irritated by pains in his bones giving him 'jip', he:

> Put myself in the doctor's hands and submitted to an exhaustive examination and treatment with a Moritz bed [metal bed used in sanatoriums] and special food. I was weighed the first day and made 9 stone, 2lbs, 12 ounces. A few days later after much weight producing diet I topped at 9 stone, 1lb, 12 ounces! This was to the great despair of the chemist who sold me the food and weighed me. The doctor, on the other hand, was amused. I have also consumed various nasty medicines and had mustard baths and am almost completely well again – except for the pains in my shins. I will return to my regiment by the 18th after first visiting my Provincial in Preston and recruit for chaplains. And now we have lost Fr Doyle, God rest his soul. He was a great friend of mine and a devoted priest.[46]

Fr Fitzmaurice won the Military Cross with the 2 Royal Irish Rifles when he was injured in 1917. He was also captured on 22 March 1918 in the German Spring Offensive as were Fr Duggan and Fr Casey. Fitzmaurice wrote from a PoW camp in Beeskow [22 miles south west of Frankfurt] on 4 October 1918 and finally on the day after the Armistice was signed, he informed Rawlinson that he was safe in the Prince of Wales Hospital, Marylebone, after a severe bout of Spanish influenza. He recovered and died of natural causes in 1945.

The painful condition of lumbago, reported earlier by Fr Crisp, was not uncommon in the damp and cold conditions of trench warfare. Fr Gwynn SJ with the Irish

43 DAA, Bickerstaffe-Drew to Rawlinson 22 January 1916 from Liverpool Merchants Hospital, Étaples. He was born in 1858.
44 SDA, Gillett Diaries, 1-13 April 1917.
45 JAL, Steuart Diaries, 8-30 January 1917 in total.
46 DAA, Fitzmaurice to Rawlinson incorrectly dated as 24 August 1916, should be 1917, a week after Doyle's death.

Guards interdicted a sense of humour, or was it mundanity with this condition? When reporting his 'lumbago' to Keatinge he remarked that his condition: 'Is now rather acute and the MO is sending me to hospital, someplace where I can get Turkish Baths and suggested Paris as I would be bothered and get no rest in London or Dublin.'[47] After some wrangling from Keatinge, Gwynn had his wish and was transferred to No. 4 Stationary Hospital Versailles, where his condition was diagnosed not as lumbago but as a 'touch of rheumatism or a slightly trapped nerve'. This was confirmed in a letter between Gwynn and Keatinge. At Givenchy: 'I was going along a trench when a shell burst some two yards from me the other side of the trench. I flopped down at once and may have trapped a nerve in my thigh.'[48] Lumbago is a lower back ailment.

Nervous and Mental Problems

When nerves, fear, weariness, and mental anguish are reported, the psychological components become entangled and probably not correctly, if at all, diagnosed or treated. The study and practice of psychology was in relative infancy. Psychological effects may be visible but the causes almost certainly not. Shell shock was only slowly being accepted and post-traumatic stress disorder had yet to be discovered, hence, an appreciation of these difficulties is necessary. Whilst explaining his pre-war and present state of his mind, Fr Walker whose paintings feature throughout confusingly grasped for a medical explanation for his insomnia:

> The difficulty is sleep. I used to suffer a good deal from insomnia before the war but had not been troubled out here. Perhaps the retreat on the Somme had something to do with it, as it entailed many nights without sleep dealing with the wounded. After I could not sleep at all. I wrote to you [for a change] but since we have been shelled and I am out in a tent and sleeping better. Consequently there is no need for an immediate change.[49]

Many priests confessed to being tired and weary and in need of a break. Typical was Fr Joseph Woodlock SJ whose brother features later: 'I find myself on the edge of a breakup (sic) and feel there is no good in trying to drag on till things get less busy. I will get leave and ask you [to extend it] to a month, it may patch me up. I am on the edge. I will be going to St. Buenos.'[50] Rawlinson refused to countenance a month, suggesting

---

47 DAA, Gwynn to Keatinge, 14 May 1915.
48 DAA, Gwynn to Keatinge, 27 May 1915.
49 DAA, Walker to Rawlinson, 2 May 1918. He is referring to the German Spring Offensive.
50 DAA, J Woodlock to Rawlinson, 27 March 1917. St Buenos is the Jesuit Seminary in North Wales and a Retreat Centre.

fourteen days.⁵¹ During the German Spring Offensive of 1918 Woodlock became estranged from his unit. Papers reveal that: 'He subsequently turned up at his brothers (Frank) office in Boulogne at Base. Fr Joe had been behind the German line and had managed to elude the enemy. Frank kept asking him how he managed to escape. He refused to talk about his time behind the lines'.⁵² Joseph Woodlock explained in a letter to Rawlinson: 'I hear from my brother Frank that I was officially reported missing – I am glad to say it was an exaggeration!'⁵³ Was this a case of leaving one's post and being open to charges of desertion? Why the mystery, was it a subterfuge, confusion, or was he suffering from mental health issues, possibly depression or PTSD?

Fr Byrne's inability to work at the front any longer was supported by the medics: 'He (MO) says that I am quite sure that I won't stand the strain of the life and that any attempt to, will lead to breakdown.'⁵⁴ There were more serious cases to report. One incident, which received scant empathy from his own authorities, related to Fr Cagney, which if it was not so tragic would have been comical. After an exchange of letters Cagney's situation is summarised by Rawlinson to Monk at the War Office:

> The Rev W Cagney, an Irish Redemptorist has been reported to me as having left his post [*he was last seen tearing down the road on his horse shouting "save yourselves while you can"* – in the original but omitted in this official report] when there was a rumour that the Germans were through. He next turned up at Boulogne [in hospital] where I have tried on two occasions to get a coherent story from him without avail. He owns that he went completely 'off his head' [sic], and might have got into serious trouble spreading alarm and despondency. A private soldier acting as he did would have been 'shot at dawn'.⁵⁵

If contemporary acceptance of mental health issues was limited by lack of institutional empathy and knowledge, there were sanguine voices at the Front urging compassion: 'Fr Potter tells me that Fr Cagney was very upset the day before he left Brigade not to be allowed leave. His nerves were also very bad in consequence of the shelling.'⁵⁶ Even the CO of the Ambulance attached to his Brigade said that Fr Cagney was: 'of a very nervous temperament and absolutely unfit for the front line.'⁵⁷ The General of the South Midland 34 Division, where Cagney had ended up after he had been confined overnight as a spy, had the good sense to: 'tell him off and let him go'.⁵⁸

---

51 Rawlinson did not officially grant leave – this was an army matter but it is likely that he intervened with the relevant CO in an unofficial capacity.
52 RCBFA, *Obituaries*.
53 DAA, 3235, Woodlock to Rawlinson, 6 April 1918.
54 DAA, Bourke to Rawlinson, 21 April 1916, doctor's note attached.
55 DAA, Rawlinson to Monk, 20 April 1918.
56 DAA, Carden (Hessenhauer) to Rawlinson, 5 April 1918.
57 Op.cit.
58 Op.cit.

Other cases were more obscure. The mental anguish of Fr Trew's family was acute. His sister Clara wrote to Bishop Keatinge in June 1918 about his whereabouts:

> We have neither heard from, or of, my brother for the last three months. He had written very regularly so the prolonged silence is causing great anxiety to us all, more especially his aged parents. Having lost our younger brother in the 1st year of the war, our eldest last January…… Fr Trew is the only brother left to us, at least we hope and pray that God in his mercy will spare him.

God had spared him, yet it remains a mystery why Trew did not contact his family, a diagnosis of temporary amnesia caused by stress never apparently being considered. Keatinge was informed that Trew had relinquished his commission in February 1918 at contract renewal. He reapplied in May 1918, but the Keatinge enquiry had set off alarm bells prompting the Army to instigate Fr Trew's compulsory attendance at the 'Special Candidates Medical Board,'[59] on the grounds that he had not contacted his family in arrival back home in London. The report concluded that he was generally fit but '*mentally unusual*.' Offered to Rawlinson, his response to 'crocks' was inevitable: 'Under the circumstances I certainly don't want him back in France.'[60] This case suggests a degree of Army medical concern over his mental health but they are unable or unwilling to diagnose further. Rawlinson may have had other knowledge of Fr Trew but there is nothing in the records. The change in the Allied position and therefore stress levels from early to mid-1918 needs to be considered. France was a very dangerous posting in 1918. His contract expired in February before a large German assault was imminent but he applied again in May in the middle of it, therefore, fear or cowardice are unlikely, anxiety or trauma would seem more probable candidates. Serious mental health issues should be disregarded as evinced through his lucid arguments when appealing for a gratuity which demonstrates that he was far from unusual. He argued on the basis that if the diagnosis is correct then his mental infirmity must have been caused by the war as he was initially passed fit by the Army in 1917, and then unfit in 1918, hardly the reasoning of the unbalanced mind. We do not know the results of this claim but he was still an active Southwark Diocesan Parish Priest at St Bartholomew's until his death in 1938: 'The Church was first extended in 1929, back to the extant west end with a small choir loft added, when Fr Alexander Trew was Parish Priest (1926-1938).'[61]

Military intervention in the area of mental health issues was clearly tentative but beginning to be taken seriously as experience was gained. It is worth noting that the precise time of this refusal to re-engage Trew coincided with the period of greatest need as the Allies reeled from German assault and severe chaplaincy shortages.

---

59 PRO, WO 374/69489.
60 Op.cit.
61 <http://polychoir.co.uk/The_Church.htm> (Accessed 18 April 2014).

Rawlinson remained adamant, for without any other navigational lights he adhered to his tried and trusted formula of steering Catholic England away from the potential disapprobation of the authorities which may have resulted from of a mentally 'unusual' chaplain. In conventional areas such as alleged drink and sex abuse, no margin of error was afforded the mindset of the accused, any resultant action relied on moral, political, and legal judgements.

Sex Scandals

Sex scandals were rare and difficult situations which had the potential of devastating the Catholic good name, and if they surfaced had to be eradicated. As with drink and bad language, if dereliction of duty could also be alleged, then the accused was on a very slippery slope. The results were devastating for the accused if judged guilty; and equally devastating for the organisation if ignored and scandal spread. Fr Mortimer J. Galvin [not to be confused with Fr Jeremiah Galvin mentioned earlier] was one such case. He was accused of poor morals and dereliction of duty, Carden [Hessenhauer] wrote a letter 'Private and Confidential' on 20 August 1918 to Rawlinson:

> He returns very late to the Presbytery – sometimes as late as 2.a.m., apparently he plays cards. The parishioners have complained to the Curé that he walks about with a particular woman – sometimes in the evening, and even in lonely places. This the Curé has not seen himself but it is common talk in the village … the woman in question is a refugee much sought after by officers and thought to be charming. Fr Galvin is supposed to have taken her out to dinner at a neighbouring village [during Mass he arranged for a collection to be made] and much to the scandal of the Curé and the village Fr G. gave these bags to *this creature* in the church. He rushed through Mass and got off his vestments quickly and was at the door to offer Holy Water to this creature before she left. To choose out a woman of *that kind* to make a Civil Collection during Mass is a gross offence. An interpreter priest said it was common talk about an English priest [Galvin was Irish from Kerry] who was always with a woman and that he may have been seen kissing this woman. I then visited a very good woman in the village who said she had seen nothing personally and could only say it was the talk of the village. It would be impossible for such stories to get about unless Fr Galvin had been indiscreet.[62] [Author's italics]

This episode gives the impression of being petty, unproven, and deceitful. Yet Hessenhauer's track record was good, and Rawlinson's even better. Did Galvin go astray or was he the victim of malicious gossip, perhaps sexual envy from officers?

---

62 DAA, 3234, Hessenhauer to Rawlinson, 20 August 1918.

Was it her status as refugee or her demeanour that defined her as *that kind*? Was *this creature* in question a prostitute, and if so was Galvin under her spell, or simply acting in a remedial priestly manner? Could he have fallen off the chaplaincy pedestal and simply fallen in love? It is impossible to be sure but staggering that a proper enquiry was not afforded Galvin. The allegations amount to hearsay and rumour but sufficient for Rawlinson to require Galvin to resign his commission.

Galvin, originally a Kerry man, was loaned from the Glasgow Diocese and given that he went missing and does not appear in post-war Catholic Directories, it is reasonable to assume that he also gave up the priesthood. He may have had mental health problems, eschewed his religion, or simply had enough. His father offered his own plausible explanation for his disappearance. Whilst trying desperately to contact him in December 1918 he wrote: 'I am quite certain that he is suffering from shock and loss of memory not having written for several months to me'.[63] Galvin's address was unknown but he did pick up mail at the Charing Cross Hotel, ironically a favourite haunt of Fr Steuart. The hotel provided this extraordinary sketch and description of Galvin which resides nervously in the Public Record Office.

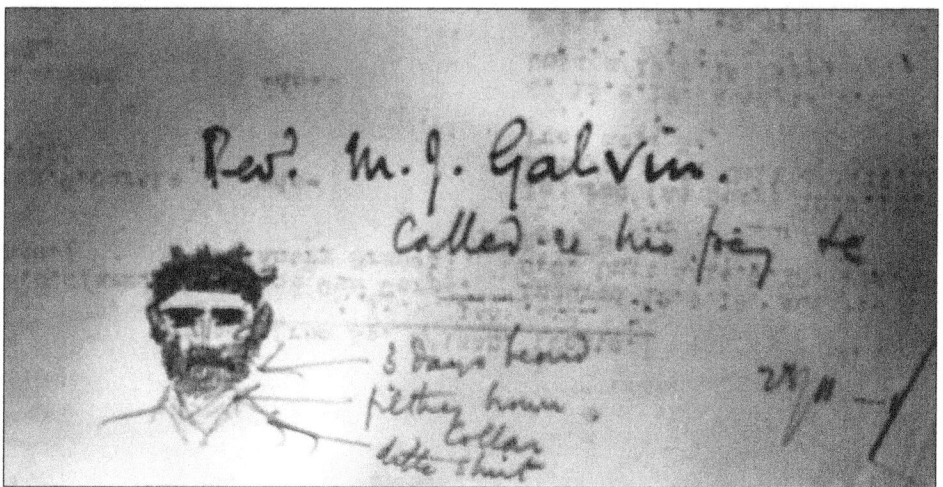

Sketch of Fr M J Galvin. (PRO, WO 374/26288)

Whatever the reason this was a personal tragedy for a priest with three years good service. His testimonial read: 'Character – Fair. Health – Good. Suitability – Not Suitable'.[64] Evidently Rawlinson in his coded summation had pointed the finger at his 'character' and his demise was therefore inevitable, even though 'fair' suggests Rawlinson was not entirely convinced. Galvin may well have been completely innocent

63 Ibid.
64 Ibid.

but the bar was set very high for Catholic priests and human transgressions were not permissible for a chaplain who carried the Catholic good name on his Captain's shoulders. Rawlinson's judgement was usually sound and Galvin became yet another unknown casualty of war.

Sex and Alcohol Scandal

Galvin's case was sad and perhaps harsh but there were justified cases of Rawlinson's interventions to protect Catholicism and the following example of Fr Richmond is a strong one. Access to post-war documentation confirmed him as a clandestine habitual sex and drink offender, who both during the war and after, portrayed all the hallmarks of denial, exhortations of innocence, and cynical manipulation associated with this type of miscreant.

The case started when Fr D Hughes SJ, SCF, reported: 'I have to write to you on a painful subject. It is to ask you to take Richmond away; if he was sent home it would not be amiss. It would be too bad to unload him on another Division'.[65] Then Fr Joseph Brown SJ CF reported that: '…Captain Constable, Divisional Headquarter staff complained to me that he (Richmond) horrified everyone by his vileness of language which was loose and blasphemous when he visits the mess and we have to keep the whisky locked up. He then charged him with being a drunkard'.[66] Fr Hughes SJ the Senior Chaplain to the division wrote the same day 10 July 1918: 'Lieutenant Colonel J Davis says he could not believe that Fr Richmond was a chaplain so vulgar was his conversation'.[67] However, doubts crept in, Richmond was a calculating man and not the naïve person he purported to be.[68] He was convincing throughout his defence and even his accusers had second-thoughts. Cunningly he was beginning to win support from his immediate colleagues in 38 Welsh Division, so that after reflection the accusers reassessed their opinion of Richmond and back-pedalled to try to limit the damage. Late in July Fr Brown lamented: 'I feel sure he would prosper by a new start, I venture to state this side of the case to you. After all we have no school of Padres. Frankly I like him as I now find him, positive guidance is what he requires'.[69] The SCF of the division Fr Hughes commented:

> I hear that Father Richmond is leaving and I sent a note to him to say that any mistakes were entirely due to ignorance of army ways, he thought it was the ordinary way of going on in the army. In new surroundings he will do great work

---

65   DAA, 3234, Hughes to Rawlinson, 23 July 1918.
66   DAA, 3235, Brown to Rawlinson, 10 July 1918.
67   DAA, 3235, Hughes to Rawlinson, 10 July 1918.
68   He continued with this evasiveness when he returned to Nottingham Diocese post-war and was an evasive priest to dismiss. Richmond Papers NDA.
69   DAA, 3235, Brown to Rawlinson, 12 August 1918.

and completely retrieve the mistakes made by ignorance of this I am quite sure. In his new division you will certainly find this to be the case. Certainly during the last fortnight when he has seen he was on the wrong method, he has worked hard and well among men, impressing them with his fearlessness and got on well with both officers and men.[70]

Fr Hughes continued in a more desperate tone:

I rode over to see Father Richmond on Heavy Siege Guns and found him much perturbed at leaving. The great cause of his fear is due to a strong letter he got from his Lordship his own bishop [Thomas Dunn]. I beg you accept the letter of penitence he brings you and put him somewhere else and not let his career be ruined. He is a capable and brave man so I do hope he gets another chance.[71]

Charles L Perry, Senior non-Catholic chaplain wrote to Rawlinson:

He got it into his head that the way to become popular and influence officers and men was to conform to their method of doing things. He has had a rude awakening and the experience will be of the utmost value to him. I am confident that if you have a straight talk to him he will still be a valuable worker, officers and men testify to a complete change already.[72]

These were charitable yet wrong-headed attempts to mitigate. On first reading it appeared that Richmond was a victim of an unfair conspiracy and had been harshly treated. Was it a simple misunderstanding or lack of empathy from senior chaplains most notably Rawlinson? If so it suggested a flawed system and unsound personalities not worthy of the Catholic mission, seriously undermining faith in the system and Rawlinson. Additionally he might also be accused of prostrating himself in the face of Army criticism, whilst revealing a lack of man-management skills. These questions occupied my mind until I researched the Nottingham Diocesan Archives where the files on Richmond provided all the evidence to exonerate Rawlinson's abilities, character, and methodology. Examination of Richmond's post-war records confirms that criticism of the Principal Chaplain could not be further from the truth, if senior chaplains had been hoodwinked Rawlinson had not. Richmond was a disreputable minister and forced to resign from the priesthood. Scrutiny of the *Ad Limina* Reports[73] to Rome in the 1920s has confirmed his unsuitability for his vocation thereby confirming Rawlinson's sound judgement. This was a man who continually transgressed, and as

---

70 DAA, 3235, Hughes to Rawlinson, 12 August 1918.
71 Ibid., 15 August 1918.
72 DAA, 3235, Perry to Rawlinson, 12 August 1918.
73 Each bishop is bound every 5 years to provide the Supreme Pontiff with a report on the diocese entrusted to him.

perpetual fraudsters habitually do, he was incredibly persuasive in his attempts to appear as the victim himself. Rawlinson was wiser than those around him. Richmond had not convinced him and he was rapidly sent home. On 7 August Rawlinson wrote to Fr Brown: 'I do not propose sending Fr Richmond to any other unit. He has done already sufficient harm out here'.[74] The die was cast, *iacta alea est*. Rawlinson wrote to his bishop, Thomas Dunn, whose response, was:

> I am distressed and surprised beyond measure to read about Father Richmond. He is a gentleman and a convert and ought to know better how to behave himself. As a matter of fact I allowed him to join up only because he begged very hard to allow him to do so. He represented to me that he belonged to Old Army stock; many of his relations having been soldiers and that his mother who had practically repudiated him when he became a convert was ready to be reconciled with him if he became chaplain. Don't show any consideration in his case but if he should come home in disgrace he will have a bad time at my hands.[75]

Dunn confirmed his own apparent hoodwinking by Richmond: 'I know him well, he is not by any means a knave, but he is a great deal of an ass'.[76]

Rawlinson did not agree. On Richmond's Army testimonial he wrote, 'Character – *Peculiar*. Fitness – Good. Suitability – Not suitable at all'.[77] This testimony was for Home Office consumption and usually contained guarded language, but these remarks are the harshest for an outgoing chaplain researched in the Public Records Office. The term peculiar speaks volumes and is not difficult to decode in the vernacular of the day. The manner of his removal was the effective but disingenuous device of ill-health. Richmond wrote from Derbyshire 31 August 1917: 'I have the honour to request your permission to tender my resignation of my chaplaincy. In view of my nervous collapse and its subsequent consequences I am given to understand by Bishop Keatinge that you were prepared to grant my request'.[78] This doubletalk offered a convenient way of allowing both the recipient and the organisation to avoid bad publicity and further disciplinary action.

In Nottingham Richmond came back to create difficulties after the war. Further indiscretions, further enquiries, yet more unsuccessful attempts at rehabilitation, and finally dismissal from the priesthood. Despite Richmond's deception Bishop Dunn did get to grips with him, even though it took time and a deal of patience before the Church could rid itself. Rawlinson showed no such qualms.

---

74 DAA, 3235, Rawlinson to Brown, 7 August 1918.
75 DAA, 3235, Dunn to Rawlinson, 29 July 1918.
76 Ibid., 24 August 1918.
77 PRO, WO 374/60980, 29 November 1918.
78 PRO, WO 374/57411.

Richmond was dealt with by Rawlinson instinctively, ruthlessly, and correctly and his decisive action restricted any political fall-out.[79] The removal of this disgraced man reinforces confidence in Rawlinson ability and commitment to weed out problems. Experienced priests who had developed a good understanding of people and character from their work at home were the filters, Rawlinson the high judge and executioner.

Gas and Related Illnesses

Gas caused horror for the troops and consternation for those occupying the moral high ground. Predictably such issues were brushed aside when similar retaliatory measures were adopted by the British Army.[80] In practice poisoned gas of whichever mutation was a severe problem throughout the war. Respirators were often inefficient and an impediment to freedom of movement, seriously hampering spiritual intervention to the wounded and dying. Gas created various degrees of affliction. Fr Roche SJ reported to his Provincial Fr Nolan that he was in hospital in Exeter having been evacuated and expected to stay for 2 to 3 months: 'I am still partially blind not being able to see anything more than a few yards away, my throat too has been affected and my voice has partly gone. They do not think there will be any permanent effects. I will do my best to get out of here as soon as possible'.[81] A speedy return was a commonly expressed desire.

Fr William Gallagher serving with the 2/8 Battalion Kings Liverpool Regiment, [Liverpool – Irish, Fr Gillett's original deployment], was damaged for the long-term and any opportunity to return was denied him through his injuries and subsequent illnesses. Gassed at Armentieres on 30 July 1917, the local newspapers published the mistaken statement that: 'It was at first feared that he had been dangerously injured, but letters from two brother chaplains proved that this is not happily the case'.[82] Unhappily it was very much the case. He was hospitalised for 5 months with respiratory damage which developed into pulmonary tuberculosis and dysentery. Retiring to his home in Nenagh co Tipperary after being in various hospitals in Ireland and England, he continued to receive treatment at home as his illnesses continued. In July 1919 he was still suffering from acute bronchitis, anaemia and breathlessness. Aged 27 when gassed he was unable to be moved from his home until March 1920. Analysis of his sputum by University College Dublin revealed there are 'neither leucocytes, red corpuscles, nor pigment to be found. The chief organism is diplococcus which is

---

79 I was granted unlimited access and permissions to these papers from both the bishop and archivist, for which I am grateful. My purpose was to examine the system rather than the individual *per se*. Although given permission to use in this thesis, citation is not given to respect the sensitivities around these topics. This is purely the decision of the author.
80 The same applied to liquid oil flame throwers and aerial bombing of civilians.
81 JAD, CHP 1/53 (58) Fr Daniel Roche SJ to Fr Nolan SJ, 22 October 1918.
82 *Tipperary Nationalist*, 8 August 1917.

encapsulated and which I believe to be pneumococcus. If a vaccine is required culture can be made.'[83] Fr Gallagher's claims for essential medicines and doctors' visits was first agreed as reasonable and then without explanation rejected as not appropriate. This was despite the nearest suitable hospital being over 100 miles away, being unfit to travel and his case being supported by the medics. He appealed with the words: '… as my injuries are permanent, I respectfully request that you will take into account that I am a clergyman, to whom of course, bronchial trouble is doubly unfortunate.'[84] Ireland was in a state of war, external or civil, in the early 1920s, a period of unprecedented political revolution leading to the foundation of The Irish Free State in 1922. Without dates the reasoning behind the compensation claims and counter-claims remains speculative, nonetheless, it draws attention to the sometimes bizarre culture of British bureaucracy: the left hand denied him essential medical support but the right hand offered him financial recompense.[85] A document of 1980 regarding his death [90 years of age] shows that although he was by now a long-time Irish citizen, he had received a British Army Pension of £2106 p.a., a Comfort Allowance of £172.86 p.a., an Unemployability Allowance of £1287.86 p.a. and finally an age allowance of £427.55 p.a.

Not all priests who were gassed suffered badly: Fr Adamson SJ had only temporary effects whilst Fr Jack Fitzgibbon played down his ordeal: 'You may hear I have been gassed, well it's true, but I think only slightly. I was under it for over 4 hours. The after effects have been strange, I am being evacuated to the Base for the moment.'[86] Fr Steuart was particularly unlucky being gassed thrice, the first occasion:

> Maj de Berry, and I, while leaving the town, were gassed (slightly) with gas shells which came up behind us & followed us up Rue de Gambilla from the station. Had difficulty in putting on my respirator, so got some mouthfuls. Luckily no serious effects, but every cigarette I smoked for the rest of the night tasted filthy.[87]

He continued to be unlucky:

> Moved up to the Ecole, other side of Ypres. Just as we were nearing it we were gassed by shells. I found that with my box-respirator on I couldn't see at all & got separated from the platoon and found myself alone. By shouting I found one of the men who was also lost & we sat down to wait. In 5 or 10 minutes the Doctor came back and found us.[88]

---

83 Dr Mc Weeney PRO, WO 374/26235.
84 PRO, WO 374/26235.
85 Albeit the former was probably discretionary, the latter a legal requirement.
86 JAD, CHP1/21 (14).
87 JAL, Steuart Diaries, 31 March 1917.
88 JAL, Steuart Diaries, 22 July 1917.

The third and more serious event occurred on Monday 20 May 1918, note the almost nonchalant approach: 'Nothing doing. Casual shelling. Gas shell strafe started at 10:30 p.m. and went on without stopping until 3:30 a.m. Mask was almost intolerable: was sick in it. Got a certain amount of gas by taking off mask.' Next day:

> Hot sun & gas streaming out of the ground. MO, Sgt. Henry, McLellan and Taffy all down. I took over MO's job and evacuated 43 until at 4:30p.m. I had to give up as my eyes were shut & I was sick. Went down to details with Watson. No better so went to FA at Toutencourt, thence to Clairfaye, thence to 3rd Canadian CCS at Doullens. Four air-raids during the night.

He was hospitalised the following day: 'Off to Rouen at 9 a.m. Amiens at 6 p.m. at No8 where I was in Jan 1917. Am in same ward as Watson, Burton & Bethune; & Sister Temperley was here when I was in that ward in 1917, is still there. Eyes very bad,' and with no improvement he was evacuated to 'Blighty' on 24 May 1918.[89] He went to hospital in Manchester and very soon began his recovery which was mainly to his sight. His gradual recovery allowed him to recuperate in the social circles with which he was familiar and he soon enjoyed the countryside of his Perthshire home. Posted to Blandford by the War Office he had already campaigned for a return to the 12 Highland Light Infantry and his request was granted by Rawlinson.

Fr Gillett was fortunate not mentioning gas whatsoever. Another chaplain who left a diary, Fr Drinkwater was not so lucky:

> Fr Drinkwater was badly gassed ten days ago at the front. For five days he was quite blind and suffered a great deal, but he is now very much better and has practically no pain. He is still suffering from the cough but I believe out of danger. He was extraordinarily cheerful and made very light of his trouble the same as he did when he was seriously wounded two years ago. He is really a splendid man, and has done first rate work out here for the past three years and a half.[90]

There is no doubting Fr Drinkwater's injuries or cheerful disposition but the eulogising tone may have represented the more subtle side of Rawlinson appealing to the Archbishop of Birmingham. His footnote asked: 'I suppose you have no more men available for the front? Our shortage of 90 priests in France alone and makes the work impossible, and is exceedingly harmful for our cause.' Appealing to McIntyre's sense of duty he then let it be known that next month he was going to Rome, 'where I last met your Grace'. The whole letter appeals to moral and political justice in meeting Catholic general and chaplaincy requirements with more than an intimation of flattery [for the Archbishops priests, especially Drinkwater].

89 JAL, Steuart Diaries, 22 July 1917–24 May 1918.
90 DAA, Rawlinson to Archbishop Mc Intyre (Birmingham), 14 October 1918.

Injuries from Hostile Action

Was Rawlinson exaggerating Drinkwater's injuries for the greater cause? The answer is definitely no, if anything Rawlinson under-played Drinkwater's injuries and courage, maybe he ought to have mentioned Drinkwater's humility, the first injury on 5 October 1915 demonstrates:

> The whizzbang had a mark on our corner [Neuve Englise] and one burst just over me, so that I felt it warm on my neck. I was just going after a badly wounded boy who complained of the cold, with some idea of lending him my British warm, when another whizzbang came and laid me out, besides killing a signaller and wounding a stretcher-bearer, I felt a violent blow in the middle of my back, and felt sure that I was dead. After a few seconds I decided I wasn't dead and might as well get up. I felt very stiff and asked someone if there was a hole in my coat; and he said "Yes". Felt a bit feint all day, and lay down near a stretcher-bearers dug-out, and they fetched me in, and discovered and dressed my wounds. It would be a six weeks job.[91]

By 7 October he reported, [To the Rubery Mental and now Military Hospital in Birmingham – he only remembered the slow boat and rail journey to England and not the Base Hospital in France]: 'They took some more bits of metal out of me, [though a sizeable piece which worked its way to the surface painfully some years later and had to be removed].' 20 December he returned to the Front in Beauval at 4 CCS.[92] His gassing incident was reported in similar down-to-earth fashion ironically three years exactly to the day from his shelling experience:

> Wakened at 3 a.m. by rapid fire of 4.2's such that we were bound to get one sometime and finally one landed in the doorway. The cellar was filled with what I was sure was gas and put on my box respirator, but the others didn't. I had to take it off a bit when the wounded came in: I also went out of the cellar to the road but of course there was gas there too. About 8 a.m. I had bad eyes and sickness, and my eyes got rapidly worse.

Next day: 'stayed at HQ at Vendelles still quite blind'. The following day Drinkwater was moved to 12 CCS at Tincourt and in the evening by train to 2 Stationary Hospital at Abbeville where: 'I am getting my sight back but a cough is developing'.

Underplaying ones hand is a characteristic emerging from chaplains' evidence. Fr Moran MC is such an example:

---

91   BRM, Drinkwater Diaries, 4 October 1915.
92   BRM, Drinkwater Diaries, 5 October–20 December 1915.

I was wounded on the 17th July [1918] at the show at Rheims. There was an officer and corporal killed by the same shell and we were side by side at the time. So I have a lot to thank God for. I was hit in four places in the right arm, one serious in the upper right arm but all the bits are taken out now. I won't go to hospital contrary to the directions of the ADS doctors. I just got a few injections and went back to my old post. I'll soon take my arm out of the sling when all pain is gone. Time will tell but I have not yet realised what happened. I was unconscious for a few hours and came round suddenly.[93]

Fr W Ryan a priest from the Hexham Diocese is another example:

AA shell burst into my dug out last night and knocked me out. Thank God I escaped very lightly with 4 or 5 wounds. Two men, one on each side of me, were killed. Could you spare a man to relieve me? I will long to get back as soon as possible. I am sorry to give so much trouble. Hoping you are well.

Other serious injuries included Fr Nevin a diocesan priest from Galway He was visiting the men in billets when a shell burst wounding many, as a result he was: 'seriously wounded and had his leg amputated and also has a wound in his arm, and is suffering considerably from shock. Although not out of danger there is a good hope that he will recover.'[94] He did recover. Fr Nevin became an outstanding success running a club for Catholic soldiers at Lourdes where he expediting visits and pilgrimages before starting his new life in Sydney, Australia in 1920. He won the Recompense Militaire for his work in France.

Fr Bouchier, a Servite priest from Lismore co Waterford, was injured on at least two occasions, on 19 April 1917 and again in March 1918, when his right arm was under threat of amputation. He was awarded the MC after he received head wounds mitigated by the opportune intervention of an object: 'On one occasion his life was saved by a silver cigarette case in his breast-pocket stopping a bullet. [Now preserved in Bagbroke Priory]'. After the war Fr Bouchier remained in hospital for a considerable time. A silver plate had to be inserted into his head. Fr Bouchier plagued with ill-health still managed to say Mass until his death in 1957.[95]

Other injuries which were only minimally recorded included Fr Northcote losing an eye and subsequently appealing for 14 days leave because the glass eye he had received had been broken,[96] Fr Bouchier an arm, Fr N H Brown damaged lungs, Fr F M Browne thigh, and all things in between including Fr Legros who gallantly saved a nursing sister by shielding her during a bombing raid on 11 CCS and received shrapnel

---

93   DAA, Moran to Rawlinson, 11 August 1918.
94   DAA, Rawlinson to the Bishop of Galway, 5 May 1917.
95   Army Bishops House Aldershot, Catholic Chaplaincy Papers.
96   DAA, Northcote to Rawlinson, 12 May 1917.

in his buttocks for his noble efforts.[97] The Chaplain's Department never accurately or systematically recorded injuries; the evidence presented above is from correspondence to Rawlinson and is probably the tip of the iceberg.

The weaponry which inflicted the 22 Catholic chaplaincy deaths buried on the Western Front is as follows: 2 were killed by bombs dropped from aeroplanes, 17 by shells and three thorough illness,[98] 0r 9, 77 and 14% respectively. There are differences between these and the overall figures of those admitted to Casualty Clearing Stations which are for wounds only, but give a modicum of comparison:[99] 2% for bombs 58 % for shells and 39% for bullets and grenades. Chaplain's bullet wounds were quite rare whilst shell injuries common. This might suggest that Catholic chaplains were not in machine-gun fire and therefore not supporting the troops over the top but there is sufficient evidence to contradict this hypothesis.[100] In all probability injuries, like death, owed more to circumstance than simple suppositions. If any personnel were in the firing line then they stood more chance of being victims than those further back, but as high explosives, bombs and stray bullets were indiscriminate killing methods, then analysis is problematic and furthermore rather pointless. Fr Scully for example reported a bullet in his knee and Fr Forrest received a stray bullet to the head, both men left no further evidence and subsequently returned to post, Father Bouchier's escape from a bullet has been mentioned.

Accidental Injuries

These were few but unusual. Fr Looby was knocked off his bicycle suffering a ruptured right patella, on 13 October 1915. Fr McBrearty was injured playing football, various priests fell off their horses or were injured building huts or chapels, and famously Fr Lane-Fox blew off his hand when adolescently amusing himself with live ordinance in the form of Mills bombs.

Deaths

Twenty two Catholic chaplains are buried on the Western Front. Fr McAuliffe died on the way home and is buried in Limerick. Fr McIlvaine was killed at sea returning to France after injury. He is buried in Hollybrook cemetery Southampton. Each grave at the Front will be visited in later chapters.

---

97 DAA, General Standing to Rawlinson, 9 July 1917.
98 S. Bellis, The Cult of Fr Willie Doyle: Rebalancing the Unrepresentative Historical Treatment of Catholic Chaplains in the Great War. Presentation to University of Liverpool, May 2014.
99 Gordon, *Lifeline*, p. 161, 659 injuries analysed – sickness was not recorded as it was more probable for these deaths to occur later in hospitals.
100 When deaths are analysed then there is ample evidence that some chaplains were killed going 'over the top'.

Diminished Post-War Personalities

This is an area which might produce valid and interesting research results. As it stands it can never be known how many early deaths or cases of diminished life fulfilment resulted from men's exertions at war, although the example of Fr Myerscough may show the way to further studies in these areas. Despite Fr Francis Woodlock's derisory remark that Fr Myerscough was a 'little insignificant man' he was in fact a popular chaplain at war. In spite of this his obituary suggests that his post-war mental condition was somewhat strained. Described as: 'a man of sterling character, he was subject to depression… unfortunately he gained a reputation for undue severity, terrorising small boys who now have unhappy memories of him'.[101] The change in character is marked but the true extent of war trauma on these men, probably oblivious to its effects, is unknown.

One successful Preston born chaplain [MID] Fr T Kelly from the Liverpool Archdiocese continued his service after the war but suffered a cerebral thrombosis in 1923.[102] After extended hospital treatment he never fully recovered and died after much distress in 1937. He was ill for three years up to 1910 but never faltered as a chaplain except for varicose veins, despite: 'I was treated badly by the authorities [his leave to attend his dying mother was delayed by bureaucracy] and for my poor mother in Southport it was even more hard, from what those around me told me on my return home.'[103] There are four competing elements in Kelly's case: pre-war illness [undefined], good health albeit with varicose veins and their possible link to cerebral thrombosis, the stress of war on his later health, or simply natural causes and age [54 at time of thrombosis].

Catholic chaplains suffered and endured appalling conditions and deprivations. They were not alone, and it can be readily argued that compared to infantrymen or gunners, for example, their officer-clerical status gave them some advantage in the material world. Yet it was the spiritual world that these chaplains were concerned about and it is abundantly clear that their survival assisted the spiritual well-being of all who requested their services. The conditions they braved were readily and willingly accepted in order to complete their tasks which they achieved with remarkable consistency.

The preceding chapters have paved the way for a closer examination of the day-to-day life of these men through the accounts of Fr Gillett and Fr Steuart which follow.

---

101 JAL, *Remarkable Men of the English Province*, pp. 212-217.
102 PRO, WO 374/39049. This long official account of Fr Kelly's disabilities, treatment and care, would interest both military and medical researchers.
103 DAA, Kelly to Rawlinson, 6 August 1918.

5

1916: À Partir De La Belle Époque À Folie

From the beautiful time to the madness, neatly summarises the surreal and bizarre juxtaposition between Boulogne's relative isolation and the carnage on the battlefields, within earshot in mid-1916. Fr Gillett was welcomed to Boulogne on 28 June and Fr Steuart briefly 13 October. They diligently recorded their experiences in personal diaries, which will be corroborated by individual correspondence mainly to GHQ from other chaplains. Basic progress can be followed by markers on the map in each chapter. Note they do not include their daily routines or brief interludes such as leave, such mapping would be a worthwhile but a complex task not necessary in this story. Their accounts complement each other and develop an appreciation of life for a Catholic chaplain 'on the ground'. Differences of personality provide individualism, whereas constancy and resolve in conducting their mission remained steadfast.

1916 is commonly remembered for the Battle of the Somme, an altogether inadequate description of many military operations in the northern central area of the department of Somme. General Haig's 'Big Push' which opened 1 July 1916 was the major battle in a zone around and between the rivers Ancre and Somme, mostly north of the town of Albert. Fr Gillett and Steuart's diaries describe this area of activity, regardless that both men arrived after commencement. Other battles were being conducted particularly at Ypres, and in subsequent chapters these will be reviewed as the chaplains followed their army units to which they were attached, in essence a realistic reflection of military action as it happened. The war was not one of single decisive battles, but rather a continuum of skirmishes and major attacks punctuated by rest periods. Talk of a quiet zone on this front is unquestionably relative: there was constant danger even 'at rest'.

By the summer of 1916 a curious state of affairs existed between those places in France seemingly untouched directly by war and the Western Front. Paris was enjoying a period of outward frivolity, despite or because of, the underlying fears of invasion. In Boulogne too, civilian life went on much as usual, whilst those on the battlefields were experiencing a scale of carnage never before imagined. These situations may be considered a period of 'phoney war', the situation which precedes many 'real wars'. It happened in Britain in the early part of the Great War and has become a common term relating to Britain in late 1939, describing the period between the

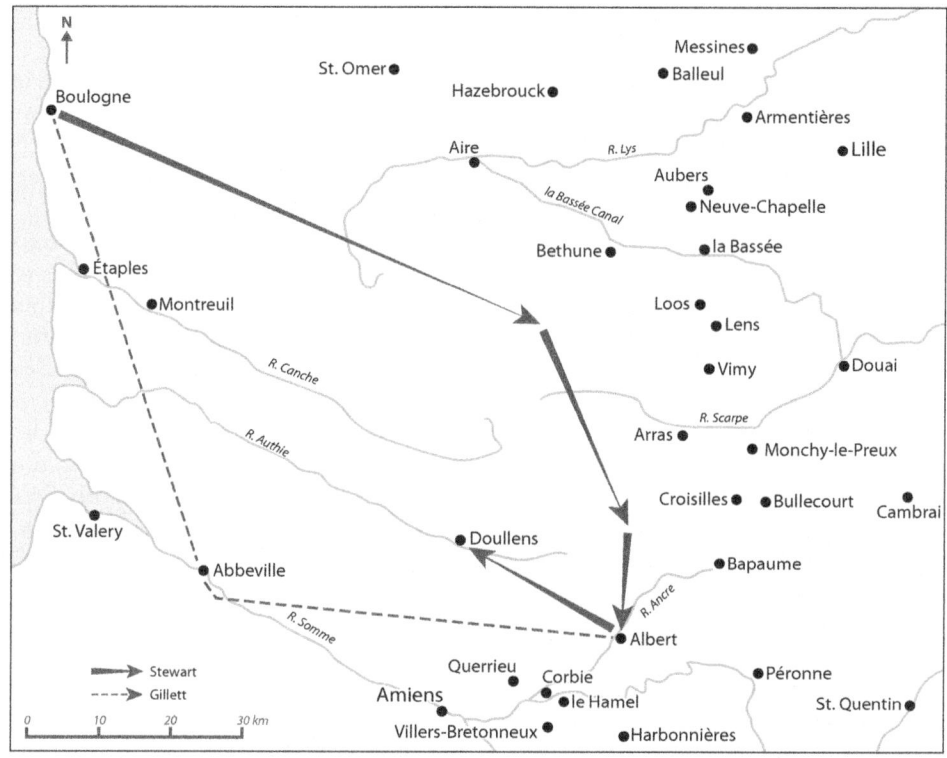

Map of Frs. Gillett and Steuart on the Somme 1916.

declaration of war and the inevitable impact of subsequent engagement. In both scenarios initial civilian incredulity was gradually replaced by the reality of forceful, violent German military action. As the dead and mutilated arrived home, shock and grief replaced any lingering attempt, subconscious or not, to become distanced from the truth. Returning soldiers themselves attempted to subvert the truth for various reasons, but the casualty toll could not be hidden. Gillett's observations, made as they were at the point of impact, allow an insight into the complete naivety of the newly arrived soldiers, their chaplains and French civilian associates. Steuart had not yet arrived and when he did went immediately into action only briefly passing through Boulogne. Fr Gillett's testimony for mid-summer 1916 will, therefore, be utilised.

So what did this era look like in Paris and provincial Boulogne in mid-1916? The term La Belle Époque discerns a flavour of the times: one of contemporary bourgeois indulgence in Boulogne, if not the exaggerated romanticism of fashionable Paris of which Renoir famously painted and the remnants of which Gillett would embrace in 1919. Instead, in mid-1916, Gillett captured its essence in certain quarters of Boulogne whilst simultaneously becoming aware of the violence as war encroached. The term La Belle Époque describes the optimism of France, and particularly Paris, between the end of the Franco-Prussian war in 1871 and the early part of the First World War. The expressions La Belle Époque and indeed the First World War were not yet in usage, nevertheless, the optimism generated after the 1870 creation of the Third Republic is self-evident. Regional peace, economic prosperity, and the fruits of increasing colonial expansion gained pace alongside technological and scientific developments, all of which encouraged a rise in secularism, materialism, and national confidence. Even if the loss of Alsace and parts of Lorraine in the Franco-Prussian War still ate at the heart of most Frenchmen, the collapse of the Second Republic propelled forward a new way for the French people. Cultural innovations were embodied in artistic expression, gentility of fashion and manners, and café life. Those able to embrace this golden period considered themselves modishly liberal. Notwithstanding these shifts, France had a strong traditional and cultural Catholic backbone. In literary circles the influential writer Émile Zola spanned this crucial period. His personal beliefs in many ways mirror the contradictions within the French experience. Predominantly he was a chastening critic of Catholicism but also at times a devotee, thus reflecting the ambiguities of the period. His harsh literary realism or naturalism, reminded others of the abject poverty and desperation of life beneath the surface of current social veneer. This inner turmoil would soon be over-powered by military events, yet the dichotomy between Catholicism and secularism was clear and Fr Gillett was quick to observe and comment throughout his time in France.

In reasonably prosperous Boulogne Zola's darker side of urban life eluded Gillett, but throughout his travels in France he repeatedly remarked on French rural poverty. His admiration for peasant grit and resourcefulness was deeply felt. He recorded the genteel and gay atmosphere in Boulogne in the summer of July 1916, a town displaying an air of sophistication associated with Parisians who sojourned there to enjoy the sea, nearby beaches, golf, theatre, restaurants and hotel life. But it was also a busy commercial and trading centre which functioned in the war as both occasional Army headquarters, and as a vital port of entry and exit for matériel and personnel. Gillett chronicled both the *petit bourgeois* society he witnessed plus the exacting reality of the arrival in Boulogne hospitals of wounded British soldiers, and their forward transference to British hospitals if they had survived so far. In religious circles he understood that Catholicism as a universal religion shared similarities in liturgy, rubrics and doctrine across nations, but local variations based on historical and cultural differences intrigued his English customs. Conversely, he was not always a complete devotee of French ways. Some British chaplains found the French versions of services too long, especially sermons. Was Fr Gillett lamenting or being droll when in late November 1916 he commented: 'Exposition in Drucat church, attended Vespers in afternoon but never again – too long – Vespers – hymns – sermons and the French sermons are some length – more hymns – in all 2 hours. *Golly my piety was exhausted* and it was freezing in the Church'?[1] In general Gillett was a passionate supporter of French Catholicism

---

1   SDA, Gillett Diaries, 30 November 1916. Author's italics.

1916: À Partir De La Belle Époque À Folie   93

to which he referred throughout. He shared his priesthood with French and Belgian civilians to great effect throughout the war, but his main occupation was to alleviate the spiritual deprivation of ordinary soldiers of whom he became a great admirer.

Recognising the seriousness of the situation was a phased affair for both the general population in Boulogne and Gillett. He spent seventy days there before entraining to the Front. The scale of the war and its tragic consequences gradually made inroads into the psychology and practicality of the citizens of Boulogne, deeply affecting this French town. Gillett's diaries reveal this mounting sense of tension carrying along a new realism. On arrival at the Western Front he was able to witness the stark metamorphic transformation from the beautiful time to madness, replicating his own transition from a parish priest in peaceful times, to a chaplain on the Western Front. His apprenticeship was coming to an end: he was in Zola's language having to 'step up to the plate'.[2]

Fr Gillett at Boulogne

Fr Fred Gillett's accounts initially show his un-readiness for what was to follow, he was not alone. The acutely contradictory situations existing at Boulogne and Albert, a mere 90 miles away by wartime rail, encapsulate divergences and contradictions which will be repeated continually throughout the war. His enthusiasm is captured leaving Folkestone on Wednesday 28 June 1916, he reported:

> Altar rails crowded with communicants. Belgian sermon for the people, the people all sing in simple Gregorian right through the Mass. Pyric, Gloria, Sanctus, Agnus Dei, very inspiring. At 11am, on the boat which is full of troops. Before leaving lifebelts are issued. At 11:15 boat swings out, bevy of all sorts of folks on board. Nurses, Red Cross people, VAD's, officers and troops of all shapes and sizes, of all nationalities and rank. Arrive Boulogne about 1 p.m. put up for the night at the Hotel Louvre. The passage was gloriously smooth – thank God for that'!

The next day marked a shift from comfortable normality towards the effects of war:

> 19th June, Feast of SS Peter and Paul. At 7:30 a.m. said Mass in St Vincent's Church close by. One of the nurses that had come over on the same boat attended my Mass, which was offered for the nurses. Nurse Harrington informed me that she knew Sister Louise of Beacon Lane – great! Visited for the first time 13th General Hospital up the hill near the Casino. My first site of the wounded, phew

---

2   Émile Zola's, *La Bête Humaine* (Oxford World Classics, 2009). A reference of progression from fireman to driver.

what crowds and what sights and what stories to tell. Received my appointment to Boulogne for hospital work until my time comes for the line

Assigned as Fr Grobel DAPC's assistant, the next day he witnessed more soldier suffering: 'Watched several train loads of wounded arrive; poor fellows'! Moreover, on Saturday 1 July the 'Great Push' on the Somme had begun whilst he:

> Strolled around Boulogne and got acquainted with the town. Saw the Cathedral Church in the old town where there is great devotion to Notre Dame de Boulogne – a glorious cathedral. Strolled out to the CWL hut and found it well organised and very comfortable, fitted with a chapel for Sunday use. Close by is the famous statue of Napoleon with his back to England, presumably a token that he despised her BUT what would be his thoughts today as her best and bravest rallied to defend his fair France? In my stroll, many fine houses were pointed out as having been occupied by nuns previous to their being expelled by persecuting laws.

On Sunday he: 'Said a public Mass in St Nicholas's at 8:45 a.m. which was the children's Mass. Afterwards I went off to the cemetery to conduct the funerals of my boys to be buried'. His empathy and awareness increased, Monday:

> Some 4 trains of wounded arrive from the line. Apparently the first effects of the great July push. The walking wounded look awful, vacant and nervous, tunics torn to shreds some with blankets around. The stretcher cases are screened off. The French mourning strikes me of being very impressive and neat. Much more so than in England, although their church services, owing to the men being called up, are not too impressive after England. The singing is makeshift except when the congregation take it up. High Mass is continual with them.

Tuesday was: 'a quiet day, beyond a run around the hospitals'. Next he gave an insight into the Catholic chaplaincy organisation on the ground: 'Every Tuesday the chaplains confer with the 'Boss' for appointments etc. etc. Fr Rawlinson (OSB) comes down from GHQ and sees everyone. In the afternoon we all meet in the club for tea'.[3] Day by day the war was looming into the consciousness of those in Boulogne: 'Airships and aeroplanes scouting round on the lookout for mines and submarines. Today one could hear the roar of the guns. Not an unusual thing when the wind was favourable'. He remarked 5 July that: 'Funerals always at 8 in the great city cemetery of Boulogne. After breakfast the rounds of the hospital – now packed with wounded in consequence of the severe fighting going on'. Fred Gillett was a frequent and avid social observer with a distinctly compassionate outlook. He wrote: 'Fri 7th July at 9 p.m. a huge hospital train

---

3   Tea or more commonly 'clerical tea' may have been a euphemism for something a little stronger and appearing in the early months.

arrives – most walking cases but pitiable to watch the poor fellows hobble along – arms and legs and hands bandaged. Taken off to the hospitals for wash and clean and then most of them boated for 'Blighty' to leave the hospitals free for stretcher cases'.

8 July he integrated religious and social observation: 'Stalls are clustered around the church and the good people pop in and out of the church making their visits and in the midst of their work remembering their boys at the front and the cause of their country. What fun strolling around amongst the great crowds and listening to their bargaining'. The to-ing and fro-ing between the routine of civilian existence and the horrific casualties of war continued: 'Sun 9th Mass in Detention Barracks and Rosary there in the afternoon at 3:30 p.m. Around the hospitals – the jaw cases an awful site, poor Pat has lost both his legs'. Tuesday 11 July 1916: 'Funeral Mass in St Nicholas's – bearers in shiny hats – a Franc given at the offertory when the crowd of mourners go up to kiss the paten or crucifix – a continual jingle of coin. After this little ceremony all but the chief mourners leave the church'. On his return from hospital he experienced a minor explosion which: 'Popped off – gave me quite a fright', but found it was only practice on a target out at sea: 'Gee whizz what a roar, quite deafened me'. Some few months later Fr Gillett would surely have smiled at this recollection, as he sheltered in trenches in full battle mode replete with cacophonous sound track.

French Republic Day 14th July restored Boulogne to something like normality. He observed: 'Bunting all over the town. Shops all bedecked on the river. A half-holiday for the townspeople'. The next day he: 'Took a car for a spin to Le Portel. What a glorious view one gets from here of the sea and Boulogne. People all about very early – shopping all done in the early morning in these big towns. Quite a buzz of life'. Two days later the sense of Belle Époque temporarily re-emerged after Mass at the Detention Barracks, he noted: 'Shops open much as other days. Cafes do a great trade on Sundays. Folks all sitting out sipping their lemonade or Pernod and taking stock of the passers-by. Benediction at the club in the evening. Folks quite dressy – white stockings and white shoes all the rage'.

Contrasts continued: '17th July, Mass and hospitals – this morning received a soldier 'extremis' into the church at the Canadian hospital at Le Portel. One noticed all the French drinking houses have a billiard table but without pockets – the French game is all canons'.

20 July the sense of 'phoney war' reappeared:

> Mass of Blessed Sacrament at 8 a.m. – lots of school children there – evidently a French custom to come to this Thursday Mass – the organ blazing away was very fine. Strolled back from hospital in the afternoon. A glorious sunset and crowds of people around the Plage – lots of revelling and sea bathing. French band playing for an hour or two on the Plage.

Bands playing, revelling, and sea-bathing are normal holiday time pleasantries but by contrast they resided uncomfortably within the earshot of soldiers suffering and dying. The concept of total war had not yet taken hold, but as the days continued even this French idyll would collapse under the assaults of death, illness, and German bombing; this was merely the transition stage. The shift from normality to civilian engulfment in the war was gradual and erratic, but also inevitable. As the Somme battles raged, in Boulogne on 21 July it was a:

> Gorgeous day – as we went to Mass the boom of canon was very audible. 3 or 4 planes pass overhead on the way to see what's on. During the burials the firing was very distinct. One learnt later that the continual 'boom' was the explosion of an ammunition dump destroyed by the Boche aircraft. At 6:30 went into church and found St Nicholas's crowded.

One of the least attractive aspects of war was the execution of British soldiers for transgressions, some justifiable and others not. Gillett's empathy extended to a man shot at dawn. As a protegé of Fr Grobel a fellow Lancastrian chaplain and DAPC, Gillett commented on his mentors spiritual duties: '25th July – Cemetery and there I see the grave of the poor man Fr Grobel had attended in the very early hours of the morning. He had been shot at 4:30 a.m. – resigned and had received all the last rites of the Church. Mass was said for him in his cell – at it he communicated'. Fr Gillett never attended an execution in person but Fr Steuart and Gill will later testify the sadness surrounding these events. Whilst this soldier was being buried Gillett observed that: 'On my way up noticed French playing tennis on the hard dry sand and quite a good time they were having'.

On the 28 July we are reminded of the differences between French and British Catholic priests at war. British and other nationalities chaplains, under the jurisdiction of their bishops, were forbidden to take up arms; in secular France the government controlled its bishops ensuring that taking up arms was compulsory for French Curés. It did not appear to cause Fr Gillett much soul searching: 'The French priests as soldiers are quite numerous in the Army – they inspire confidence in the men and infused a great spirit into them. On all sides one hears great things of them. Many of them are receiving promotion. The French law forbids the attendance of the minister in the hospitals unless a request in writing entered in the man's pay book or prayer book'.

By 29 July the now familiar routine of normality laced with potential danger occupied his mind: 'Mass and hospitals. It is amusing to see how the French use dogs; they strap them to simple handcarts and make them pull them along'. Next day:

> Glorious day – blazing hot, strolled around the old city, how glorious the trees are and the green plots around the old ramparts make a walk very pleasant. What thoughts came to mind as one watches the crowds going to and fro to the churches? Masses going on at all hours. Attended High Mass at St Nicholas's and very good singing by a special choir of boys. Lots of torpedo boats around today – rumours of a submarine in the neighbourhood.

In the 'roasting heat' of early August he wrote: 'Zepp's reported over Boulogne'. This was unconfirmed yet they did cause destruction as late as August 1918 as we will see.

On Friday he remarked: 'Guns again very audible today. Found the hospital in good time and then went for a dip in the sea – lovely; crowds about doing the same'. The illusion of La Belle Époque continued: 'Sat 5th August. Mass, then lolled about, great fun watching the marketing. Mistresses all out with their maids, who parcel things up and toddle away at the heels of their mistresses'. On Sunday his mind was focussed on his religion particularly French customs:

> Mass at 13 Stationary hospital then at Detention Barracks. All morning the bells are chiming away, calling God's creatures to pay their homage. And the streets are full of people hurrying to the churches to fulfil the highest of obligations. Attended the 11:30 Mass in the church of St Nicholas. This is the lazy folks mass and what crowds of them there are. The church is more than packed. They say France has lost its religion? But what about the crowds then at Sunday Mass – it is wonderful. And during the day there is a constant stream of visitors. The behaviour in the churches is novel to the English mind.

The King passed through Boulogne on 8 August. It was dutifully noted as Fred Gillett embraced the present, but he was now being lured towards the Front himself: 'Wed 9th. Weather holding out beautifully, how nice to be lolling about with a glorious sky overhead – the vast sea one huge glistening expanse and a roaring, scorching sun taking every drop of moisture out of one and with all this pleasure and repose at Boulogne what scenes further in land'? He was slowly acclimatising to his forthcoming fate informed by not only the deluge of early Somme casualties, but two-way traffic of those being rushed up to the Front. This drew another empathetic comment in mid-August: 'Strolled into the station to find a long train packed with lads for 'up to the line'; carriages too luxurious, so the men are packed into the vans and travel much like cattle'. Good solid empathy and admiration of the 'Tommy' continued throughout the war. Fr Walker painted such a scene with equal pathos, reflecting kindred spirit with Gillett:

The Locon Express. (JAD, Paintings of Fr Leslie Walker)

Religion and war were now competing forces within his development as a chaplain attached to the British Army. A researcher's duty therefore is to ascertain if he tended towards being more an officer than a priest, or vice versa? Fr Gillett was consistently and emphatically the latter. To replace the officer dimension we might consider him to be a cultural geographer cum historian. He combined his cultural fascination of French secular and spiritual customs by observing the activities of people and places within these war scenarios and across time. He was provoked by his sense of social injustice and particularly the legal secularisation imposed on Catholicism by the French Government. His diary entries repeatedly capture his thought processes, for instance: 'Fri 11th. Crowds of Australians move up the line; transport wagons all massed and great heavy guns. Quarant 'Ore[4] in St Nicholas's crowds of communicants, spent half an hour in watching and praying for our lads and our cause. At 8 p.m. public devotions – some very beautiful and direct singing'. Contrasts within the same diary page are not a regular feature in Fr Steuart's account where it will become evident that being an officer held great import, hence defining his demeanour. Gillett continued 14 August noting that: 'French soldiers and a General decorated on the Plage. Wild and stormy and the cars in consequence unable to run along the promenade'. He was more comfortable within his own culture and the following day, on the important Feast of the Assumption, he celebrated:

> Mass at hospital. Cathedral Church the main church today – High Mass sung by the Bishop of Arras, who now lived in Boulogne as his palace and cathedral at Arras were no more. High Mass at 9:30 a.m. everything carried out beautifully. In the afternoon solemn Vespers and Procession round the old city walls, the dedication of France to Our Lady. Procession very fine – all the little children in white. Bishop walks the streets in mitre and rochette. Keeps leaving the procession to bless the little children presented to him. The whole week to the 23rd taken up with pilgrimages from neighbouring churches to Our Lady's shrine. The Assumption and France's national fete day and a great birthday chosen I believe by Napoleon. City is full of life and excitement.

He continued in this vein until 20 August: 'Pilgrimage day for St Nicholas' parish starts at 6:30 and everybody makes for Notre Dame Cathedral'. Thursday: 'Visited the Cathedral and saw crowds at their devotions. And they say that France is losing her faith. Don't believe it. Church gaily decked with bannerettes and around the altar of Our Lady, crowds are moving all the day through'. The next day: 'Mass and hospital, and another run up to the Cathedral. Still crowds coming and going indeed all through the octave of the Assumption the church is continually thronged. On Saturday he officiated in the Cathedral at the Sacred Heart altar, a forerunner for next day:

---

4   40 hours of prayerful devotion in the presence of the exposition of the Blessed Sacrament.

> Mass in hospital and prison. Great ceremonies at Cathedral today – procession in afternoon through the streets of Boulogne. The town is bedecked. Masses of people turn in from everywhere and the soldiers stand and gaze in amazement. Procession very long but not that order and precision one sees in Preston and Manchester processions. Bishop takes part on foot wearing mitre and rochette and carrying a staff, accompanied by the chapter and many clergy. The day closes with solemn Benediction in the Cathedral. Quite a day of piety and an eye-opener to the British soldiers. What a blessing must come to France through the piety of its many devout women.

The next day he observed guns on the quayside waiting to be delivered which he described as: 'huge, ugly, fearsome monsters'. Tuesday was time for reflection, something that he achieved throughout. We will see that Fr Steuart's contemplations are more militaristic and formal, but Gillett's tend towards the intuitive and introspective.

> Mass. Visited Wimereaux – a beautiful seaside place, some 2 miles from Boulogne. Searched round for the golf links which I couldn't locate at all. Weary with my search squatted down just off the roadside and stared across to England. Quite a clear day and the Dover cliffs in sight in the distance. Ah England, the power in the war and yet her soil untouched and her people unperturbed. What a contrast and France in turmoil and strife and she peaceful and restful. The boom of guns was telling of the noble sons of England and France.

Time was passing slowly, consequently he relished the opportunity to meet and socialise with other chaplains and acquaintances. On Fr Grobel's birthday at a chaplain's weekly meeting, he stumbled across Fr Haney: 'Lunched together at the Deveraux and had a great chinwag'. This was the calm before the storm. He would have known that four Catholic chaplains had already perished fulfilling their duties in this arena. John Gwynn SJ, serving with 1 Battalion Irish Guards was the first:

Fr Gwynn of Galway died of shock due to severe wounds on 12 October 1915 aged 50. This was not his first encounter with danger:

> It is nearly alright now [a recent wound] – thank God. I had a very narrow escape and I know it was prayers that saved me. It was the day the Irish Guards took Brickstacks and trenches at Cuinchy [near Bethune]. Several shells burst where I was, but I was not touched. The last thing I remember was seeing the Guards get to the top of the ridge, where a lurid red blaze seemed to crash in to my eyes with a deafening crash. I was hurled back some five yards or so. When I came too I felt my face all streaming with blood, and my leg paining me. I was suffocated too with thick, warm, vile gas from

Fr John Gwynn SJ.

Headstone at Bethune Cemetery. Age 50. 1 Battalion Irish Guards. KIA 12 October 1915.

the shell. Although I was sick and dazed for two or three days, I never had to give up, thank God.[5]

To add to his worries on another occasion he was dug out of the mud when a shell exploded nearby, and has been described, he spent some time in hospital with rheumatism or a trapped nerve. Finally, on 11 October 1915, whilst in a dug out with fellow officers evading heavy German artillery, a shell landed in the doorway causing many injuries. Fr Gwynn was hit in several places but particularly the left lung and died next morning.

As Father Gillett was settling into his new life at Boulogne the battles on the Somme intensified. Fr Donal Vincent O'Sullivan from Killarney in the diocese of Kerry attached to 1 Irish Rifles was killed in action on 5 July 1916 at Bouzincourt, aged 26. Fr Gill wrote in his diaries:

> No words could be strong enough to express our sorrow at the death of Fr O'Sullivan. Not only keen about his own brigade he was always anxious to help in all directions. He had gone up to the ADS which was receiving wounded from several units of his Brigade. This was a dangerous place in the midst of gunfire. By one of those accidents during the war, a battery of howitzers was placed just alongside the dressing station. Of course this battery attracted counter fire. Fr

---

5   JAL, *Our Catholic Chaplains Experiences* p. 257, retold from *Catholic Times*, July 1916.

O'Sullivan was talking to some men near the dressing station where a shell killed him and several other soldiers. One of the other chaplains took the funeral service and the soldiers made a special cross. The Curé of Bouzincourt provided a coffin. We were in the thick of an attack when the funeral took place. By his kindliness, cheerfulness and self-sacrifice, he had endeared himself to all, I do not speak of his courage for that goes without saying. Personally I never met a better chaplain and one whose sole ambition was to be attached to an Irish Regiment.[6]

This was a glowing testimony from a man not known for issuing plaudits.

At Bouzincourt Cemetery.

Headstone. Fr Donal V O'Sullivan. Age 26. 1 Irish Rifles. KIA 5 July 1916.

6 JAD, Fr Gill Diary, pp. 55-7.

On 17 August whilst Fr Gillett was commenting on French devotions in Boulogne, Fr Denis Doyle SJ, attached to 2 Battalion Leinster Regiment was fatally wounded on the Somme. He was buried two days later. As the Leinster's advanced towards Longueval, Guillemont, Combles, and Ginchy a shell exploded at the ADS. Fr Doyle was of Wexford descent but born in Kimberley South Africa. Displaying the attributes of the Jesuit's military founder St Ignatius of Loyola, Doyle was described as a man who demanded strong discipline and 'the son of a true soldier-Saint'.[7] He won the Military Cross which the Commonwealth War Graves recognise but which is curiously not mentioned in his obituaries.

Fr Denis Doyle SJ. MC.

Headstone at Dive Copse British Cemetery. Age 39. 2 Leinster Regiment. KIA 17 August 1916.

The underlying desire for most chaplains was to join the action and to achieve their spiritual missions as priests despite the realisation of the enormity of suffering and the challenges facing them. It should be emphasised that it was not Fr Gillett's wish to be part of any delay in working at the Front. Some chaplains pulled ecclesiastical rank to get there but even if he could have done so it was not in Fr Gillett's character to ask favours. His life was based on obedience and humility and he was prepared to wait even though it took seventy days before he was attached

---

7   *Dublin Review* 1919–20. *Chaplains of the Great War*, pp. 187-9.

to a Division.⁸ Not all new chaplains had the same notion and some like Fr Henry Gill SJ were able and prepared to pull rank. Henry Gill's family owned the Gill and Macmillan publishing business and he had earned a reputation as a prominent scientist having studied under Cavendish at Cambridge. Based at Rouen for a mere 16 days, his annoyance at being detained at a Base Hospital was expressed via a direct request to Keatinge, then the Principal Chaplain in 1914. He wrote to his Provincial: 'I enclose a copy of a formal request which I have sent to the Principal Chaplain. The letter explains itself'. Gill was expressing his frustration of not being with a Division: 'There are a great number of sick and wounded [Rouen Base Hospital], and at times some are to receive Extreme Unction. I do not consider this to be the kind of work I came out for'.⁹ In the early days of military chaplaincy Fr Gill was exhibiting his own inexperience. It *was* an absolute necessity to look after the sick and wounded in medical facilities as well as trench work. Instead strings were pulled to liberate Gill, surely a divisive and unnecessary course of action among brothers? Fr Grobel APC described Gill as: 'dissatisfied and awkward to deal with'.¹⁰ The arrangement to release Fr Gill was clearly of mutual benefit. Fr Gillett kept his thoughts to himself but expressed his own frustration as relief when finally released for the Somme: 'Mass. Boss comes down and I receive orders to go up the line – HURROO! I am to report to the 54th Brigade 18 Division.'¹¹

Fr Gillett at the Front

Fred Gillett captured the transition from Boulogne's relatively calm *Belle Époque* environment, to the *Folie* or insanity of the devastation on the Western Front. He arrived at 11:35 a.m. on 6 September first at St Pol, west of Arras:

> where we had a halt of 2 hours and watched train after trainload of men pass through – cavalry, artillery, Canadians, Australians, all sorts on the road. Depart 2 p.m. from Tincques which was our railhead. From here we tried to get off in search of our regiments. The roar of guns told us we were in the vicinity of the line. We were roommates in a very filthy farm house – phaw! After reporting to brigade HQ I was attached to 11th Royal Fusiliers, 12th Middlesex, 7th Bedfordshire's and 6th Northants then R E Coy, M G Coy, and lastly 54th Field Ambulance.

---

8   SDA Fr Gillett's War Diaries, 29 June to 6 September 1916.
9   Here it is only reasonable to presume Gill meant Base work rather than Extreme Unction – a vital sacrament in war and a key denominational discriminator.
10 DAA, 3234, Grobel to Rawlinson, 23 November 1914.
11 Op.cit.

10 September, Gillett agog with his new military surroundings still found time to observe both spiritual and domestic cultural signifiers: 'The French Crucifixes at entrance and exit of the village very conspicuous. Houses seem to be all 1 storey buildings – in the farms, the houses are all back to back and built squarish-like – the centre land being usually the manure dump – and around this the buildings seem to be put up'. This farming narrative was accurately painted by Fr Walker, a good example of cross-referencing the written word with an artist's eye, suggesting a somewhat symbiotic or intuitive response to shared experiences. Such overlaps are repeated throughout although they apparently never met each other.

Four Stages in the Growth of a French Farm. (JAD, Paintings of Fr Leslie Walker)

Fr Gillett spent the next few days becoming acquainted with troops and civilians amidst surrounding tumult. This period of acclimatisation was brief but allowed Gillett's philosophy to emerge, combining his desire for both the corporal and spiritual welfare of the troops. His observation and admiration of the troops is self-evident. 11 September:

> What a sight to see the whole Brigade on the move. And what thoughts came to mind as one looked on these strapping lads and wondering what the future held

in store for them. But they sang and joked apparently never giving the future a thought. They seemed happy in their roving life and richly enjoyed the present.[12]

Two days later, as the men trained and edged ever closer to Albert and the ferocity of the Somme, he compared good and evil. God and the peaceful village represented by the church spires and trees represent good; hideous fighting, brawling noise and death their antithesis:

> Mass at 7:30 then Rosary. Raincheval was a cosy little village – there she lay nestling is a huge hollow and surrounded with woods. The church spires, tower up above us, the tree tops bespeaking the war of God and peace. All silently watching over the peaceful village. Yet this village of peace and quiet can tell its tale. In it, hides away some 1200 men, training for the hideous fight, awaiting for orders to go forward, some must go to death, others are spared for the victory. The peaceful village now a dumping ground for men going up to action and its peacefulness is disturbed by the brawl of noisy Tommies.

Fr Gillett gained his experience as a parish priest in a working class district comprising many Liverpool-Irish and was familiar with the social habits of these men. His observation encompasses both sadness and reality. 14 September:

> Mass at 7 p.m. then Rosary. Men billeted all around the church but few come to church. After the day's work and training they love to gather in estaminets for their beer over which they smoke and chat and the church is forgotten. Here they are, many preparing for the slaughter. Any minute they may be ordered forward. Yet thought of duties before their venture never seems to come home to them. They let slip the chances God put in their hands and have no remorse. God's mercy and goodness receives no recompense, yet many of these men are soon to court death.

It is worth noting that Gillett's army units contained few Catholics which influenced these early observations. When in the midst of a strong Catholic presence, such as Lancashire, Irish, and American troops, he would view their religiosity in an altogether different light.

The time for rumination was rapidly fading and ten days later he was involved in the Somme action: 'Mass at 9 a.m. At 10 a.m. everybody is moving up the line. And I get my first sight of the ravages of war. Through Bouzincourt away left, then right, through the woods and here we come right into a mass of our heavy guns. The shots are whistling over our heads into Thiepval'. It continued two days later. The variety

---

12   In Gillett's file in SDA there are photographs of some of his units pre-battle but unavailable for publishing.

of a Divisional chaplain's *modus operandi* is neatly packaged in this seamless account linking the trenches and advanced dressing stations:

> Thiepval. Up the line in the trenches at 12:30 when the barrage opened – what a din. Over the top and in a short time prisoners were being brought down the line. Up went their hands whenever they passed any of our men. Spent the day and night in the ADS but not overworked, the wounded were getting to other hospitals. What a hideous sight right with the roar and flash of guns. Just by some 4 huge South African guns were belching forth and the Boche retaliated. The bridge over which our wounded were taken was struck and we had to seek some other road. Took the ADS up to one or two posts and we had some going.

The fighting was now intense and continual, units being rotated between the rear and the front lines. 28 September he remarked:

> To Albert to look around and see the wonder of the leaning Madonna. What a place Albert is. It was really my first site of a ruined village, terrible. German shells were falling a little way off. Trudged off to Lancashire Dump in Aveluy Wood and watched the boys fighting their way over the Thiepval Ridge, to the left of the village. The Boche guns were very active and all kinds of stuff were bursting over our troops.

The next day:

> Dr McElvey was killed and awaiting burial at Paisley Corner. I wasted 4 hours hanging about and that after a long and weary trudge along the trenches. In due course got a grave dug and piously buried the poor doctor.[13] All the while shells were falling around and several times we had to seek shelter. But finally we got through with it. It was a filthy wet day and the trenches were awful. Poor men were lying on the top, knocked out – arms and legs were butting out of the trench sides and here and there a dud shell was sticking out. I was glad to have done with it all and get back to our wee shelter in the woods.

As the battles continued he:

> Visited the line at North Bluff beyond Lancashire Dump – by railway bridge at Authuille. A prisoner of war cage there, where prisoners are searched and then sent right back to established cages. At 7 p.m. Boche opens fire on the wood in search of our guns. A squeamish business as the shells were falling around our camp. Men ordered to stand-to, ready to bolt. Everyone on edge. Whizzy, plimp,

---

13 See Appendix VII for Burial Directives. DAA, Ephemera.

a dud, everybody in a cold sweat. After about half an hour the firing stops and nobody is sorry!!

Later, on 24 October, Gillett described the situation north of Albert: 'Got into German shelling – two or three large crumps came over, but got away untouched. Mules and transport stampeding – I was glad to get clear. The Courcelette area was under observation by the Boche, he was always trying his luck around about.'

Fr Steuart at the Front

Fr Steuart entrained to Albert from Boulogne via Abbeville on 13 October, arriving two days later. On 25 October, after a brief familiarisation behind the line, he joined his battalion 12 HLI near Countalmaison. [Close to where Gillett was working]. 27 October:

> Re-joined Battalion in '26th Avenue', a support trench in Le Sars. Heavy shelling and machine gun fire all around. Took Blessed Sacrament with me. Wore my tin helmet for the first time. As I got into the 26th Avenue I was going to steady myself by resting my hand on what I thought was a sandbag but found it was a dead man's head sticking out of the parados, also found a leg, and most of a body in a similar position further on. Slept in very narrow dugout.

Other chaplains were enduring their own specific encounters and deaths mounted. Fr Guthrie was the next Catholic chaplain to die. Serving 8 Battalion East Lancashire Regiment, this Benedictine chaplain attached to St Mary's Abbey Quarr, Isle of Wight, died of wounds near Varennes, between Albert and Amiens, 21 November 1916. Originating from France, little else is known of him.

The arbitrary nature of this war was emphasised by comparing the same day's activities across Guthrie, Gillett and Steuart. They were serving in a circle of less than 5 miles diameter when Fr Guthrie was killed. Gillett was at Warloy: 'At last out of the line for a rest – move out of Albert to Warloy trekking through Millencourt and Henencourt, a lovely walk'. Henencourt is a mile from Varennes where

Headstone. Fr David Guthrie OSB. Age Unknown. 8 East Lancashire Regiment KIA 21 November 1916.

At Varennes Cemetery.

Guthrie perished. Meanwhile Fr Steuart at Talmas approximately 4 miles apart was seemingly in a different world:

> Mass and renewal of vows at convent. Funeral (9 to 12!). A very sorry business. Slouched thro' the streets in an alb just below knees, two 'chantres', two servers & a beadle, Missa Cantata and burial. All very casual and irreverent to my mind. Benediction in Convent at 3:30. Officers Club opens in town room for my billet. At 5 p.m. went to church for Confessions. Heard two and gave Communion.

Chaplains spent much of their time with the fighting men: fluctuations between routine and action applied to both clergy and military:

> For the average soldier on the Western Front, very little happened on a day-to-day basis. Even when soldiers were at the front line, they watched and waited. Boredom was a major problem. But the prospect of action gave soldiers plenty of opportunity to feel not just boredom, but fear. Both could be relieved by humour. And The Wipers Times was partly a product of soldiers' need to tackle both the boredom and the fear.[14]

---

14 Richard Grayson, 'The Wipers Times: The funny side of World War One' <http://www.bbc.co.uk/history/0/23931340> (Accessed 4 June 2017).

Being somewhat divorced from the social life of the military in secular terms chaplains did not have the *Wipers Times* as consolation. Nonetheless, their spiritual and pastoral duties practically brought them into contact with troops and officers, offering a stark reminder of the question: what should a chaplain be, an officer or priest? Of course he had to be both but degrees varied between individuals. Fr Gillett tended towards the latter whilst Fr Steuart was disposed towards the former. Distinctions were derived from pre-war cultural and pastoral deployment which had been defined by their backgrounds and the needs of the Church. Gillett from a thriving but economically disadvantaged Liverpool-Irish parish was comfortable with the common man, but less so with the officer class in general to whom he was ambivalent. He could fulfil his mission with the common man/soldier rendering military status as simply another obstacle to overcome. Steuart had lived a more isolated life confined mainly within the Society of Jesus' headquarters at Belgravia. Not having been a parish priest, and unaccustomed to the working class hampered his integration with troops. Although it is evident from his comments that *he* felt at home with senior officers, their cordiality was not, alas, reciprocated towards a Catholic chaplain with the junior rank of a 'small fry' captain. Instead he found his niche with other captains but significantly did not go out of his way to fraternize with fellow chaplains. Unlike at home his social status could not be used effectively which caused him personal angst, particularly in the latter days when he craved official recognition. His orientation towards the military officer class, reinforced at Stonyhurst, was attenuated by both his status quo within the Army and the restrictions of the chaplaincy remit. Both men were good priests at war and their daily spiritual routine was much the same, but their own outlooks, interpretations, and demeanours were in every other sense different. The social range across chaplains reflected the pre-war Church's need for men from all walks of life: but their effectiveness as chaplains was ultimately shaped by the realities of war. Any comparisons between chaplains have to take this into consideration.

Sensitivities and traditions apart, both chaplains continued supporting their troops. As the winter wore on activities were necessarily scaled back if seldom in absolute safety. Gillett lamented that 13 November: 'Troops up the line for another wretched spell, when is it going to cease?' His spirits rose when he declared a successful operation at Beaumont Hamel with 2,500 prisoners. Steuart claimed 4,000 on the same day, a day when: 'A black goat strayed into the camp and subalterns spent most of the night moving into one another's tent'. Three days later: 'Find that the goat and two more dogs have joined us permanently'. Animals appear on occasion, from Steuart's goat to Gillett's 'wee puppies'. Possibly the most amusing animal story was at Adruicq, between Ypres and Calais. A Catholic hut had been provided in the village run by Fr Carey SJ. As troops went back and forward it was an opportunity to exchange messages and provide spiritual succour. Confessions were conducted by relays of chaplains: 'Father Devas, a later arrival, loved this exhibition of religious licence and threw himself into it – he and his inseparable dog – who wouldn't, for all the efforts of the army, be thrown out of the Church but squatted happily beside his master and must have become an expert in military confessions'.[15] The dog, like the chaplains, was unable to divulge the secrets of the men.

There was always attendant danger at this time even if these chaplains were not actually in the trenches. Bombing, shelling, and aerial machine gunning continued even if ground fighting was interrupted by the weather and fatigue. Gillett 9 November: '9 p.m. enemy planes over and machine gun bullets flying, 6 in our attic'. The next day: '… planes up all through the night bombing and when folks run into the street, rat-tat-tat of machine guns'. Then 14 November: '4 bombs dropped more or less amongst us. 2 bombs not nearly 20 yards away'. Steuart missed the excitement being billeted at Naours at this time. In contrast to the dangers in Albert, Fred Gillett moved to Doullens towards the end of November and was billeted for a short while in a chateau to which he exclaimed: 'Great swells what, what'!? St Riquier was his next destination and he was delighted to find: 'A glorious old abbey church there with convent. The church looked as though it had been recently renovated'.

In just three months on the Somme Fr Gillett had clearly revised his opinion of war. The initial naiveté of La Belle Époque had dissipated, incredulity was well and truly a memory. His initial 'Hurroo' when he was first deployed on 6 September had been full of innocent enthusiasm: 'Spent the evening with Fr Prescott and Fr Appleby.[16] Sat up in billet till about 2 a.m. chatting about a hundred and one things and a hundred and one persons – lovely night it was. Yarned no end, the three of us and drank not a bit'! By 2 December, the naiveté of September had been replaced. He succumbed to an outpouring of joy and relief when he exclaimed: 'my first leave, hoop-la'! He left next day and arrived at Liverpool on 6 December visiting his family in Lytham, but he rarely commented on his leave, in complete contrast to Fr Steuart who provided great detail. He returned on the 15 December. Both chaplains' diaries are routine until Christmas approached. After midnight Mass, Gillett 'entertained the boys to coffee and Cognac in café. Two canny fellows pocket a bottle each'. To this he makes no further comment but continued to note that: 'All the day spent in feasting, the men all dine about 12 o'clock and very long and good it is too. Then in the evening the officers join messes and have a rare blow out. Some real fun today, everybody in the best of moods'. In such conditions and after so much peril who could begrudge such celebrations? Fred Gillett remarked on St Stephen's Day: 'Rested to get over our previous celebrations – my servant away – unable to get up to attend me'. In any case

---

15   K. Finlay, 'British Catholic Identity during the First War: The Challenge of Universality and Particularity', (unpublished Master of Philosophy thesis, Oxford University, 2004), p. 239. Her brief case studies of Devas and Drinkwater, reveals an outline of their personalities, and is a welcome inclusion into Catholic chaplain historiography.
16   Appleby possibly Canadian, Australian, or Navy CF.

1916: À Partir De La Belle Époque À Folie

St Riquier Abbey, 5 May 2012.

Gillett does not provide any diary entries until New Year's Eve leaving the inquisitive to read between the lines. This festive period suggests a relaxed relationship between this cleric and the men and toward alcohol ordinarily. This is consistent within the Catholic Church who: 'took a relatively relaxed view of such classic Protestant taboos as drinking and gambling, vices which were as prevalent in the army as they were in contemporary working class life'.[17]

Steuart reported on 18 December that he: 'Went up to join Battalion in the line. Lost my way and had a close shave with a dud. Found the HQ at Seven Elms'. He quickly established himself as an enthusiastic manager of the Regimental Mess at HQ, performing various activities. Note Fr Steuart did things for the men but not with them, revealing his general personality and *modus operandi*. 20 December: 'Went in search of beer for men's Christmas dinner, found it in Corbie 800 litres – 543 francs'. Next day he: 'Went out again looking for pigs for men's dinner. After great trouble found two at Toutencourt'. 22 December he: 'Drove to Toutencourt in Mess Cart to fetch the pigs. Paid 277 and 401 francs respectively. Brought back pigs to Q.M.s store at La Boiselle'. He celebrated Midnight Mass in a marquee for 60 men and: 'started wearing a Balmoral'. He then noted: 'The Doctor said last night at Mess "It's a funny thing that men in the army put themselves down as C of E, Presbyterian and all sorts of things, but the only Padre that they are all pally with is the RC Padre"'.

---

17   Snape, *God and the British Soldier*, p. 22.

As ever a sort of normality was interspersed with danger. Steuart had a close shave on St Stephen's Day when searching for a billet: 'A bomb fell in the courtyard just across the street and killed two me. One was not quite dead and I had time to give him his absolution'. His Sottish regiment went into the line ironically on New Year's Eve.

Epilogue – 1916

1916 introduced both Gillett and Steuart to the frightening horrors of modern warfare. Gillett from a background of urban parish work did not display the slightest interest in military strategy or the officer élite. However, he would later find that his lack of familiarity and negotiation skills with the higher echelons in the British Army created an obstacle in the pursuit of his duties. For now, he had settled gently into France before being thrust into the Somme cauldron around common soldiers with whom he constantly empathising, as he did the plight of civilians. On the other hand, Steuart's institutional background inclined him towards the military officer class. Without the benefits of a parish background or of gentle immersion into the action, his meagre fortnight's 'on-the-job' preparation on the Somme ensured that he was completely unprepared for his new role within the army. Sadly, he never really understood that any social advantages he may have to offer would not be of benefit; these had no purchase at war. He was a chaplain, a captain class 4, and in common with the mass of other chaplains, nothing else.

Both men had survived 1916 without any serious mishaps. Their eyes were now firmly wide open not only to the challenges and horror of war, but also the opportunities for delivering spiritual sustenance amidst both the excitement and routine. The robust life of a divisional chaplain was dangerous and at times wearisome; but it also offered fulfilment and challenge. Their commitment would be tested to the full in 1917, as they accompanied their troops in other battle zones around Arras and Ypres. As a measure of the intensity of the year to come, nine more chaplains would lose their lives in 1917 compared to four in 1916. Many survivors would never be quite the same again.

6

1917: 'Bah! What a game… The world is supposed to be civilised'

Fr Gillett's observations in January 1917, quoted in full later, reflected the mood felt by many as this war of attrition continued. Many thought the conflict would be over by Christmas 1914, some Christmas 1915, but by Christmas 1916 that dream had been buried in the stinking dark mud of Ypres, the sewers of Arras, the slag heaps of Loos, and the chalky slime of the Somme. The term static war used by most historians is to a large extent true. Trenches stretching from the English Channel coast to Switzerland were, given the odd land snatch and usual retaliatory measures from both sides, unchanged much at this point in time. The Germans did make a tactical retreat to their pre-prepared Hindenburg Line between 14 March and 5 April 1917, which gave an illusionary and temporary cause for optimism, then all settled down and returned to the continued slog of recent years. Yet this strategically correct version of static warfare is incomplete, troops throughout the war constantly rotated between the line and areas behind, they also moved between battle zones and chaplains moved with them. The lines may have remained virtually static but the soldiers and their chaplains clambered onto buses, carts, horses, bicycles, dilapidated railways, or else wore their boots out to reach their latest war zones.

The interchanges between the three major battle zones of the Somme, Arras, and Ypres, were supported by adjacent training and rest areas in less hostile places. The shifting military deployments between these relatively static areas are most recognisable in 1917: the bulk of 1918 fighting took on a different, more mobile nature. Divisional chaplains followed their battalions but when possible did as much as they could for Corps troops in their vicinity, stragglers, and troops passing through without a chaplain. They were not always in the line, but if not, they were located nearby and could minister their services when soldiers were available. This meant continuing to employ local churches where possible, else utilise makeshift premises and improvised facilities when closer to the action. The Universal Church had a wide remit to provide all types of spiritual sustenance, this included soldiers from any geographical, cultural, or social background, including prisoners of war: and Belgian and French civilians where local French priests had gone to war. Nurses, doctors, veterinarians, labourers, artillery, and all the many stray Catholics temporarily disconnected from their regular units were also assisted and appear in both Gillett and Steuart's diaries. Divisional

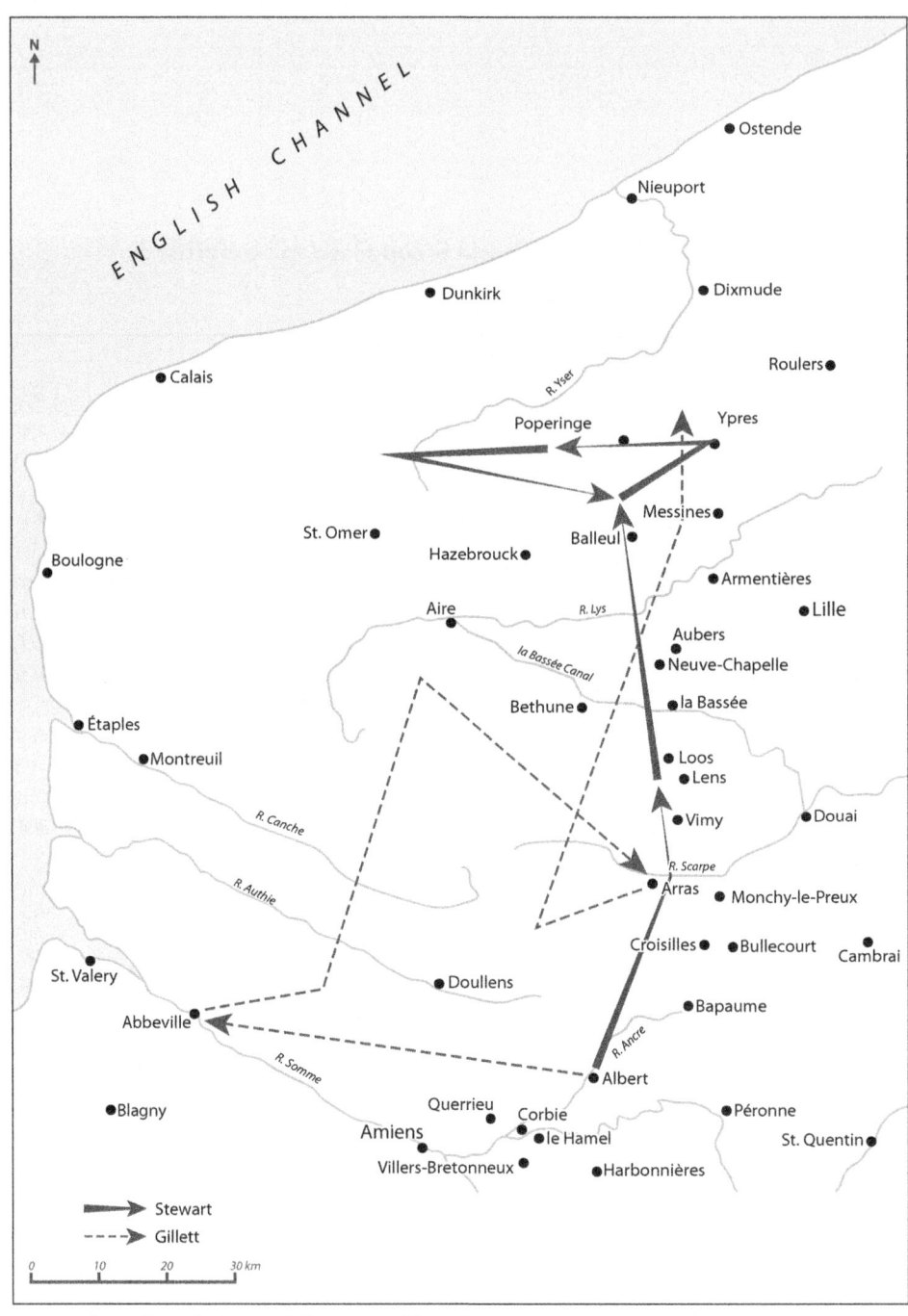

Map of Frs. Gillett and Steuart on Three Fronts 1917 – Somme, Arras, and Ypres.

and Corps chaplains offered all these services in addition to their core work looking after British personnel. This pattern of duty was repeated across the whole chaplaincy enterprise. This was the Catholic Church in being and in 1917 nine of its chaplains attached to the British Army paid the ultimate price for their beliefs and devotion.

Both Gillett and Steuart spent early 1917 on the Somme before going their separate ways, frequently zig-zagging without ever meeting.[1] In chronological order, Gillett went to Guarbecque midway between Arras and Ypres and out of the firing line. Then to Arras and Ypres, which were very much in the firing line, but they also enjoyed quieter periods. He spent Christmas 1917 at Ypres. Steuart went first to a quiet section near Arras, then action through the sewers of Arras, west of Arras at rest again, before moving to Ypres and returning to Arras for Christmas 1917.

If Christmas had been a time of celebration last year, the New Year of 1917 was non-eventful. Both men reported a quiet time. Fr Gillett embarked on 2 January to Abbeville and wrote: 'Put in 2 or 3 days at Officer's Club. Away without leave. Put in a happy 3 days with Wilfrid Pickering'.[2] Fr Steuart had less luck, on 3 January he: 'stayed in bed with a bad cold' which led to him being hospitalised and 'evacuated' until 30 January 1917. In spite of this, his diary mentions that he was not too bad throughout except for loneliness which was somewhat dissipated by one amusing fellow patient: 'An old Naval Commander (Thompson) turned up during the night on his way thro' to Blighty. He has a cage with 9 Algerian birds in it. Must be eccentric. In charge of transports at Marseilles'.

Fr Peter Grobel the DAPC in Boulogne and Fr Gillett's early chaplaincy mentor became the first chaplaincy victim of 1917. Originating from the Salford Diocese, he had been a Naval Chaplain in the Boxer Rising in China at the capture of Tientsin in 1900. Despite his previous service he was only 52 when he died of pneumonia

Headstone. Fr Peter Grobel. Age 52. DAPC Boulogne. Died of Pneumonia 1 January 1917.

---

1   This is debatable. Steuart did claim to meet Gillet [sic] in Albert on 26 October 1916. Gillett was in Albert on that day but does not record meeting any chaplains, being engrossed in the welfare of the troops.
2   Fellow CF from Hexham Diocese and alumni of Ushaw College.

At Boulogne Eastern Cemetery.

on 1 January. His grave at Boulogne Eastern Cemetery was a place of commemoration he knew too well, shown below.[3]

The ebb and flow of war meant that these relatively cosy early January scenarios of Frs. Gillett and Steuart would not last. On 12 January Gillett returned to his philosophical analysis of war: 'Every village one passes has its bevy of soldiers all training for slaughter – some to slaughter others, others to be slaughtered. BAH! What a game – and this when the world is supposed to be civilised'. Four days later he was with his regiment but the intervention of his Commanding Officer is interesting [author's italics]:

> 8 a.m. waiting for the busses, 9 a.m. and 10 a.m. still hung up waiting – hour wary! At 11a.m. we get embussed and get going. Through Val de Maison, Puchevillers, Toutencourt, Martinsart Wood to Aveluy then an hours march to huts way out beyond Crucifix Corner; in the desolate shell ridden area, toward Mougnet Farm. *Late at night sent back by CO who wouldn't have me up with them.* Got back to the Transport lines about 12 p.m. and had to doss down on the floor in some broken down farm building. All night long the guns are roaring and we have left the secret silence of the rest area for a bit. The bussing was the most beastly cold job and lasted a deuce of a time.

3 Sandy ground necessitates the gravestones being laid flat.

Throughout, Gillett testified of obstacles in conducting his spiritual duties through army indifference. As late as 1 January 1918: 'Army recognises anything and everything except religion – godless lot of authorities I have to deal with in 18th Division and 54th Brigade – too fond of other things'. Whist some commanders had a negative view of chaplains 'getting in the way' most had followed General Haig's example and recognised the benefits to morale that might be gained by a good relationship between the army and the chaplains department. An alternative interpretation in this case might be that the CO's actions were a duty of care, a compassionate intervention. In any case Gillett did not object. This was not a matter of religion and Catholic chaplains were duty bound to follow the legitimate demands of the authorities in non-spiritual matters.

Whilst Steuart was recuperating from his cold, Gillett oscillated between reflection and danger. The cold weather had restrained military action and caused great physical hardship. Gillett reflected in his 31 January entry: 'Horses falling all over the place, and yet they carry on – marvellous really. Frost very keen – hardest frost for years, how the poor lads can survive a spell in the trenches in the intense cold beats me. And yet a little grouse and they are all smiles – their hearts and spirits are wonderful'. On 4 February he: 'Visited RF's in afternoon. A stunt on last night – guns started about 11 p.m. and went at it pell mell for an hour. Fighting W. E. of Beaucourt – 3 trenches taken – HURROO!'

Deployment in battle has been explored but how did it work in the real world? The model for the majority of chaplains' of which Frs Gillett and Steuart are typical, was to offer close support before, during and after battle, but not to actually 'go over the top'. Support was still a highly dangerous mission and most deaths occurred in the close proximity of the actual fighting. The three days from 8 February amply demonstrate this. From villages behind the lines where he had conducted pre-battle services Gillett illuminates the scene:

> Last night from 11 onwards awful fighting going on – scrapping somewhere. What a hideously frightful whistle the shells have at night and the roar of the guns seem intensified in the quiet of the night time. Action took place from Pys. Bombing taking place owing to the clear moonlight – on the Aveluy Dump – phew!

The following day he went in search of the needy, and in particular advanced along a communication trench to help with the rations. A dangerous mission but an excellent opportunity to tend to any men injured or dead, it also endeared chaplains to soldiers and showed courage and a willingness to 'get one's hands dirty'. Fr Gillett played down the incident:

> Tramped over the old battlefields of Sept 1916 again and reconstructed the scene. Followed the line of the attack right up to Thiepval, dead still lying about – trenches one mass of equipment and broken arms and small ammunition

– MG bullets and coils very conspicuous. At night went up with the rations to Grandecourt setting off about 7 p.m. and getting back about midnight. Adding to the excitement one or two shells came over. But no one caught. In the dark we tramped over anything and everything even dead bodies lining the road side.

Life was a mixture of excitement and routine. On 10 February he prepared services on Sunday for the men and civilians. Afterwards he 'toddled up' with the rations, as ever playing down the danger:

> Quiet day. Hung about Martinsart and saw to Service notices for Sunday. At night toddled up with the rations again. What a display. Very lights going up here and there along the line all the night through; and the belch of the huge guns – a large flash and a roar and along speeds another iron ration.

Reports of chaplains being 'up with the rations' were ambiguous, being unclear as to whether they physically assisted or simply escorted the men doing the labouring. Fr Gillett was a man well-used to the common soldier and played football with them on occasions, so for him helping his 'poor boys' was second nature. Furthermore, chaplains were treated in a mature manner by Rawlinson and his senior colleagues who respected and encouraged individual responsibility and decision making, safe in the knowledge that their long years of disciplined mission-based education could be relied on.[4] By taking the rations Chaplains made themselves useful at a mundane, if dangerous level. This acted as both an opportunity to render spiritual assistance if required and as a means of showing solidarity with the troops, the rations being a cherished and much needed source of soldier contentment. The scene of 'taking up the rations' is recreated by Fr Walker SJ Painted on location in February 1916, near Givenchy, west of Arras.

Gillett's time remained varied. 17 February in the Battle of Boom Ravine[5] he assisted in escort duty:

> Made my way to Quarry Crossing. Wounded lying about along the road side, difficult to get away owing to rail facilities being limited. German prisoners made to do the heavy stretcher bearing and very keen to work, they work. Evidently they were glad to be out of the firing line. Wounded not serious fortunately. Took a prisoner down to cage myself – to the amusement of overlookers. 4 of our lads turn traitors and give away our plans – consequently get badly cut up before attack commenced. At night the transport were badly trapped and came in for an awful time.[6]

---

4   That is until they crossed the disciplinary line in more serious circumstances.
5   The last battle on the Somme/Ancre before the Germans withdrew to the Hindenberg line.
6   Traitors have been attested see </westernfront1917.wordpress.com/2017/02/17/boom-ravine-somme-1917/> (Accessed 14 April 2017).

Taking the Rations – Givenchy 1916. (JAD, Paintings of Fr Leslie Walker)

Steuart had benefitted from a quiet time recently but on 22 February he marched at 3:25 p.m. to Arras: 'Pitch dark, arrived at Arras about 8. HQ about 1,000 yards from Boche lines. Some places our lines are only 12 yards from theirs. Steel helmets and gas helmets de rigeur. All the firing on our side'. Two days later he made the following observation:

> Mass at 9:30. Went up the line with McHardie in afternoon into front-line trenches. In some places less than 30 yards from the Boche. Saw one of our own aeroplanes just after it was brought down – crumpled up like a piece of waste paper. The pilot only had a broken leg but died. At one place the remains of a house, less than 200 yards from the Boche line, a piano was being played. A man of our battalion killed today by shell shock.

He returned to a quieter quarter west of Arras.

Meanwhile things were intensifying for Gillett on the Somme as the Germans retreated to their well-prepared Hindenburg line:

> 26th March. Visited Beaucourt – Bailescourt Farm. Grandcourt, dead all over the place. Railway between Mill Farm and Miraumont badly cut up – shell holes

enormous showing careful work of the Boche to hinder our advance. Grandcourt seems to have been built on a swamp and with the winter rains and thaw following the frost – it is now simply a flood. In parts the roads were impassable – here and there a gun or waggon is trapped.

Next day he reported:

Everybody topsy turvy – Boche running like h… (sic). Puisieux – Achiet – Irles lies evacuated. Some excitement for the Boche are unsighted by our men and it is difficult to come up to them. Everybody flying all over the place. All this gives great encouragement to our brave lads – at last we have them really on the run.

This was the perceived truth at the time but proved to be a false dawn as the Germans retreat was ostensibly strategic. This temporary psychological boost was welcome and the optimism is reflected in the next day's entry. Again contrasts can be made between hopefulness and caution, violence and peace, victory with defeat:

Had a great walk with Kilduff, glorious day.[7] Took him through Athuile on to Thiepval, past Thiepval Crucifix and over the country to Grandcourt – along Artillery Valley, a German gun position. Saw there a man squatted on a huge shell – but when we came up to him we found he was dead and yet not a scratch on him. Through Grandcourt a little way on to Miraumont then over country again, back over Regina Trench and Desire Trench and Schwabben Redoubt, then on home. What a view one gets after mounting the hill north of Thiepval – can see for miles. Plenty of dead all over the place – but parties were engaged burying them. Derelict tanks and aeroplanes were here and there to be seen. Aeroplane fights going on. Altogether we had a great day.

Fr Gillett's aptitude for realism had returned. 21 March: 'Retreat finished – held up at Courcelles. Troops now taken out of line. Passed the night at Anthuille, Bepaume, Péronne, and Noyen all in our hands – everybody very 'bucked' – fancying the war is over! I DON'T THINK'.

At this juncture both men were having it relatively easy. Yet the striking contrasts continued. 26 March, Steuart in Arras: 'Went thru' the sewers in afternoon with Major Eastern and up Stretcher Trench'. Bizarrely he: 'picked snowdrops about 200 yards from the Boche line' and later had an escape when: 'Shrapnel fell around me in the street'. Meanwhile on the 28 March, Gillett embarked for Guarbecque on the border of the Nord and Pas de Calais Departments, a place roughly equidistant between Arras and Ypres. Fr Gillett's love of Church architecture and his need for the cultivated aspects of life should not be ignored: '28th March. Guarbecque. Arrived

---

7 A Redemptorist priest from Westmeath who became a close friend of Gillett.

at Guarbecque about noon – after an hours march from detraining station. What a pleasure to feel one is going to have a few days in civilisation again. A beautiful old 11th century church here'. Walker and Gillett again sharing the same joy based on similar outlooks and values.

30 March Fr Steuart was back amidst the action:

> Went out in morning to the chapel in Catholic Club. House hit by shrapnel and bits fell into the chapel. In afternoon went up trenches with Campbell to see scene of exploded dump. Lost our way near the German trenches and came under direct observation. They opened fire on us with pip-squeaks & we ducked behind a bank while the shells burst all round us. After 12 rounds we dashed for a trench & got away. Felt very much interested and not at all windy. In the evening Maj Du Berry, and I, while leaving the town, were gassed (slightly) with gas shells which came up behind us & followed us up Rue de Gambilla from the station. Had difficulty in putting on my respirator, so got some mouthfuls. Luckily no serious effects, but every cigarette I smoked for the rest of the night tasted filthy. Battalion moved out to Habarcq.

1 April Gillett was confined to isolation in his billet due to 'Spotted Fever'.[8] Four days later he was on his feet and arranging services in time for Easter for civilians and troops which was thwarted, his frustration is palpable:

> Easter Sunday. Tramped to Thiennes for Mass where I'd arranged for the Royal Fusiliers and Northants etc – found notice had been passed out but no one turns up. Troops had all been taken out for ceremonial parade. Straffed Div HQ but no use. French make a big day of Easter. Everybody dressed up and Processions the order of the day. Quite a religious feast, so different to so called English Christians. The Army Godless, at least the section I have to deal with.

Whilst Fr Gillett was engaged with domestic affairs, Fr Steuart was dodging shells: 'Easter Sunday. Mass in cellar for 12th HLI and 10 RS and at 11 for KOSB. Gave Communion in afternoon to 10/11 HLI and the MGC and TMB Coys. A shell knocked in the barrier of the cellar while I was with the 10/11 HLI'. But worse was to come:

> Mon 9th April 1917. Got up at 4:30 a.m. Brigade started through the sewers at 6. Terrific barrage. 46th Brigade took its objective at once and numerous prisoners began arriving. Had a terrible march through the trenches & the Bosch barrage to a sunken road beyond the cemetery. How we escaped I can't understand. I had the Blessed Sacrament with me. Waited in sunken road for 2 hours. Number of

---

8   Typhus related caused by ticks, the bane of a soldiers life.

Guarbecque Church, 17 July 2013.

Guarbecque Church. February 1916. (JAD, Paintings of Fr Leslie Walker)

prisoners brought in. A tank began advancing on our right, and at once drew a heavy shell-fire all over us. Advanced at last on ground simply whistling and piping by snipers, and took refuge in shell-hole with MO, Sgt. Henry, Duffy, Palmer, Fisher, Lt Saunders SR, Lt Lloyd, R Berks, going out every now and then to wounded. Helped to dress Lt. Haldene of ours, dreadfully wounded, who died afterwards. Fr Collins killed by a pip-squeak in the Railway triangle. Heard that the objectives have all been captured, and more besides. A Coy charged and captured a battery of 77 mms; B Coy took 8 other guns. Established an aid-post in the captured Battery, but were soon shelled out of it by heavies. Had very narrow shaves. Sgt Major of 1 company urged his men by pointing to the MO and I, who were well in front. Returned to the battery, practically safe by now & established an aid post in a good dugout/full of the personal effects of the commanders of the battery including his Iron Cross ribbon, a bit of which I now have. Took many souvenirs – helmets, bayonet, trench stick etc. Walked over to Brown to see McHardie who has been rather badly, but not seriously wounded. We had to dodge a sniper on the way who had already killed 3 men. CO came over to our dugout to write his dispatches. No sleep tonight.

Arras and the locale were becoming killing fields for men and chaplains. As Steuart reported, Fr Herbert John Collins from the Westminster Archdiocese was killed in action 9 April at Blangy near Arras'. Collins was shelled whilst assisting the medical officer with his regiment 9 Black Watch and is buried at the formidable cemetery of Cabaret-Rouge Souchez, some 3km north of Arras town.

10 April Steuart continued:

> Consolidating. Several tanks knocked out. Cavalry coming up: too late in my opinion. Strolled about yesterday's battlefield. Boche trenches smashed flat. Many must have been buried in their dugouts. Strange to look back and see Arras behind us. Very few dead Boche lying about. About 7 or 8 thousand prisoners. Occupied in interrogating prisoners. Weather fine in morning, but snow and hail and rain in afternoon. Cavalry, RA and Transport streaming up.

Headstone. Fr Herbert Collins. Age 35. 9 Battalion Black Watch. KIA 9 April 1917.

Steuart's accounts regularly tend towards the militaristic and help confirm him as more of an officer than priest. His reference to 'interrogating prisoners' is confusing. He was probably referring to translation rather than to cross-examination, way outside his remit as a Catholic chaplain. Fr Steuart was apt to exaggerate his military competence and involvement. He continued in this vein:

At Cabaret-Rouge Souchez Cemetery.

Wed 11th. Orders from CO to follow him in front of Monchy about 8am. Went off with MO and Capt Henry. Had hairbreadth escapes. Several times had to dash into shell-holes and lie there whilst sniper and machine gun bullets whistled over the top. In one hole we lay one on top of one another. Heavy crumps and shrapnel all around us. Went right up to the front of Monchy and then had to fling ourselves into a shell-hole as a machine gun spotted us. He fairly put a lid of bullets over our hole. At last we had to leave it, & we jumped out 2 at a time and got safely back, about 100 yards to where the Somerset's were lying under a bank. Found a dug out and made an Aid Post. Tons of Boche explosives lying about, and the next two dug outs blown in. The wounded exposed to the snowstorm but erected enough shelters and made tea for them on the M.O's primus stove. MO, I and CO, Adjutant, MO of Somerset's, Fry of the RA & 2 liaison officers in dugout. Tea at intervals. Meals consisted of biscuits, bully, and chocolate – sustaining but rather cloying. Emerged at intervals and looked after the wounded. Gave them my cap comforter and Burberry. Very cramped and uncomfortable in dug-out. No sleep. Awaiting for relief (W.Yorks) at 5 a.m.

In stark contrast Fr Gillett operating near Guarbecque and still not officially fit for duty, was ministering to the Royal Fusiliers and Sussex Pioneers undergoing retraining and rest. 9 April he celebrated: 'Mass in barn at Papote for Sussex Pioneers – Confession and Holy Communion of the troops. Got breakfast in pub close by, then tramped back home. In afternoon was dead beat so rested'. Next day he: 'Strolled about and generally put in time – supposed to be still isolated. Rumours reach us of the great push at Vimy and Arras'. A day later: 'Visited by APC and Foubet – glorious day – put in my time strolling about'. Playfulness continued on the 13 April when Gillett said: 'Mass again – lunched today with Mr le Curé. Went to Lillers in afternoon. Met APC who ordered me to buy a new hat mine was so disreputable. Thought twice about it – but he was insistent'. Humour helped this temporary but much needed respite.

The presence of both peaceful and violent sectors within such short distances from each other creates remarkable and surreal parallels. The trivial nature of Gillett's existence, as opposed to the seriousness of Steuart's at this moment in time is illuminating. These experiences repeatedly alternate to reveal the converse nature of military life. By the 12 April the Arras 'stunt' was over for Steuart and life returned to relative peace, but the cycle of death continued elsewhere in the current Arras campaign. 18 April, Fr Mathew Forster Burdess was killed less than 40km from Arras, when sheltering with other officers in a newly captured cellar which the Germans had booby trapped. All were killed. Burdess, a priest from the Hexham Diocese knew Gillett from Ushaw. Burdess also had a distant link with Steuart through Jacobite connections being a descendant of General Thomas Forster who led the Jacobite Rebellion of 1715 and known for his: 'unswerving loyalty to the Stuart cause'.[9]

9   UCA, *Notes from Ushaw*, July 1917.

Fr Mathew Burdess.

Headstone at Villers-Faucon Cemetery.
Age 40. 6 Gloucester Regiment.
KIA 18 April 1917.

The carnage continued and was shared across the clergy. Five days later 23 April 1917, Fr Leeson from the Liverpool Archdiocese, attached to 13 Battalion Royal Fusiliers was the next to be killed, aged 40. Fr Jim, the son of a dock labourer from Plum Street, Litherland, Liverpool, was a bright boy and able to overcome his disadvantaged early life. The Society of Jesus supported his education at St Edwards College Liverpool and his seminary training for the priesthood at Upholland. Initially Fr Leeson, as we have seen, was treated shabbily by other officers echoing Fr Gillett's experiences in this regiment. Were the problems he faced purely poor appreciation of his religions needs from a regiment which had few Catholics and presumably little knowledge of their traditions: or were they based on social exclusion, perhaps a mix of both? Fr Leeson was ignored in the allocation of billets and denied basic foodstuffs which forced him 'to beg for some dried bread and water'. He then stated to Rawlinson: 'I do not mind roughing it, but I feel I must make known, and keep my position up as Catholic chaplain. Would you let me know [the correct procedure] before I take any steps'. The Army were unconsciously or not testing his mettle, but he was from tough stock and soon won them over. Major General Williams 37 Division, recommended him for a Mention in Dispatches in March 1917 shortly before his death:

> For exceptionally good service with the 111th Infantry Brigade since June 1916 and particularly the operations on the Somme and Ancre. He has shown a persistent disregard for danger at all times during the execution of his duties, and has won the esteem of all ranks by his bravery and practical common sense.

During the engagements on the Somme he was constantly up in the front line, and in the Ancre he "went over" with the men ... his influence for good has been felt by all, regardless of creed'.

This example challenges earlier suggestions that in a regiment with few Catholics the chaplain did not usually 'go over the top'. It may be that at this time his regiment had been back-filled with Catholics but that is highly unlikely. A more probable explanation owes more to his personality and the fact that he was from a strong Catholic community at home, as noted chaplains had affair degree of independence in these situations. He was killed in action by shell whilst ministering to men fallen in open land during a diversionary action, aged 40. No photographs could be found of Fr Leeson.

Fr Leeson's earlier difficulty with military personnel was not an isolated one. Fr Charles Wright CSSR served for a time as chaplain to 8 Battalion, (Liverpool-Irish) KLR and forewarned GHQ that [owing to a new CO 'kicking him out' of his quarters]: 'I only hope the Catholic men from the Scotland Road district of Liverpool [where Frs Gillett, Higgins, Leeson and others served pre-war and the epicentre of poverty and sectarianism] would not regard the unprecedented action of a CO as an insult to their RC padre (The CO is a Protestant Irishman) as I believe they would be capable of raising hell. Sectarian trouble is nowhere more bitter than the North End of Liverpool'.[10] There were a number of concerns here, from personal insult and inconvenience of Wright, to a sense of entrenched protection of their Church, and a forewarning that these soldiers *would* cause trouble by defending their chaplain. These occasions help to explain the Catholic perspective which can hitherto seem skewed. Sectarianism was not theoretical: it was an evil which seeped into every nook and cranny of daily experience and contaminated all those within.

Headstone. Fr Jim Leeson. Age 40. 13 Royal Fusiliers. KIA 23 April 1917.

10   DAA, 3235, Wright to Keatinge, 21 January 1916.

The timing and location of death was unpredictable and depending on individual belief, a matter of luck or Divine Providence. For example when Steuart went on leave between 17 April and 7 May, he embarked from Boulogne. Arriving in the evening he found: 'Officers Club and Hotel d'Louvre full so went to Hotel Dervaux in Grande Rue'. His stay was unremarkable. If he had taken leave and been in the same hotel 1 August 1918 then his chances of survival would have been slim. The Germans, even this late in the war, managed to bomb and destroy the Hotel Dervaux. So much for La Belle Époque.

With Fr Steuart on leave it was Fr Gillett who would take his share of the Arras punishment. 27 April:

> Entrained at Pernes, or should have done – engine disrailed so had to march lower down and entrain at Bryas. A lovely little march. Got to Arras about 6 p.m. and we were greeted by a shell straight away. Then marched, marched, marched; it seemed endless and in the twilight and on into the night with power and bite. All slept in open trenches. Slept for an hour myself in a shell hole – but too cold and got up and walked about – about 4 o'clock watched the guns belching forth along the Arras front. Everything topsy-turvey – no one knew where we were – land all old battlefields – no grub all day. My poor stomach felt it.[11]

At Neuville Vitasse next day, just south of Arras town, he demonstrated the fortunes of war and the bravery that often went unnoticed: 'Confessions of different units due up the line. Just after I'd heard a crowd in one shell hole – a shot came over and enlarged the hole – lucky us – we had gone barely an hour before the guns were active on this sector. No billets here – no houses in fact – bivouacs everywhere'. The contrasts continued to the next day:

> Walked off to Arras for Mass – no chance for the troops. Met Fr Harker[12] and did Arras with him – Cathedral – Hotel de Ville – etc. etc. – met several other chaplains during our tour. And we did well, did ourselves well. Met Haney and what a day I had. But poor Arras, what a site. She had always been under the guns and it looked like it. Great underground passages where all lived – one could stock an army underground. It was the only safe method to live like rabbits and burrow underground. Visited Beds and Middlesex in evening, a man or two killed close to his billet. Plenty of old iron flying about. Just jumping into a car when plump came a shell close by. We got off 'tout de suite'. Interesting to watch the Boche shelling of the Arras – Cambrai road – one wondered if anything at all could be left.

11 Fr Gillett suffered from gastric problems from the time he volunteered to the end of his life.
12 Fr Thomas Harker, HEX, Ushaw, Catholic Club, 63 Division.

Fr Gillett often made light of his situation as the next two entries demonstrate:

> 2nd May. In evening toddled up to the Aid Post ready for tomorrow. No accommodation so up all night to fill in time up line with troops and rested with them in the trenches. Snatched a wee sleep in Boche dug out – but up at 3 a.m. to watch barrage. Beds and Middlesex over the top, Fusiliers and Northants in reserve – about 7 a.m. trudged back to aid post to attend the wounded, who were now coming down. Had to pass through our own guns – and they seemed to spit fire all the while.
>
> 3rd May. Over the top at 4 a.m. The guns making a h… [sic] of a din. At dressing station all day battle going badly – being horribly beaten. Bits of shelling falling through canvas of dressing station. 1:30 rumours we are retiring but false – we come back to original line that's all. Troops were to have taken Cherisy but fail. Up all night at hospital – din and guns hideous. 1st Northants thrown in to save our position.

By contrast, Fr Steuart on leave between 18 April and 6 May spent his time: 'Mouching [sic] about, fishing and walking. Tea at Fintryvale'. He: 'Went for motor ride to Sma' glen, Crieff, St Fillans, Killin. Aberfeldy'.[13] Not being part of a diocesan parish life he had no religious obligations on leave and consequently enjoyed the relaxation which his comfortable background afforded. Gillett did not have formal diocesan or parish duties on leave either, though he was happy to say Mass on occasion in Liverpool.

Back on the Western Front Gillett was experiencing Arras as so many would:

> Mon 14th May Héninel. Moved to Héninel – but only transport – to stay with Battalion. In bivouacs. In evening went up with working party at night. Got beans going through Hemel – but got through alright. On return at 3:30 a.m. more shelling – some 4 of our lads knocked out. Gun dumps are fired and everyone runs for it. Was glad when we got to our quarters again.

He did get some respite, of sorts. The Medical Officer sent him to Boulogne for four days to receive dental treatment. Humbly he did not criticise but had to wait over a year until the Americans arrived to be properly treated. 10 July 1918 he confirmed that: 'Visited American dentist in the wood and had some good work done', in sharp contrast to the British Army when on 19 March 1918 he: 'Thought to get dental treatment in CCS but they wouldn't touch me'. So much for camaraderie!

Steuart returned to join his units in the relative safety of Barly some distance west of Arras. From early May to mid-June Gillett's chaplaincy duties were largely routine, despite the occasional aeroplane attack. Meanwhile, he indulged his talents as

13   Perthshire.

interpreter and keen observer of French tradition in the relative peace of Warlincourt – lès Pas, simply referred to as Pas, where he arrived on 19 June. A week later:

> Mass at 7 – village all astir – Bishop coming to confirm. Kiddies all in white and early about crowding in from villages – huddled together in traps and carts of a sort. 9:30 a.m. Bishop rides up in a motor car – 10am. 10am Mass – 2 soldiers of mine are confirmed but later were killed R.I.P. Vicar General examines the children, the Bishop addresses them, then Holy Mass. After dine with the clergy – a great spread. In evening Bishop addresses my soldiers and I interpret for him and then after gives short Benediction. He speaks of the impression the English Catholic soldiers have made in France and thanks the brave men for all they are doing.

Ypres – Preparation and Reality

Once again the cycle of violence and peace completed another revolution. It was now Steuart's turn for excitement. His battalion marched to Ypres 17 June. Ten days later:

> Heavy shelling all day and night. Air-fights without result. Boche plane barely 800 ft over our camp. Got away unharmed. Palmer and Kennedy killed. Went to their funeral with Cox. Another of our balloons brought down' then two days later: 'Went up at night to Ypres with rations. Night fairly quiet, but we were held up for about 3/4 an hour at a very dangerous corner, where the Boche was putting over 9.5s, most of which burst about 100 yards from us. Arrived back at Erie Camp at 2:30 a.m.'.

Ypres, 1 July: 'I came under very heavy shelling, six of them bursting within 50 yards and closer, of me. One of these caught an 8th Seaforth subaltern wounding him badly just over the heart. The APM Grindley and myself did what we could for him, but I think he must have died before he reached the ambulance'.

Fr Gillett's destination was unknown to him, but he was also about to march to Ypres. Demonstrating his virtue on 1 July he: 'Preached in French "pour les agonisants" and delighted the people on direction for the dying'. The next day he marched out to Godwersveldt near Ypres claiming: 'My two weeks in Pas have been lovely, the old Doyen kindness itself'. These experiences with the French clergy and civilians are unique to the universal nature of Catholic chaplaincy. After Mass at L'Abeele 'a lovely church' he reflected on the political domestic situation in France with respect to the resistance of locals to French secularist laws, noted earlier.[14] 3 July, Steuart and Gillett were within 10km of each other. Steuart billeted in a cottage in Watou, whilst at L'Abeele Gillett: 'Billeted in a farm, where there is only one room I eat and sleep

---

14   SDA, Gillett Diaries 5 July 1917, Chapter 3.

in – so some 7 or 8 of us officers doss down as best we can'. 6 July, both men in close proximity to each other reported the King had passed through.

The Battle of Messines Ridge 7-14 June anticipated the third battle of Ypres fought from 31 July to 10 November 1917.[15] Like the Somme campaign of 1916, the Ypres operation was a collection of battles: Pilkem Ridge, Poelcapelle, Menin Road, Passchendaele battles one and two, Broodseinde and Langemark among many individual encounters. General Plumer in command of 2 British Army and Gough in charge of 5 Army agreed that this was the opportunity to breakout and attack from Ypres thus ending the debilitating stalemate of the trenches. They were supported by the French, Canadian, and ANZAC troops. The strategic aim was to capture the German submarine bases on the coast. As often happened the weather behaved badly being unseasonably wet. By October the battlefields became quagmires which were dreadfully efficient in claiming fatalities on both sides. Our chaplains experienced the military build-up and the weather, witnessing the horror of death and mutilation on a grand scale. Lloyd colourfully locates these battles in relation to the Somme: 'If the Somme of 1916, particularly its first ghastly day, has become a metaphor for a kind of innocence lost, when a generation of Britons faced the awful reality of total warfare, then Third Ypres is a slough of despond; a descent into the perils of Dante's *Inferno* with no possibility of redemption'.[16]

Auxiliary and less concentrated action occurred around the main battle zones throughout the war. Messines was a preparatory attack and not the main battle so that in early July the scale of the forthcoming actions would not have been known by our chaplains, but they could see the military build-up and sense the anticipation. Dictated by geography and restricted access to official information rumours abounded, but there is nothing in the chaplain's correspondence to suggest that this was not just another military operation. It was their duty to accompany the men and provide pre-battle spiritual preparation as well as during and after the main fighting, by now this was their well-trodden routine.

In July the situation as recorded by Gillett and Steuart can be teased out. Like the tides, as Gillett flowed in, Steuart ebbed out. 9 July Steuart's regiment left Ypres temporarily and repaired to Noordpene in the Pas de Calais whilst preparing to return to Ypres in readiness, as it transpired, for the forthcoming battle. Meanwhile, two days later Gillett tramped to Vlamergtinghe as his units moved closer to Passchendaele where: 'Shelling began so I turned back. Little of Vlam left – a hot spot. In afternoon saw 3 of our balloons fired – umpired for cricket match in evening. Lovely weather'. This topsy turvy world with chaplains and military criss-crossing each other; and the contradictions between violence and calm seem somewhat bizarre one hundred years

---

15 It is interesting that the blast from the detonation of 19 British mines at Messines was apparently heard in Whitehall 260k away, but not by Steuart at Rougefay 120k and Gillett at Arras 89k distant..
16 Nick Lloyd, *Passchendaele : A New History* (Penguin, 2017), p. 3.

later, but were accepted as normal by these battle hardened men. It was now Gillett's turn at Ypres, a theatre of war of which he was not overly fond. Both he and Steuart entered the Ypres sector prior to the main battle and their comments show that even outside the main fighting line life could be extremely hazardous, Gillett:

> 14th July. Up at 4:30 to go with Crisp[17] to a burial at Zillebecke.[18] Chap already buried when we got there. Anyway a lovely walk – but Zillebecke phew – a death trap. Hell blast corner was our reference – 'nuff said'. Shells flying all over the place and dead lying all around – here men, there horses and waggons and limbers galore. Some health resort. Caught in hospital on our return for an hour's bombardment – sweat all over and was glad to get away at last. Poor Crisp he didn't quite relish it either. In afternoon went to Pop; which is constantly shelled. On signal being given people all shut down and go into cellars and no getting them out at any price.

Two days later his account is both sad and somewhat humorous:

> Visited Reninghelst. Requiem Mass going on – soldier and child from Pop. In evening a little excitement on – a Boche tackles our balloons and seemingly getting away when our planes appear from somewhere and chase him down to earth – man is taken prisoner and machine absolutely untouched, becomes ours and the driver [sic] describes himself as 'fed up'.

18 July Fred Gillett was again amongst the preliminary battle action:

> Got into a Boche straffe at Menin Cross Roads and had to sit tight for half an hour. On return journey got into another straffe on our guns and sheltered in a trench for a bit. Luckily the Boche firing was off the mark else we wouldn't have much chance. Was glad to get home alright.

It is worth noting that many of the artillery bombardments and aeroplane attacks happen outside the main battle dates emphasising the value of diary data.

Occasionally chaplains acted as 'necessary officers'. He was offering spiritual services between Steenvoorde and L'Abeele when his organisational skills were required: '24th July. Mass. Troops on the way to Steenvoorde – but the party I was with lost directions and we trudged and trudged and at last finally sat down wearied out. The details had neither food nor water so Brooks and I squared some estaminet and we finally got them fed. In evening returned to my billet at Abeele'. Catholic chaplains always tried to help as long as these duties did not conflict with or impair their spiritual mission:

---

17 Fr Charles Crisp SAL, 17 CCS.
18 Now Zillebeke.

'If the Chaplain is always willing to oblige others, and do things for them, they in turn will all the more willingly help him… St Paul's axiom: "All things to all men", cannot be too closely followed'.[19] Fr Steuart would undoubtedly have relished such an opportunity.

20 July Steuart's brigade had returned to Ypres camping at Vlamertinghe, as was Gillett. These were gruelling times:

> 22nd July. Mass in marquee of Divisional Canteen. Very fine day. Boche planes over frequently. Found a company and a half of R0yal Irish Fusiliers who had not had Mass for two weeks. Went to them in evening and gave general absolution. Moved up to the Ecole, other side of Ypres [4km North West]. Just as we were nearing it we were gassed by shells. I found that with my box-respirator on I couldn't see at all & got separated from the platoon and found myself alone. By shouting I found one of the men who was also lost & we sat down to wait. In 5 or 10 minutes the Doctor came back and found us. The Ecole is shelled night and day, but we were very deep down and quite safe. About 9 men killed and a dozen wounded or gassed.

The next day preparations for the upcoming battle accelerated: 'Went with doctor and staff to dug-out next to the White Chateau on the Potijze Road. Went up by Menin Road and Half Moon trench. Very hot time. The dug-out is not proof against heavies, and is very crowded'. As a prelude to most battles trench raids were orchestrated to gather prisoners and as much information as possible: 'Tues 24th Our Battalion & the 6th Kings Liverpool Regiment made a raid at 1 p.m. Most successful. Penetrated beyond the Boche front line, and took about 150 prisoners, not counting killed and wounded. Our casualties not heavy and wounds mostly light. One man died of wounds (Pte W Portlock) and two more died later in the CCS at Brandhoek'. British preparations and German counter measures were taking their toll in this pre-main battle phase. Next day: 'Attended to the wounded all day', and bemoaned that: 'Most days our meat ration is bad, from the heat' and that he: 'Should have been relieved today'. Two days later he commented that: 'Wounded and gassed (ourselves and others) coming in all day. Orders for relief tonight, but cancelled later on account of a report that the enemy is evacuating his front system. Patrols found that this is not true, so we wound out at about 4 a.m.' He encountered fellow Jesuit chaplains Irwin and Monteith in a brief respite before: 'At 9 p.m. the night before battle, in heavy rain and humidity, we marched up to the trenches and quartered in a '50 foot dug-out'.

26 July Fr Gillett's preparations for battle had commenced with spiritual reflection: 'Confessions at 6:30 p.m. in the Steenvoorde Church and Holy Communion – addressed a few words to them and read them prayers after Holy Communion. What devotion in those big, strong lads and how they shout out their prayers – the future has little fear for

---

19   DAA, Ephemera, *Roman Catholic Chaplains: Information and Hints*, p. 9.

them; their trust is in Providence and they have faith like children'. He was aware that 'something was brewing' and proven correct. The men were soon to be back in action requiring that he conducted a frenzied search for as many camps as possible to hear pre-battle Confessions. 27 July: 'Mass for the soldiers – who are soon to be in it all again. Visited camps which are scattered all over the place. The next day he sang Mass and: 'Gave Confessions at Winerzeele at 6 p.m. then Steenvoorde at 7 p.m. – a goodly turn up'. It seems the troops suffered no illusions as to their possible fate as the Sacraments were well attended, this time by a Lancashire unit: 'Sun 29th Troops move – after 10 Mass, heard Confessions of some Lancashire boys and gave them Holy Communion. In evening encamped for the night in Cornwall Camp only one night though, have to be up the line for the fight on 31st'. The time for preparation both military and spiritual was nearing an end. Gillett wrote on 30 July: 'Mass for the last time at Abeele – general meeting of all chaplains to be addressed by Corps General – General Jacobs. Located in Cornwall Camp and everybody tip toc of excitement great events coming. In evening move further up – tomorrow 30 Division go over the top – best of luck boys'.

The Third Battle of Ypres commenced 31 July. Steuart, forever enthralled by the military wrote:

> Zero hour at 3:50. Came up top to watch it. Magnificent sight. Just missed by a MG bullet. Number of prisoners soon came in. Gave Viaticum to one. Four prisoners carrying one of their wounded on a stretcher, killed by one of their own shells. Tanks going over, but much hampered by the heavy ground. In afternoon went up Haymarket to Cambridge trench. Fifty foot dug – out, very wet, had to be continuously pumped. Heavy rain started. Gardiner killed on Blue Line and only about 13 of his company left. Division had to fall back to mid-way between Green and Blue lines. HQ moved up to front line. Doctor and I and staff remained behind awaiting instructions. Boche sending over 17 inch and other heavies.

Gillett also witnessed the start of the battle:

> 03:50 a.m. barrage opens – 30 Division go over the top – our troops move up about 8 a.m. to go through at the given time – 30 Division lose direction, attack a failure – we come back. During attack at Cowshed Farm with Dressing Station – about 11 a.m. Boche shells falling all around us trying to get more guns close – very hot for a while. Later go to Woodcote House Farm to find Bartley[20] working like mad. It is the Main Dressing Station. Guns going like mad to maintain our position and recover ground. Regular bombardments every 4 hours, phew what a din.

Fr Bartley SJ was ordinarily based at the Main Dressing Station. As a Divisional chaplain Gillett made his own deployment decisions and clearly felt that the most

---

20   Fr William Bartley SJ, 53 Infantry Brigade.

effective place to be was with the wounded, consequently he worked alongside Bartley at the medical facility. Attending the injured and dying until the early hours was no picnic, he noted: 'Too wet to sleep, so march about and finally settle in a driver's seat and snatch a few hours' sleep that way'. There was no respite: the following day he again worked in the main dressing station but did not forget the fighting men: 'Battalion up the line again, raining like h... all night, murky and wet – wretched weather just when we want it fine. Everywhere muddy and flowing – poor fellows up in the trenches'. When exhausted he retired but found: 'bivouacs too uncomfy so get up and sleep on a bus – drier anyway if not comfy'.

1 August Steuart illustrated the deteriorating weather and quagmire-like conditions, recording officers he knew either killed or wounded:

Myles killed by sniper. Trotter, Maclean, Gregor & Bannatyre wounded, Trotter and Maclean seriously. Bannatyre died of wounds. RSF occupied our HQ Their doctor, Aldridge, shared our dug-out. Very chatty and interesting old chap. Very heavy shelling all round. Five tanks knocked out. Raining still. Ground a swamp of grey mud. Great difficulty getting up ammunition. Our heavies unable to move up. Hardie & Sutherland, severe shell-shock. Miserable time. Casualties coming in. Acted as interpreter for 4 prisoners. Counter attack defeated.

The following day: 'Heard that relief was coming to-day. Dublin Fusiliers, Munsters & Connaught Rangers came up. In afternoon moved back to Potijze. Heavy shell burst at most 10 feet from Doctor, Henry, and me, knocked us over but didn't hit us. Later, another came about the same distance from us'. Clearly his regiment were mauled and were now taken out of the line. Steuart's ordeal was over for now, moving out to the relative calm of Oudezeele where he continued his Mess functions. By purchasing 'tea and various items', the contradictions between each day defy comprehension. Hence vicious, miserable, and dangerous situations sit uneasily with the routine and normality of shopping for tea, that they are only separated by a few hours and miles adds to the drama.

1 August Fr Simon Stock Knapp, DSO, MC, a Carmelite with 2 Battalion Irish Guards died on the operating table the day after being hit by a shell. He incurred stomach wounds attending the injured at a dressing station, emphasising the precarious nature of static facilities. Fr Keatinge, later *Episcopus Castrensis*, and Rawlinson's predecessor referred to Fr Knapp as: 'He struck me as a man who loved to be in the presence of God'.[21] Fr Knapp's grave in Dozinghem cemetery near Poperinge was photographed but the lettering was unfortunately indistinct in 2013.[22]

---

21 *Dublin Review 1919-20*: 'Chaplains in the Great War', pp. 63-6.
22 The CWGC have a rolling repair programme and it is possible that Fr Knapp's grave has since been reworked.

Headstone. Fr Simon Knapp ODC. DSO. MC. Age 59. 2 Irish Guards. KIA 1 August 1917.

At Dozinghem Cemetery.

In time honoured fashion these intense bursts of activity were followed by relative peace until 10 August when violence resumed for Gillett:

> 04:30 guns open out – battle started at 7 a.m. wounded coming into hospital – strolled about saying Rosary for those fighting and asking for success. Went up to Woodcote House dressing station – nothing doing. Lots of Beds and Royal Fusiliers through Corps dressing Station. Everything going well today – thank God – held up at Inverness Copse later.

The next day sacraments were celebrated in the open: 'Heard Confessions of the Leinster's with 3 other priests in a field, a fifth priest saying Mass in the open and giving Holy Communion as they finished their Confession. Fr Clifton said the Mass'.[23]

Fr Steuart went on leave from 9 – 21 August and left a full account of his adventures in his family homes in the Isle of Wight and Perthshire. In Steuart's absence the cycle of action then mundanity continued. On Tuesday 14 August Fred Gillett remarked: 'Mass again in the farmhouse and then troops hurriedly moved up to the line again. Some hitch evidently – busses took us to Chateau Segar – rested there all night in sorts of dug outs. Guns noisily trekking forward and at 11 a.m. a crowd of

23   Fr Thomas Clifton STK.

tanks waddle up the line – clattering, huffing and snorting'. The day after: 'Mass in Noordpene – troops over the top at Inverness Copse. But no luck – repulsed'! Then he visited Broxeele: '… and then went into St Omer – bien magnifique – and replete with English history – the Cathedral is lovely and I visited the Old Jesuit College where priests were educated during the Reformation to return to England for their martyr's crown'.

On the same day 17 August, 8 Battalion Royal Dublin Fusiliers were engaged in heavy fighting at Passchendaele, accompanied by Fr William Joseph Doyle [Willie] SJ, MC. He was blown to pieces by a German shell. Much has been written about Fr Doyle; it has been argued that: 'Fr Willie Doyle is, in the Catholic recollection a seemingly magnetic attraction thus creating a void where the majority of chaplains become marginalised or ignored'.[24] True, but that is not to deny the many accounts of his bravery. It was also a moment when the predominantly Catholic Irish 16 Division fought alongside the largely Protestant 36 Ulster Division. Hit by a shell his remains were never found. Killed on 16 August 1917 he is commemorated on panel 160 Tyne Cot cemetery.[25]

Fr Willie Doyle. MC.

At Tyne Cot Cemetery Panel 60. Age 44. 8 Royal Dublin Fusiliers. KIA 17 August 1917. (Shared panel with Fr Stephen Clarke bottom left. Aged 29. 9 Lancashire Fusiliers. KIA 4 October 1917.)

24   Bellis, 'Catholic Chaplains', p. 34.
25   Panel shows 17 August. Date discrepancy understandable when body never found.

With Doyle dead, Gillett absorbed in religious history and Steuart playing golf-croquet, the absurdity of war is plain to see. It is astonishing how three men can experience totally different events in the same time frame and be blissfully unaware of the contradictions. This is perhaps the secret for the survival in this war: only deal with events in your immediate vicinity seems an apt dictum.

Meanwhile Fr Gillett continued in his efforts to get the men to their religious duties, with mixed results: 'Sun 19th August, Mass at 08:30 at Broxeele – 11 a.m. Soldiers Mass – all sleep in after previous day's march, so few present. Cycled off to Wulverdinghe for 11 a.m. Mass to catch Sussex Pioneers – all confessed and gone to Holy Communion. At 6 p.m. Rosary at Broxeele – not a devil turns in – all in the 'pub'! Exasperated he may have been but he always retained a sense of proportion with working men, recognising that the pub and a lie in after a heavy shift were not entirely new phenomena.

Steuart returned to Ypres 21 August and went straight into battle the next day: 'Left Bivouac Camp at 5 a.m. and arrived at Erie at 7 a.m. Left there at 10:30 to take up my battle post at Bavaria House on the Potijze road. Fearful shelling all round, the worst I have ever seen'. Then strangely nothing else of note was reported until 29 August when 12 HLI were withdrawn. He merely recorded celebrating first Mass in a YMCA hut, and secondly at Bivouac Camp at 10:30, the latter in the open. Very strong wind so at the Gospel I moved into a shed'. He then nonchalantly recorded: 'Boche planes over; some shelling and bombing. Confessions at 6.' Gillett also reported little in mid-late August. The relative quietude of their own units was due to the worsening weather conditions. 27 August Gillett confirmed: 'Nasty day so idled'.

It was a nastier day for Fr Michael Patrick Gordon, a Dumbarton born priest and professor at the Glasgow Diocesan College. He died of shell wounds received when billeted with the 32 Division Corps Dressing Station, aged 34.

1 September, Steuart's relief when departing Ypres was palpable. Gillett was the unlucky one remaining in Ypres until 1918. Steuart: 'Set out on motor buses at 4:30 for new area, everyone delighted to be leaving Ypres. Arrived WEMAERS – CAPPEL about 8:30 a.m. Breakfast at an estaminet. Waited for 10/11th to move off. Billeted with the Curés'. 6 September he arrived north of Arras after a long march.

Headstone. Fr Michael Gordon. Age 34. XV Corps ADS. KIA 27 August 1917.

At Coxyde Military Cemetery.

Stationed at Wilderness camp outside the firing line, Steuart continued the routine duties of a chaplain celebrating Mass, the Sacraments, making arrangements for same and letter writing. He also donned his Army officer's hat: '11th September. Note from KOSB detail camp to visit a man in prison on a serious charge. Wrote to several parents of men and to Washbourne for candles, wine & hosts. Bomb dropped near station at Arras. The man (Pte Alexander KOSB) wants me to act as Prisoner Friend at the Court Martial. I have had to accept'. The next day: 'Went to Dingwall Camp at 10:30 to attend the Court Martial. Proceedings very short – I spoke last "in mitigation". The President afterwards gave me a hint that the prisoner would not receive the death penalty'. Violence of a conventional manner returned the next day. He went up the line with the doctor:

> On the way saw one of our planes brought down by Boche archie. One of the wings knocked off and we could see the pilot falling below the plane RIP. A New Zealander killed near us in the trenches. He was an RC and I was able to give him absolution, tho' he probably never recovered consciousness RIP. Boche still shelling Monchy.[26]

Aeroplanes busied the diaries of Steuart, Gillett, and Drinkwater whose own brother 'Oxo' was killed when his plane was hit by German anti-aircraft fire, for which he bore responsibility having encouraged him to volunteer. Lovatt Scouts, official observers reported: 'No one left the machine and they saw Germans round it. The machine disappeared after being fired upon pretty constantly by our guns'.[27] The painting below features planes from Merville which in now the Merville-Calonne Airport between Bethune and Armentieres.

26 Monchy-le-Preux some 12km from Arras centre.
27 BAA, Drinkwater Diaries, 10 September 1918.

No 16 Flying Squadron – No 4195 (BE 2c). Leaving the Aerodrome Merville – La Gorgue – April 1916. (JAD, Paintings of Fr Leslie Walker)

Fr Gillett went on leave from 7 to 18 September, and as was his custom he did not utilise his diary, with one exception: '16th September. Said Mass at Sacred Heart Liverpool – but unable to get through – taken off the altar and put to bed where I spent the day'. He did not offer an explanation but before the war, and later in life, he suffered a succession of gastric disorders. In any case the next day he was well enough to depart for the Front. On his return to Poperinge his battalions had moved on and he spent the time fulfilling his duties to the Chinese, civilians, and random corps and divisional troops. He re-engaged with his own battalions on 20 September where he: 'Did some Lewis Gun firing – football in evening. Beds celebrated the Anniversary with terrible orgy – had us out of bed at midnight having a sham battle with them – everybody blind to the world of course'![28] October started 'wild and windy' but there were no reports of fighting. There was of course still the apparently random danger lurking from the skies. 13 October: 'Mass – filthy wet – getting fed up. Poor Buffs are visited with aeroplanes and bomb drops right at door of one of the company officers mess – many killed – some 100 or so lads wounded that night – poor Eyre badly upset'.

By early October Fr Steuart had also settled into a period of routine, taking the papers around, enjoying lunches, being inspected, purchasing books and items for the mess. 2 October: 'Wrote to Brit. American, Tobacco Coy for cigarettes for Canteen'. Conversely, the constant menace of random warfare surfaced: '3rd October. Went up line with Doctor to see Aid Post for next week. Whizbangs for us in Johnson Avenue.

---

28 Evidently more successfully than Steuart who on 13 May 1918: 'Tried a Lewis gun in the evening, caught my thumb in the cocking bolt, and tore half my nail off'.

Coming down Lancer Avenue it was heavily shelled. One man killed and one man wounded just in front of us. Got through safely home. Lunched at the Aid-Post at Fampoux'.

Whilst Steuart and Gillett were occupied in early October with basic chores, chaplains were still dying. Fr Stephen Clarke from Kilmore, Co. Cavan met his death on 4 October 1917. Attached to 9 Battalion Lancashire Fusiliers, he and the medical officer had gone forward of the ADS to attend an injured soldier in no man's land. The Lancashire Fusiliers with a strong Catholic presence would have expected their chaplain to attend one of their own, and he did not let them down. The medical officer was equally dedicated and scrupulous; alas these spiritual and humane endeavours had fatal consequences as both were obliterated by a shell. Clarke was aged 29 years and his body was never found. A plaque in panel 160 commemorates his fall at Tyne Cot, similar to Fr W Doyle.[29] Soon Fr Looby will become the third chaplain to be killed in the same way and in the same Passchendaele battle, all being atomised or blown into innumerable pieces by shell fire, whilst accompanying their men.

The details and method of Gillett's next deployment are vague although he did attend a chaplains meeting on 10 October at which he received orders. Six days afterwards he located to the Advanced Dressing Station at Essex Farm:

> Tramping, tramping, tramping, so weary at last jumped into a goods train and snatched a little sleep, and woke up just to find the train about to clear off, so jumped out and cleared off to Ypres. A gorgeous morning and how gruesome the Clothe hall and Cathedral looked against the gorgeous sun rise.

He continued: 'Walked to give time for transport to get up and landed in for breakfast about 9 a.m. – deadbeat and footsore. Visited ADS at Essex Farm and met battery there'. Advanced Dressing Stations were varied in construction and size depending on the local situation. These improvised structures being lightly constructed were not usually designed for permanency. Others such as Essex Farm which Gillett attended, must have been constrictive in operation but did enjoy the permanency of a concrete bunker converted to the task.

More routine followed for Fr Steuart. Monday 22 October he: 'Lunched with Monteith at 13th DAC [Divisional Artillery Column] on the Arras – St Pol road'. The meal apparently caused Steuart's illness when for the next two days he suffered a: 'Bad attack of sickness and diarrhoea as the result, I think, of oysters'. As if to emphasise the shifts between trivia and realism, a short time later on 27 November Monteith was killed by a random shell in a bivouac with the Transport, some miles behind the line. He was a 'brilliant mathematician with an MA from Oxford'.[30]

---

29 See Fr William Doyle, Tyne Cot panel 160 which also includes Fr Stephen Clarke.
30 Stonyhurst War Record, *Memoirs*, pp. 198-202.

St Vaast Post – Neuve Chapelle. May 1916. (JAD, Paintings of Fr Leslie Walker)

Fred Gillett was stationed at ADS Minty Farm. On 22 October his boys went: 'over the top for Brewery and Mennier Farm. Few cases though – news good – shelling guns located round hospital so we had to take care'. The next day he had a visitor: 'Poperinge. Cardinal Bourne wishes to meet chaplains – about 15 turn up – Cardinal thanks us for our devotion to the boys and we disperse'. One of the best examples of the unpredictability of the chaplaincy experience came when Gillett reported at this time: 'Knocked about – 6 wee puppies born – much admired', and yet on that very same day (26 October) and in the same geographical vicinity, a fellow Liverpool Diocesan chaplain from Cahir, Tipperary became the first man in his brigade to be killed in action that day. He was attached to a Tyneside-Irish regiment,[31] Northumberland Fusiliers and was killed in no-man's-land at the Second Battle of Passchendaele, Third Battle of Ypres. When shells burst when attacking in open ground it was not unusual that none of the body parts were ever found. Pragmatically, he was allocated a grave at Poelcapelle because: 'the exhumation of a body from a point map reference 20. V.1.a.4.3 was partially identified from Beads and Cross'.[32] His gravestone is marked: 'Believed To Be Rev P Looby'.[33]

---

31 Not confirmed but probable as he has repeatedly asked for an Irish regiment or one containing more Catholics.
32 PRO, WO 339/45506. Reference 114569/5, IWGC to War Office, 6 December 1922.
33 Poelcapelle Cemetery, CWG reference VI E 13.

Fr Looby was not alone when he persistently pleaded to be with a unit containing more Catholics: 'I feel keenly disappointed as a young priest to be in the 53rd Norfolk Brigade where there is so little of a priests work to perform'. His SCF Fr Carden [nee Hessenhauer] supported his cause:

> Rev Looby has been most gallant when the battalion have been in the trenches and in action. In fact from the Brigadier down all speak of his goodness to the men and his utter fearlessness … Now he seems a nice boy and keen as mustard. He wants badly an Irish regiment or work with Irish boys. He will do well there [16th Irish Division]. He is young and chock full of energy. He prays not to be sent to a hospital – this would be a disaster. I hope you will be able to do something for the boy whom I feel sure you will like.[34]

Fr Looby never gained his wish for an Irish regiment but his new unit, 5 Northumberland Fusiliers, did contain a strong Catholic contingent, many of Irish extraction.

In one of the coincidences of war, Fr James Shine from Ballylaffin a mere three miles from Looby at Cahir in rural Tipperary was also killed 24 April 1918.

Headstone. Fr Patrick Looby at Poelcapelle Cemetery. Age 28. 5 Northumberland Fusiliers. KIA 26 October 1917.

War Memorial Cahir, Co Tipperary. (Also fellow chaplain Fr. Shine.)

34 DAA, 3234, Hessenhauer to Rawlinson, 12 April 1917.

A letter from Fr Looby's father, held in the National Archive pleads: 'After his death in October 1917, [...] his mother died shortly afterwards owing to the effects of his death. I lost a great deal of money by the above son and I would be very grateful for some remuneration'.[35] This seemingly selfish response may have reflected the contemporary rural mindset of a hard-headed local livestock auctioneer, but sits awkwardly with his son's sacrifices as provider for others at the expense of himself. A lot was asked of these young men, continuing apparently after their death. He left a considerable fortune of 7s 11d, approximately 40 pence.

Gillett reported continuing fierce battles in this sector, but it was the weather that became his over-riding concern: 'Wed 7th November. In camp all day – what a life, officers all huddled together in a wretched little hut – waiting about and hanging on from meal to meal. And the men? Poor fellows'. The next day moving west of Ypres to the north east, he continued his concern for the troops and minimised his own discomfort and safety: 'Bussed to Boezinge and then tramped across country – roads all marked by the Boche and shelled intermittently. Got a very warm reception in getting near Egypt House – whilst inside, shell after shell landed about us. What a desolation this neighbourhood is and what poor shelter for the troops'. He was still currently occupied at Main Dressing Stations, now at Elverdinge, but as his troops the Bedfordshire's, Royal Fusiliers, Northants, Middlesex and Sussex Pioneers came out of the line, he visited them in J and H camp and said Mass. The next camps were depressing: 'Sat 10th at Dyke Camp. Moving up with Transport – near Elverdinghe – Dyke Camp and Envile Farm are filthy, dirty places. Tents all leak and yards of mud to waddle through'. Despite the squalor and bloodshed Fred Gillett managed to escape into a vividly contrasting world nine days later: 'Visited St Sixtus – where late King Edward signed the books in the Cistercian Monastery – about 30 monks live there – chapel delightedly devotional and peaceful'. He maximised cultural and religious experiences whenever he could, regardless of adversity.

Despite 'the guns being busy all these days', Fr Gillett was in an optimistic mood and announced on 28 November that: 'News through of great advance round Cambrai – feel the war will soon be over'! This euphoria at the Front was matched at home by the first ringing of church bells in Britain since the war began. Fr Gillett and the nation's joy were short-lived. Despite great early successes combining tank, artillery, and infantry, progress was not sustained. Mechanical unreliability, inability to bring up support quickly, tentative second-stage planning, and the German's ability to counter attack in strength soon negated these gains. Nevertheless, lessons had been learned. In the Battle of Amiens in August 1918 these military strategies, much refined, were put to good effect and produced startling results.

Catholic chaplain's accounts of the situation at Cambrai reveal the confusion as opposite forces became intermingled in the smoke and mayhem. Fr Myerscough SJ stumbled into a group of German infantrymen. Identified as a Catholic priest he was

---

35   PRO, WO 339/45506.

not harmed or arrested, but simply ushered towards one of their dying comrades: 'I was led to a group of Germans, who opened for me – I passed into their midst. Here I saw a German soldier lying on the ground mortally wounded. There I received a devout Confession, gave Extreme Unction and administered viaticum with the Last Blessing'.[36] Afterwards he was escorted to the British lines unharmed. This commitment to serve a dying man, regardless of nationality and at great personal danger, indicated how men could rise to the occasion despite his demanding earlier life: 'It was not generally known that from his youth, Fr John was unduly conscious of his small stature, so that he always felt on the defensive'.[37] It might be added that his German language competence was gained at Ushaw before he subsequently joined the Society of Jesus.[38] Fr Fitzgibbon SJ also testified to the confusion, losing much of his kit including his portable altar in the melee of Cambrai. This was not a trivial matter as the altar stone contained a relic important to the individual priest.

Things were routine for Fr Steuart in early and mid-November when he declared himself bored. That soon changed, on 22 November: 'Went to Watou Hut with Doctor. Ran into a bombardment and retaliation, so side-stepped to trenches to and stayed for a bit at the Field Ambulance. Buried two of the 10/11th HLI at 8 p.m. at the Chinstrap Lane cemetery. Found 3 RC's there also to whom I gave Communion'. He was quiet again until 29 November: 'Very heavy strafe round our dug out. One landed just above latrine & about a foot behind it. Had dug-out lined with canvas. The next day: 'Two sniper bullets over us in Johnson Avenue. Heard today that Monteith was killed at Cambrai'. Steuart's information was correct.[39] Fr Robert Monteith SJ was badly injured by a stray shell in the village of Ribecourt and died next day having been ministered to by Fr Keary SJ.

It transpired that Fr Steuart knew Monteith and contributed an obituary to the Jesuit College *Stonyhurst War Record*. He wrote:

> He was just the right man for the job, and he was very keen and energetic, and if he wanted anything never stopped until he got it. He was very popular with the GOC Artillery and the other two officers of the RA brigades in his charge, and was most active visiting the batteries – a thing (especially at Ypres) which involved great personal risk.

---

36 DAA, Ephemera, Post-war Recollections: a contribution made by priests after the war in response to Rawlinson's request to publish. The project seems to have fizzled out by 1925. Normally this type of material has not been employed in this thesis. An exception is made here because it is evident that Myerscough seriously played down the adventure or triumphalist nature of his work.
37 JAL, *Remarkable Men of the English Province*, Obituary 1938, p. 212.
38 Myersough did not join the priesthood directly after Ushaw. Instead he became a railway engineer in Horwich before receiving his calling three years later.
39 Some records incorrectly state Passchendaele.

Steuart was Monteith's contemporary at Stonyhurst College and in the OTC. He mentioned Monteith on occasions in his diary, but his accounts are impersonal, reflecting both his personality and diary style.

December was a month of contrasts for both men. Gillett was still at Ypres whilst Steuart had been at Arras since the beginning of September. A quiet start was interrupted for Fr Steuart suggesting at this point in time the Arras campaign was more active than Ypres. On Wednesday 5 December he: 'Found a dud gas shell about 1 foot from our latrine', and the next day reported that:

> One of our saps knocked to pieces by Trench Mortars. Six men killed, one died on the way down, two seriously wounded – one who is very likely to die. Buried two men at Fampoux at 5.p.m. Quite dark. On the way back a fearful TM strafe, killing 7 men and seriously wounding three. All in the same sap as this morning. I was out in it but nothing came near us but bullets.[40]

Headstone. Fr Robert Monteith. Age 40. 70 RFA. KIA 27 November 1917.

Two days later it was a time for burials and drama:

> Buried two more at Fampoux. On the way up from the cemetery, the Boche began shelling Chinstrap Lane in which we were. The shells burst just at the edge of the roadway and we should all have been killed if we had not thrown ourselves on our own faces. I think this was about the closest shave I've ever had.

Next day he reported a fatal accident: 'Relieved at 5 p.m. by the RSF. Fearful strafe around our post just before we left. Buried two more at Frampoux. Whilst waiting for the boat, someone dropped a bomb by mistake in the truck in which they were standing & sixteen were badly injured. Several were killed. H Cairney, Capt. Watson's servant, killed on his way down Chinstrap'.

---

40 No Catholic chaplain was killed on this front by bullets. On average a soldier was killed by bullets in 18% of fatalities as reported by one CCS.

At Ribecourt Cemetery.

Sunday 9 December was also eventful and concluded a period which had brought him close to death:

> Mass at chapel of Joan D'Arc. Went up to Fampoux by the 1 p.m. boat, to bury Cairney. Boat broke down at St Nicholas and we had to wait half an hour for another. This one again broke down just after passing through Athies lock & we had to walk up to Fampoux. All this time our batteries had been firing heavily and we just got into the Dressing Station when the Boche retaliation opened – one of the most violent I have seen. We waited a quarter of an hour after it was over & had the funeral and again we were only just back at the Aid Post in time for the second Boche strafe. When this was over we came back by the 4:30 boat (incidentally changing S Nicholas lock gates in the dark) and arrived about 6:45. Altogether I think I have seen greater dangers during the last four days than I have for a very long time past.

As things quietened, he deservedly treated himself to a meal at the Hotel du Commerce and consumed: '… two bottles of Veuve Chequot (at 24 francs apiece)'.[41] In heavy snow on 17 December, his Battalion went into line north of the Scarpe, between Roeux and Gavrelle, reporting that: 'We are in a soft, deep dug out. This sector is quiet at the

---

41 A luxury Champagne retailing between £30 and £80, April 2018.

present'. Tranquillity was temporarily shattered two days later: 'Heavy gas shelling this morning just before stand to. Twenty three casualties, all from A Coy. Of whom 5 are dead up to date. Relieved in afternoon, & living in a shelter in the sunken road called Northumberland Avenue'.

With Christmas approaching routine returned. He arranged for Midnight Mass at Blessed Jeanne D'Arc chapel in Arras, but Christmas was a slow-moving affair with only attempts to keep warm amidst the heavy snow to occupy his thoughts, and always the rats: '29th December. Battalion moved up to right sector. Am living with the American doctor, McCluce, in the Quarry dug-out which is simply crawling with rats'. Both diarists were plagued by rats on occasions, Fr Gillett wrote almost a year earlier on the Somme: 'The floor has to be our beds and what with the rats and dirt it is not conducive to a good night and to add to all this misery the rain coming down in torrents'. These were not the rats to be found at home, having gorged themselves on human and animal carcasses they could be the size of large domestic cats.

The Ypres front was less hectic than it had been. On 7 December Fr Gillett had a rare treat with Fr Crisp mentioned earlier: 'Met Crisp at International Corner and took him off to Ypres. Came back about 1 p.m. to Pop where we had a rollicking lunch – we knocked about till tea time and then went to see the 'Duds', 17th Division Pierrot Troop and excellent. Altogether had a rollicking good day'. The troops rotated between fighting in the line and at rest, and Fr Gillett was always there for them in the areas surrounding Ypres. In addition, as he put it: 'Visited odds and ends around about including divisional artillery and trench mortars'. As Christmas approached the tensions had visibly slackened:

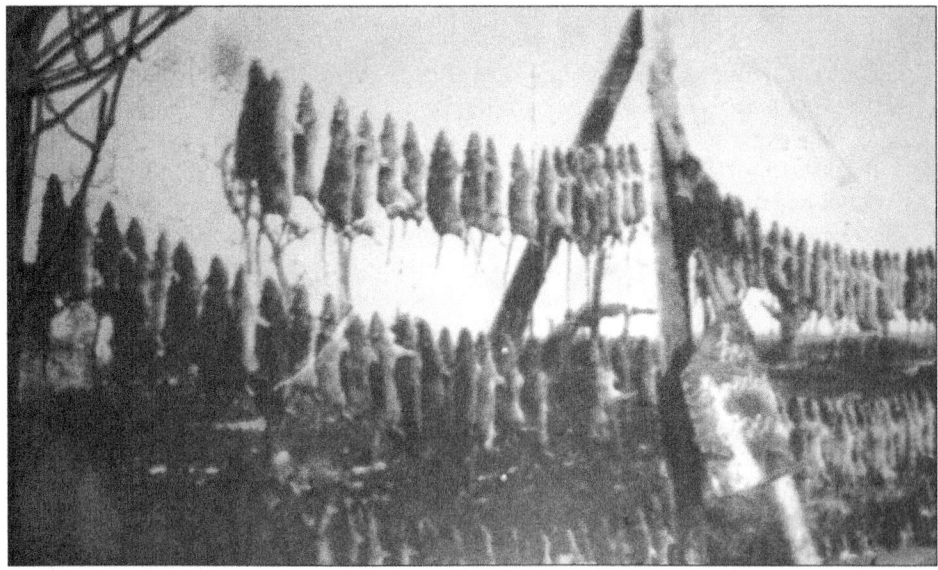

Rats on the Somme 1916. (Ramparts Museum at the Ramparts Public House, Lille Gate, Ypres)

Christmas Day – Midnight Mass a great success. High Mass before Blessed Sacrament exposed – a great exhortation. After Mass entertain officers to wine and biscuits and smokes. To bed about 02:30 a.m. At 8:30 said my Masses in a home close by the Convent. Assisted at Parish Mass as sub-deacon. Vespers in the afternoon. At 8 p.m. Battalion dinner in local estaminet – phew!

On St Stephen's Day he lunched at 62 CCS with Fr Rigby a fellow Liverpool priest and veteran of Gallipoli. After which he attended their local panto, Dick Whittington, which he thought was 'very fine'. He found real comfort the next day when he attended a chaplain's dinner at Poperinge: 'a magnificent affair; what a change to get amongst one's own'. Fr Gillett, as did Fr Steuart occasionally, confessed in their personal diaries of being lonely and it was only two months previously that Gillett had written: 'To Pop to drive away depression with a gorgeous lunch there and after the pictures – came back more cheerful'. Then again his depression was not entirely based on personal anxiety, frustration at the lack of response to spiritual opportunities by troops who lived in continual danger, perplexed him. Still when he arrived back he was 'more cheerful' exclaiming: 'Confessions in evening and did well – Hurroo'!

For Fr Gillett 1917 ended on a tragic note when on New Year's Eve: 'Nasty accident occurred amongst TMB's – trench mortar burst – killing poor Colonel Rodmore and 7 men and wounding Major Hanrahan and several others'. The appalling violence of 1917 from the Somme through Arras to Ypres had not diminished this man's compassion for other individuals. Neither had the sometimes surreal juxtapositions, which ran parallel to the violence, diminish his appetite for the more beautiful aspects of creation. If a priest was to live out his ideals then these were the most testing of circumstances to date, but it would get worse!

Epilogue – 1917

The violent year of 1917 had ended. Both priests remained on duty fulfilling their spiritual and pastoral missions with diligence and responsibility. They lived to fight their way through to another year where great changes were afoot and fresh challenges lay in wait. 1918 was to be a very different year where the balance between defeat and victory moved up and down like a seesaw. It was to be a year of increasing mobility which brought with it rising rates of carnage. Both our chaplain diarists were caught up in the major events of that year and reported events as they happened.

7

January–June 1918: 'Seesaw Margery Daw – Johnny Shall Have a New Master'

The attrition and doggedness which had so characterised the Great War up to the present time, continued into early 1918. A virtual equilibrium had existed between the head-locked German and Allied forces requiring a seismic shift in fortunes to disturb the balance between the belligerents. The prize of victory was by no means guaranteed for either side. Akin to a seesaw, the first to outweigh the other in a crude and brutal equation of industrial muscle and sheer weight of numbers, would gain control. The supply of matériel and numbers of soldiers were the significant factors and both were being drained at alarming rates. To break the stalemate both politicians and generals had their parts to play. Le Ladurie's parachutists will provide strategic and military contexts, but as the war took on a new complexion, our chaplains as truffle hunters will demonstrate what it was like on the ground.

On the battlefields, our chaplains bore witness to the mixed emotions and changes to tactics, resources, and routine. In human terms they shared many of the associated emotions: fear, despair, relief, suffering, and joy, whilst consistently performing their own spiritual and pastoral duties. Human and spiritual endeavour were inextricably linked with the fighting men, shedding light on their experiences and that of the army. Destinies fluctuated as first one side then the other sought to dominate the seesaw, the resultant vicissitudes of both the Allied and German armies being fuelled by the fresh impulses of human resources. Tactics were also refined employing greater mobility and collaborative action between the different branches of the armed forces, and armies, further increasing the rates of slaughter. Securing victory and resisting defeat at all costs now intensified exponentially for both sets of combatants. Our chaplains were both observers and participants in the reality of 1918.

The initial attempt to out-weigh their rivals went to the Germans. After Russia's capitulation in the East, a million fresh troops were available and many were launched in a huge attack on the Western Front, the German Spring Offensive. General Erich Ludendorff was confident of success: 'We must strike at the earliest moment before the Americans can throw strong forces into the scale. We must beat the British'.[1] He understood the consequences for Germany of vastly increased Allied troop numbers, and crucially also the reality of material wealth or *Materialschlacht*.[2] Ludendorff's appraisal crystallises both the hopes and desperation of the German High Command. They faced a conundrum: starvation, social and political unrest at home, and the war weariness of his troops on the one hand; and on the other the unthinkable spectre that humiliation from defeat on the battlefield, with the consequent reparations, would inevitably signal the demise of the German Empire and the Kaiser's expansionist dreams. Ludendorff craved victory, was this offensive his last concerted throw of the dice? If it failed could he to sue for peace, something akin to a respectable draw? The Allies, particularly the French who had suffered most, would not accept anything but unconditional surrender and affirmed their position in the peace negotiations in Versailles in 1919. This position was forcibly endorsed by America.

The Ludendorff Spring Offensive, or Kaiserschlacht, was an innovative attack designed to smash the British before the Americans entered the war in any significant way. He realised that the Americans would initially provide a psychological uplift for the Allies but his real concern was that a long-term military campaign could not be sustained by the Dual Alliance of Germany and Austria-Hungary, and their wavering partners. Kaiserschlacht gave him an opportunity to crush Allied hopes and at the very least force the British to sue for favourable peace terms. This approach was made possible through the release and retraining of ex-Eastern Front troops, battle-hardened but fresh, employing a range of new tactics. Stormtroopers armed with the latest technology and not hampered with the excesses of conventional support systems, used surprise, mobility, and speed as their main weapons. Ironically initial success was brought to a halt by a lack of support to the front line after it exhausted its initial energy. Nonetheless, for a few short weeks and particularly at the end of March and early April, German success followed success as the wearied British Third and Fifth Armies, who bore the brunt of the assault, were driven south and west in great disarray. With these units remained our diarists, providing their own vivid testimony to these cataclysmic events, an unusual addendum to conventional military history. For these brief days, both Fr Gillett and Steuart's daily accounts will be recorded verbatim, supported by other reports where applicable.

The Americans declared war on the German Empire on April 6 1917 resulting in the American Expeditionary Forces being formed in July of that year. They did not effectively enter battle until the French Aisne offensive of June 1918. Later in the year they conducted their own campaigns with the Saint-Mihiel and Meuse-Argonne

1 C.N. Trueman, 'The German Spring Offensive of 1918' <http://www.historylearningsite.co.uk> (Accessed 17 April 2015).
2 Britain started the war in a strong economic position but by 1917 was facing credit limitations.

Offensives. That they were able to compete at all is something of a marvel. Like the British at the start of war they had a strong navy but a pitifully small army of 80,000 with the majority of those confronting Mexico. A massive programme of compulsory registration was embarked upon and the 'lucky' 10 million new recruits drawn by lot. Their forces necessarily embarked on long training strategies and newly arriving in Europe they thought it prudent to initially resist assimilation, especially the Allied chain of command. This was a raw army, but an army anxious to prove itself with almost endless potential resources.

The strategic presence of such a potentially large new force was crucial to the success of the Allies. Consequently the landing of American troops into Europe provided new physical and psychological challenges to German morale, whilst boosting that of the Allies. Not yet a battle-hardened force they were still able to supply raw matériel and men in vast quantities. Was it only a matter of time for the seesaw to shift the Allies' way? To seize the initiative, Kaiserschlacht was crucial to German designs. The Allies were well aware of the forthcoming German ambition, if not the precise detail. Gillett and Steuart sensed the apprehension as spring approached. Their deployment demonstrated that the army was edging hesitantly towards the east and south east in anticipation, whilst their gripping testimonies illuminate the terror and panic of civilians and others amidst troop confusion. Fig 34, note the chaos of Gillett's retreat.

The Western Front had started 1918 much like each year, typified by war weariness and bad weather. Localised skirmishes within existing battles zones, including speculative, random, but highly dangerous artillery shelling continued unabated. Aeroplanes were now being manufactured in numbers and aroused chaplaincy comment. This was not merely adolescent-like curiosity; their lives might depend on it, something Fr Baines ignored when he was lured to his death from an aerial bomb.[3] The year started badly for Frs. Gillett at Ypres and Steuart at Arras. The latter was shelled on New Year's Day and suffered from the 'frightful cold, the duckboards were impassable with ice'. The former's woes were based on spiritual matters:

> Fusiliers parade and play in the New Year. Mass at 10:30 in Roesbrugge Church. Very few lads there – Army recognises anything and everything except religion – godless lot authorities I have to deal with in 18th Division and 54th Brigade – too fond of other things – attended Vespers and at night went to Brigade Cinema Show – absolutely rotten.

Not an auspicious start. The next day, despite the turn out, his task was a sad one: 'Mass. Ceremonial parade for funeral of Colonel Rodmore and the poor men killed. A great crowd of fellows there'. The next few days were spent visiting his troops and helping them pack for their scheduled move. Confusion typified this period and it

---

3   Fr Baines was killed by a bomb though curiosity, see p. 55.

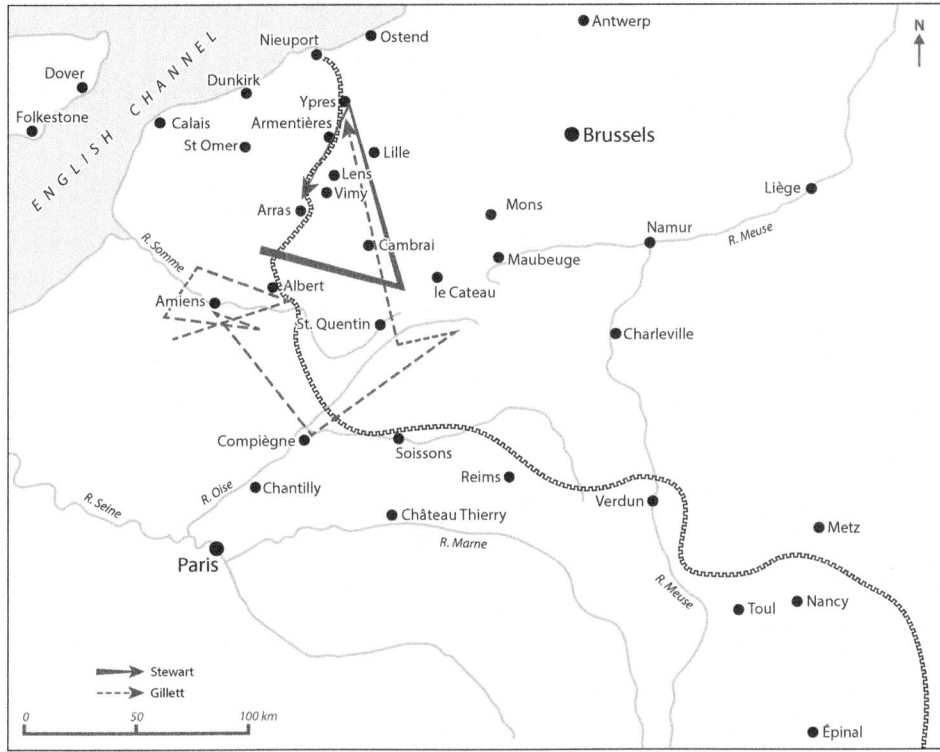

Map Frs. Gillett and Steuart January – June 1918, (including German Spring Offensive).

was not until mid-February that they marched. In the meantime he visited as many divisional and corps troops and auxiliaries as possible with very little action, seeing fit to comment on the terrible conditions 'for the poor lads in the line' at Ypres.

On 25 January Fr Gillett received a wire that his mother was gravely ill. He: 'Managed to secure a pass at once thanks to Acock. Entrained at 12 in the night'. He did not leave any further information until 14 February when he reported that: 'Mother still lingering'.[4] On 16 February in transit in London he experienced an air raid, something to be repeated by Steuart later. Arriving in France on 18 February he commented not only on his own discomfort but the general confusion caused by the reduction in strength of brigades from four regiments to three:

> Reached railhead, Flavy le Martel about 8:30 a.m. then searched out Brigade which was at Bussy. Found Middlesex had dropped out of Brigade being now

---

4   'Poor Mother dies. RIP'. She died on the 3 March with no further comment, although he did say Masses for his parents on occasions throughout.

reduced to 3 units instead of 4. I was consequently without attachment and was pushed about all over the place. Division is at Baboeuf so had to trek there and then on to Middlesex to claim my things: got to Battalion at last about 7 p.m. at Mirancourt. A deuce of a day's walking I'd had.

Being unattached was no minor matter and meant being without a cashier, billeting, transport, or messing arrangements. Until he could find a donor army unit, he would go without food and shelter, each unit being responsible for those attached to it but no others, the treatment meted out to Fr Leeson earlier shows the harshness that could apply to clerics by certain army units. Despite his annoyance and confusion he was fortunate to become reattached to his regiment. It is worth noting that on his return, the Middlesex regiment was at Chauny, some 30km south of St Quentin and south east of Amiens. This is a significant shift south from Ypres and is clearly in preparation for the anticipated German offensive. He remained here until hostilities started on 21 March. His duties were light, routine, and included services for Italian troops. This was unquestionably the calm before the storm. Whilst Frs. Gillett and Steuart were readying for further battle situations one chaplain, Fr McIlvaine from Glasgow was drowning off the Cornish coast on the hospital ship *Glenart Castle* which had been torpedoed.

Meanwhile, on New Year's Day after being relieved by the Grenadier Guards, Fr Steuart's unit marched to Bernaville about 8 km south west of Arras. On 8 January he received a warrant for three days leave in Paris before leaving for home leave six days later. Before eventually succeeding in seeing his family, he had to overcome heavy snow in Perthshire which had left many of the roads impassable.[5] On his return on 31 January, similar to Gillett, he heard that things were moving afoot: 'Heard to our consternation, that we are to be transferred to the 35th Division: the 10/11th to 40th Division. The 35th is at Elverdinghe, near Ypres!' As the 10/11 HLI moved out: '… sent urgent DRLS to Rawlinson at GHQ imploring him to let me remain with the 12th'. Burial frequency increased, he noted: 'Many graves gaping open and bodies showing'. 13 February he celebrated 25 years in the Society of Jesus whilst waiting anxiously for the Principal Chaplain's answer. This came 6 March: 'Letter from Rawlinson to say he has arranged for me re-joining the 12th HLI Hooray'!

What follows is a verbatim account describing the disconcerting situation when a fellow British soldier faced the firing squad. Fr Steuart did not question the morality of the offence or sentence, his actions and thoughts are singularly for the soul of the offender whilst acting as compassionately as possible. Consistent with the common mores of the day for many of the officer class, Steuart was not given to exhibitions of emotion or sentimentality, nonetheless, this account is praiseworthy for his humility, so often submerged by duty.

---

5   Fr Steuart frequently mentioned friends and siblings but never once his parents.

Fri 8 March 1918.

Russell called to tell me an RC Seaforth's man is to be shot for desertion to-morrow morning and I am to attend him. Went to him and spent the night with him. He made a splendid Confession and received Communion, & became quite calm and even cheerful. I can't realize even now, after I have seen him killed, that it was a man with only a few hours to live who spoke and behaved so quietly & cheerfully up to the last as he did. He prayed most fervently, received absolution again and again and Communion before midnight & again, just before his execution.

Sat 9 March 1918.

Woke him up at 5:15 and gave him breakfast. Heard his Confession again and gave him Communion. Then he smoked a couple of cigarettes and after a small tot of whisky we said some prayers and talked together. At about 5:40 he was identified by a NCO of his battalion, and then the APM and an MO came in and his eyes were bandaged and a piece of white lint pinned on to his tunic above the heart. Then he was led out, I holding his arm and helping him to make ejaculations, until we came to the pole to which he was to be tied. The firing party stood with their backs to him. When he was tied up I gave him absolution again and gave him my crucifix to kiss. The APM then told me to stand back: the firing party then faced about at a signal and took aim: at a second signal they fired & he slipped down as far as the ropes would let him, dead instantaneously. He had five bullets through his heart. I buried him at once in a cemetery close by & went off and said Mass for him immediately. He died like a hero and I am as certain as can be of anything that he is saved.

Important though this incident was, momentous events were about to unfold after the customary false alarms: '10th March. Tremendous wind up. Great Boche offensive, expected this morning. I have been allotted a battle position at Feuchy Chapel. Nothing came of it, however'.[6] He was less than charitable towards Fr McGrath: 'Mass at Club at 9:30. McGrath preached the evening, a terrible, long and dry service'. He then followed his regiment to Ypres arriving in Poperinge on 13 March reporting very little activity, a purely temporary respite. He visited the Cistercian Abbey of St Sixtus at Westvleteren north-west of Ypres without comment, unlike Gillett who enjoyed spiritual serenity there as noted. Steuart carried out a succession of religious services for a variety of units which was common practice for chaplains pre-battle. There was still time for sports despite the intermittent but perilous shelling:

6   Feuchy is a small village some 3km east of Arras centre.

> Mon 18th March 1918. Boxing (teams) competition in the morning. NF's won the match, but our Lt Capt. McLellan knocked out the Divisional heavyweight champion – who is said to have stood up for several rounds to Wells and Carpentier, in 50 secs.[7] Our Pte Young also scored a knock out, but Connolly was beaten on points & Ratcliffe knocked out. The 18th HLI beat the 35th DAC by 3 goals to 0 in a fine match.

Two days later he reported: 'Heavy shelling at Railway & Camp – but no casualties. The natives de-camping in every direction. Tremendous barrage at night and in the morning. Heard that the 32nd Division went over last night. Railway track hit plum in the centre'. The Spring Offensive was on its way.

Kaiserschlacht[8]

The inrushing tide did not fully reach Fr Steuart until 23 March. It almost drowned Fr Gillett immediately.

Gillett: Thurs 21 March 1918. Baboeuf, near Noyon 25 miles south east of Amiens.

> German Great Push Starts – at 4:30 guns fairly roar – troops all day are hurried up to the line. British line broken, guns taken, an awful scare. At 11:30 had to trek to Villiquier to report to ADS – but found no dressing station going – all on the run – got back to Baboeuf in Colonel's car – Villiquier all topsy-turvey – GHQ hurrying to get away – a debacle up the line. Up all night – no attempt to get down – in fact trekked till about 2 a.m.

Steuart: Thurs 21 March 1918. Ypres.

> Heavy shelling all the day, luckily none fell right in the camp, but two labour men were wounded in the wood. Took the C of E man to the Abbey in the afternoon. On our return, shells fell beside the road on both sides within 20 feet of us & we were covered with bits and mud but not hurt. Civilians decamping. Went to 18th HLI camp in evening. The great Boche attack is reported to have begun between Arras and St Quentin.

---

7   Bombadier Billy Wells, British heavyweight boxer and sergeant in the Welch regiment, and Georges Carpentier, French heavyweight boxer and First World War pilot.
8   Kaiser's Battle.

In Jaroslav Hašek's book the *Good Soldier Švejk and his Fortunes in the War*, Švejk bumbled towards the enemy whilst trying to reach his own line.[9] In the chaos Fr Gillett, by no means a bumbler, was unfortunately repeating Švejk's unintentional meanderings by heading directly towards the German advance. His eye witness account describes the general situation.

Gillett: Fri 22 March 1918 [Towards the advancing Germans]

> 'Visited Neuflieux – Caillouel – Bethancourt – roads packed with civilians evacuating. Chinese and Italians of Labour Corps scurrying all over the place – terrified of the advancing Boche'.

Steuart: Fri 22 March 1918.

> 'Orders to go south to-morrow. Packing up. No one knows where we are to go'.

Gillett: Sat 23 March 1918.

> 'Boche advancing – excitement tremendous. French being hurried up the line to assist our men – all marching through Baboeuf. Tried Confession at Baboeuf – no go!

Steuart: Sat 23 March 1918. Bray-sur-Somme is 10 miles east north east of Amiens, 3 miles south east of Albert

> Got up at 2 a.m. marched out at J Camp at about 7am. To Proven. Entrained at 10am. Stewart, Gillans, Tomkin, Hall and Brown with me in the carriage. Arrived at HEILLY about 10:30 p.m. March off to BRAY, 10 kilometres off. On the way met the civilian population, labour battalions and some heavy guns in full retreat. Boche have taken PERONNE and advanced beyond and are now reported six miles off Bray.

The panic was understandably intense. For some it was too much. Fr Cagney's wild alarm roaring up the road on horseback shouting 'save yourselves while you can' has been noted and could hardly have assuaged taught nerves. Our diarists were made of sterner stuff.

Gillett: Sun 24 March 1918. [The present position was indefensible; Baboeuf was now the point of retreat towards Noyon and away from the onrushing Germans].

---

9   Jaroslav Hašek, *Good Soldier Švejk and his Fortunes in the War* (William Heinemann, BCA ed 1973). A constant theme throughout the book.

Mass in Baboeuf – orders of civilians clear. What a bustle – off to the church at 12 midday to consume the Blessed Sacrament, risking nothing – everybody has to clear. Aeroplanes over and air fights over our very heads. Baboeuf full of troops and civilians coming from forward villages. Roads a mass of moving men and transport. Moving out about 8 p.m. Held up at Noyon for about 2 hours – what turmoil – civilians gathering their little parcels and making for the stations, others on the tramp.

Steuart: Sun 24 March 1918.

Arrived at Bray at 5am. Marched out to MARICOURT at 7 a.m. Passed through Maricourt & arrived at HARDECOURT about 3 p.m. Battalion immediately attacked, MO and I just behind them. Failed to establish contact with the enemy, and finding ourselves being enveloped, had to retire. We were desperately crumped on the way back. During our halt we could see the Boche Staff on the skyline watching us. Reported that we are being outflanked on both sides. We have no other British troops on either flank & have to retire further. Orders received to hold a valley halfway back to Maricourt. We had hardly taken up our positions before we were rushed by the Boche. MO, Mackenzie, Gillans, and I cut off from the battalion and had to retire hastily, pursued by Boche and machine-gun fire. Bullets whistling around us. Got to Division and reported, I remained at Bray with Hall that night.

Gillett: Mon 25 March 1918. [Dive de Franc, 3 miles south west of Noyon]

Get to Dive de Franc about 3 a.m., snatch a short sleep – morning quiet – met Wilkin[10] and McMahon.[11] In afternoon make towards Noyon; but find Boche guns on it, so stay in the distance and watch. Moving out to Dive de Franc about 4 p.m. and make for the fields short of Compeigne. Everybody windy – preparing to evacuate – no food to be got, however, got beds so settle down comfy. Poor Fr Wilkin dead beat after his few days up the line.

Steuart: Mon 25 March 1918. [Morlancourt 3 miles south of Albert]

Tried to re-join battalion, but stopped at ADS where there was no RC chaplain. Was able to do a lot of work. Noble, our only RC officer, severely wounded in shoulder and chest. Anointed and gave him Communion. Also Neill, Dunlop & Bryson who are less severely wounded. ADS had to be evacuated owing to heavy shelling. Retired to Bray. There re-joined by the MO & tried again to re-join

---

10   Fr Charles Wilkin SAL 53 Infantry Brigade.
11   Fr Francis McMahon, 142 Field Ambulance, 9 Infantry Division.

battalion. All stopped at ADS whence we were sent further back to near Bray. Hardly had we settled in the new ADS when we were told that the troops were to evacuate Bray. Retreat began about 10 p.m. the MO Hall & I, bringing along the band and Details. Terribly long march: roads crammed with troops for miles, transport and guns. Reached Morlancourt about 2 a.m.

Gillett: Mon 26 March 1918. [Compeigne 12 miles south west of Noyon]

Mass in Compeigne – then sauntered around and later tried to regain transport, but heard they had been moved suddenly so tramped to Estrees St Denis – what a mix up – parts of Staffordshire's here from everywhere – but no one knows anything of moves. In Compeigne I had a good look around Napoleon's Palace – a gorgeous place – used for GHQ for a long while – grounds beautiful. Held up for a German spy only my Sacred Heart badge convinced the French police I was a chaplain.

Steuart: Mon 26 March 1918. [Henencourt 3 miles west of Albert]

Rested in a field at Morlancourt till 6 or 7 a.m. and had some tea and bully. Marched off again under same conditions and reached LAVIEVILLE, where we camped in a field between that village and HENENCOURT. I fell asleep several times as I walked along. Here we were re-joined by the rest of the battalion. Our casualties are 340. Among Officers are KILLED: Col. Anderson, Capt. Johnson, Capt. Hannah, Lt Wuensch, Lt Brown, and Lt Stewart. WOUNDED: Capt. Taylor, Lt. Noble, Lt Neil, Lt Dunlop, and Lt Bryson. MO, self, Tomkin, Hope and Bryson with details went to Warloy for the night. Since Last Friday I have only 1 night's sleep.

Gillett: Wed 27 March 1918. [Nampcel 6 miles north east of Compeigne]

Little sleep all night – stuck on couch until MT move off with rations and in this way am able to find my unit again. What a bitterly long, cold ride – set off about 5 a.m. and get to our dump about 9 and here get in touch with 152 ASC again – hurroo. Everybody full of strange talk. Put in the day in Nampcel – hung about waiting for next move. One continuous shunt at the present. Moved about 6 p.m. and about 9 p.m. settled for the night in the fields, dossed down on the goods waggons.

Steuart: Wed 27 March 1918. [Buire-sur-Ancre 3 miles south west of Albert]

Roused up at 6 a.m. to re-join battalion at Lavieville. After lunch there we moved off to BUIRE which was reported to have fallen. I went round the three battalions and saw each RC individually and gave them absolution. No longer had we advanced over the ridge above the Amiens-Albert road than the Boche opened a frightful barrage on us. Lt Forsyth was badly wounded (and died a few days later at Warloy), Mackenzie slightly, and many men killed or wounded. MO, Tomkin, Sgt Henry, L Cpl McLellan and I got into a hole by the roadside and attended to the wounded. Very heavy crumping all the time. About 6 p.m. we followed the battalion to Buire, which we had taken over from the Sherwood's & which, we found had not been taken by the Boche. HQ in a cellar not more than 20 yards behind the front line. Here we are holding the river Ancre, our men lying along the railway embankment with advance posts forward. Went to the deserted YMCA, looted tobacco, tea, candles, & some books. The village cellars are full of wine – red & white, & champagne & everybody is helping himself. Our Mess is well stocked.

Gillett: Thurs 28 March 1918. [St Christophe-à-Berry 6 miles east of Compeigne]

Holy Thursday. Hung about all morning awaiting orders. At 3 p.m. on the move – to St Christophe[12] – All nestle down on the floor – poor Toogood [servant] out with rations, lost. At 4 a.m. roused up to know where Toogood is – getting ready to move.

Steuart: Thurs 28 March 1918.

Several terrible bombardments on our village. Many casualties. Also some of our own heavies fell short and caused us about a dozen casualties. Buried a Leicester man who was killed yesterday.

Gillett: Fri 29 March 1918.

At 6 a.m. on the move – trekking to Choisy – close by Compeigne, through Vic[13] to the Soissons – Compeigne road – a glorious march and a glorious day. Sleeping in the fields.

Steuart: Fri 29 March 1918. [Warloy-Baillon 4 miles west north west of Albert]

More heavy bombardments. The village is melting away and the church is now in ruin. After dinner Tomkins & I & Taffy went back to Warloy as Bttn. is relieved tonight. Arrived Warloy about 10:30 p.m., most of the civilians have gone. Billeted near what used to be Brigade HQ in Feb' 17.

12 St Christophe-à-Berry.
13 Vic-sur-Aisne.

Gillett: Sat 30 March 1918. [Canly 3 miles south west of Compeigne]

Attended Mass and received before moving off – French chaplain said Mass for some of his men. Moved away before the troops, looked round Compeigne. Held up for a while by French police who mistook the chaplain's badges for the Iron Cross, soon rectified. Saw effect of Wednesday's bombs on Compeigne. Moved to Arsy and then told to go on to Canly some 3 miles further. Beastly wet day – everybody soaked through – poor Toogood in very bad spirits. However, we all got beds and finally got snug for the night.

Steuart: Sat 30 March 1918. [Corbie 7 miles south west of Albert]

Bttn. relieved today. Went with Williamson to Lahoussoye to get billets. Were moved from there to Bonnay & from there to La Neuville near Corbie, where we arrived drenched to the skin after a six hour march. Established billets. Battalion came in about midnight. Spent a restless and almost sleepless night on a very small, narrow and lumpy settee.

Gillett: Sun 31 March 1918. [Le Neuville en Hez 12 miles west of Compeigne]

Easter Sunday – Holy Mass before moving – then trekked along through Clermont to Le Neuville en Hez. Got troops billeted comfortably – attended Vespers in afternoon. Transport extending 8 to 10 miles along the road. Rare, nice little dinner in the evening and me appreciating it.

Steuart: Sun 31 March 1918. [Heilly 1 mile north east of Corbie]

Easter Day and impossible to say Mass. Town under fire. At 6 p.m. moved off to Heilly where the whole Brigade is billeted. Had a good night.

Gillett: Mon 1 April 1918. [Auchy-le-Mantagne 25 miles south, south west, of Amiens]

Easter Monday. Holy Mass then moved on to Auchy[14] – a glorious day – everybody alarmed, rumours about the Boche cavalry in the neighbourhood – nothing happened. What a long line of Transport it was. Auchy full of French troops from Italy – met a French soldier priest who wanted to go to Confession and say Mass. 3 Masses tomorrow, myself, McMahon and the soldier priest.

---

14 Auchy-le-Mantagne.

Steuart: Mon 1 April 1918.

Mouched about. Fine day and nothing doing.

Clearly the worst was over and this initial phase absorbed, albeit with sporadic and intense returns of violence. This signified a major turning point on the Western Front, even if this would have been unknown for those in the thick of things. The outcome of the war was far from settled and many more were yet to suffer and die. Through our diarist's escapades the period between April and June will now be assessed. This was a phase of adjustment to the troops' geographical and military restructuring, and demands of an increasingly mobile war. Chaplains' increasing optimism is an insight into morale in general, and in the case of Gillett a revitalisation of *joie de vivre* presented by the Americans.

Fr Gillett had two major impulses after the retreat: to return to celebrating Mass, and the natural urge for rest. He remarked on 5 April from Saleux: 'Mass now regularly – idle day – resting after our wearisome trek'. Next day he said Mass for the 16th Irish Division which he described as 'smashed to atoms – division done in'. Two days later in the 'glorious church' at Saleux he celebrated a deferred Feast of the Annunciation, preached in French and English, and announced: *'Alors, vous recommendous, nous anjourd! Hui aux prieres de Notre Dame pour la armées pour la Victoire et pour les agouisants'*. Guns and fighting could be heard not too far away but when he visited Amiens the next day it was his reflective and compassionate manner which emerged: 'What a contrast Amiens is today to my first visit in October 1916 – then full of life and everything busy – today everybody has quitted it – all shattered – streets covered with debris – poor Amiens to be broken after 4 years of hope'! Despite random shelling into Amiens, relative quiet ensued until 24 April when Gillett claimed that: 'Second Battle of Amiens begins at 4:30, huge bombardment'. It appears that Fr Gillett was not the greatest military historian, maybe repeating hearsay. What he heard was the Second Battle of Villers-Bretonneux during the Battle of the Lys, 24-27 April, a successful repulsion of German advances. Gillett remained in Saleux until he went on a 'devil of a long trek' to Belloy-Saint-Léonard'.[15] April ended in Soues: 'Where we have a happy few days – just the ADC[16] a good billet and a nice church close by'.

The period since the retreat had been more difficult for Steuart. He had moved out from Heilly, roughly halfway between Albert and Amiens, to Mesnil-Martinsart. This was the area of the 1916 Somme fighting, north of Albert, west of Thiepval and south of Beaumont-Hamel. Before moving, at Heilly Church on 2 April he exclaimed: 'First Mass I have said since March 17th, i.e. 15 days'! The Germans began to shell Heilly and Steuart's unit was relieved by the Australians on 6 April:

15   22 miles.
16   Army Dental Corps.

At Beuvry Cemetery.

Marched out of the line with a London Bttn. of the 47th division. New line is in Aveluy Wood just in front of MARTINSART and MESNIL. Heavy rain all the time: road ankle deep in mud and water. MO and I have a very good elephant dug-out in the valley. The valley is partially under Boche observation, and is frequently shelled & swept by machine-gun fire.

In other zones Catholic chaplains, like their military counterparts, continued to fall. Fr McDonnell from Co. Cork, aged 41 was killed attending the wounded under fire at Givenchy-en-Gohelle on 9 April.[17] He served with 55 West Lancashire Machine Gun Company. A Vincentian priest he worked in Lanarkshire. His death prompted Rawlinson to reveal his hand in canvassing for conscription for ministers: 'A wire last night tells me that Rev J J Mc Donnell was killed on the 9th. Our deficit as you know was 71 on 31st March. If the present idea of bringing Ministers of religion into the Services matures, no one would be more pleased than myself'.[18] In the event this never materialised.

Headstone. Fr John J McDonnell. Age 41. 55 West Lancashire MGC. KIA 9 April 1918.

17 Some 77 miles from Gillett and 30 from Steuart.
18 DAA, Rawlinson to Monk, 11 April 1918.

Fr McDonnell's brother wrote to Rawlinson:

> He was posted to the Machine Gun Company [55th West Lancashire Division] because he could not remain in a post where there was little work when chaplains were desperately needed up the line. Although to his confreres he expressed a presentiment of death he never did to me or his or his sisters but asked them to pray that he might have the courage to carry out his sacred duties, the only fear he had was of being afraid.[19]

Thirty miles away from Givenchy it was comparatively quiet albeit with the customary erratic episodes of violence. Steuart's entry for 10 April: 'Nothing much doing. Aeroplane strafing all day. Spud Samson sniper, shot through the head. McCulloch HQ runner also killed. We have done great execution against the Boche and advanced a few yards. Royal Scots have pushed them back 100 yards'. Contrasts were never far away, on 12 he wrote:

> Beautiful hot sunny day. Lounged about. Met Fr Sheridan (now attached to 10th Lancashire Fusiliers). Had to break into the Church and sacristy. Found there everything necessary for Mass. Maj. Mortimer, D157 Battery called to ask me to visit his men. Mass in Church at 8:30. My 44th birthday. Today I complete my 18 months in France with this Battalion.

Fr Steuart's respite was not to last long. The German's increased their gas campaign from 17 April 1918: 'Gas last night, eleven men gassed, but none seriously. 18 April: 'Strong gas shelling at 11 p.m. Had to wear respirator for half an hour'. Next day: 'Pretty heavy casualties. Sgt Haughey, Lt Cpl Thomson, Pte McMahon killed. Stretcher bearers Lanry and Chalmers severely wounded & others'. 23 April:

> I re-joined the Bttn. at Hedauville Camp. Attack on a large scale last night, resulted as far as I can learn, in a state of "as you are". Two of our men, one who has just got the Military Medal killed last night by a bomb. Went into the line again on the AVELUY road sector, relieving the 15th Nott's & Derby. A very lucky relief, as there were several heavy bursts of fire which just escaped us. One bad casualty, of the Sherwood's, bullet through the stomach, is sure to die.

Kaiserschlacht was still taking its toll. On 9 April Fr James Shine was badly wounded in the legs and flank. It was hoped he would pull through but died at Calais base hospital on 21 April. Born in Kilcommon More North, Cahir, Co. Tipperary he was serving with the 21 Battalion Middlesex Regiment aged 37. On loan from Dunkeld parish in Dundee Diocese, Scotland, Bishop John Toner wrote: 'Fr Shine

---

19 DAA, 3238, 18 April 1918.

was deservedly popular in Dundee. We earnestly pray God that his death will justify peace. Public prayers are to be offered up here and in Perth for the sufferer RIP. "A Life Consecrated to God Sacrificed on the Altar of Duty".[20]

May and June offered a chance for Fr Gillett to enjoy countryside walks and indulge in French architecture: 'Crouy – saw glorious old monastery from which monks were expelled by the devilish Combles laws – now all in ruins', next day he: 'Called in at Belloy Chateau – where people were in residence – phew! A great walk entirely'. The next day he was roused at 4 a.m. and marched towards Amiens. As he came within reach he acclaimed: 'How gorgeous the Cathedral is as one approaches the town'. Then reality returned: 'Spent night on roadside – slept on a waggon, then under, then marched about to get night over'. He next

Headstone. Fr James Shine. Age 37. 21 Middlesex. KIA 21 April 1918.

At Boulogne Eastern Cemetery.

20 This was an epithet sometimes inscribed on headstones in the First World War.

Contay Church, 24 July 2012.

Bavelincourt Church, 10 April 2013.

marched towards Albert and billeted in fields at Behencourt clearly in high spirits, 5 May: 'Behencourt, where troops were very thick. Australians very numerous, so mind your stables! Another litter of puppies'! He remained in this area visiting several churches in Baizieux, Bavelincourt, and Contay to celebrate Mass. On the 18 May, he took time out to remember his father: 'Dad's anniversary. Holy Mass for him at Bavelincourt. Confessions in evening – no good'.

He described moments of joy as he rode a bicycle to Doullens with a fellow priest Fr Wilkin, or when he 'lolled' about' [this typically Lancashire phrase was unexpectedly also used by Fr Steuart], or sometimes 'trotted about'. By contrast, he still encountered obstacles getting the desired religious response with men from units with poor Catholic representation or from army administrative intransigence. He bemoaned the turn out for Confessions which might be for a variety of reasons but it was army laxity or worse which irked him most. 26 May: 'Expected a great number at Mass as units all out of line – but bitterly disappointed – men even not warned. Go up to Brigadier tomorrow about it'. This he did but returned empty handed: 'Visited units and interviewed Brigadier and a fat lot of use'. Fr Gillett had been trying to break the occasional impasse between himself as a clergyman and the army. He had written to the Principal Chaplain a year previously and received this considered and thoughtful, yet apparently ineffective reply on 5 April 1917:

> The difficulties you mention are by no means a rare occurrence. We have had a good many complaints from various parts of the field, and they form some of the most difficult to contend with. As a rule it is more a matter of tact on the part of the chaplain than anything else. It is almost impossible to bring a CO or even a GOC to book for preventing Services, as they can always claim that the duties [that is secular] performed by the men are necessary. At the same time it becomes most heart-breaking after a time. Unless there is some quite flagrant case that can be officially reported, or at any rate unless the fact is established that it is rarely possible to hold Services for the RC's of your Brigade (in which case of course we could bring the whole matter before the AG) I think the only other course is to approach tactfully the GOC of the Division through your Senior Chaplain. There is one thing you must certainly not do, and that is to give up heart. Perhaps on the whole I would suggest you putting the matter before the APC of your Army, Father Hessenhauer. He will doubtless do all he can to help you, and may possibly be able to see your Brigadier, or the GOC for the Division. Fight tactfully for what you want, and you will get it in the long run. Meanwhile you have my sincere sympathy.[21]

Other chaplains had similar experiences but occasionally a lack of social cachet dealing with an alien body of men limited chaplaincy success. In spite of this even those

---

21 DAA, 3231, Rawlinson to Gillett, 5 April 1917.

At Bagneux British Cemetery. (Situated on the site of former CCS.)

with social kudos such as Fr Steuart also incurred snags, on 11 June 1919 he wrote: 'Went to Mŭngersdorf in afternoon but no one turned up. I heard that my notice was not put in orders after all'. Rawlinson tried to circumvent any local hitches by nominating the Senior Chaplain as an intermediary. As a rule, disagreements had: '… resulted in some early friction between Catholic chaplains and the military and Anglican religious authorities, although not to the point of institutional impasse. As the war continued these teething troubles evaporated to permit remarkably good relations between the authorities and Catholic chaplaincy, albeit with occasional blemishes'.[22]

Fr Gillett never gave up hope despite provocation, amidst the sadness of regularly losing colleagues. On 29 May 1918 Fr Carl Whitefoord, some 16 miles distant,

Headstone. Fr Carl B Whitefoord. Age 33. 6 London Regiment. KIA 30 May 1918.

22 Bellis, 'Catholic Chaplains', p. 15.

was struck by a shell fragment in the thigh. Taken to a CCS he died the next day. Whilst laying in repose, the CCS was bombed by German planes and Fr Whiteford's body incinerated. His remains were buried by a Canadian Catholic chaplain at Gezaincourt adjacent to the CCS, 2km south west of Doullens.[23] Fr Carl Blaquhoun Whiteford served with 6 Battalion London Regiment [City of London Rifles]. In many ways he was an unusual priest, bearing out the variety of the Catholic project. Described in the *Dublin Review* of 1919 as a tall [over 6ft 1] quiet Englishman: the background of this Shrewsbury diocesan priest was distinctly different. Educated at Rugby School and Merton College Oxford he lived in a Tudor Manor near Ludlow, Shropshire, his father is described as a 'gentleman of means'. Like Fr Steuart he was descended from Scottish lineage. He was 33 when killed.

Gillett was having a relatively comfortable time despite occasional official vexation, but the spiteful nature of war always lingered: '31st May. Mass during which huge shell fell close by and the roof rattled with debris – 28 lads knocked out -Visited Molliens[24] and Mirvaux. Shelling Boche threaten Paris'.[25]

Labour Corps at La Gorgue February 1916. (JAD, Paintings of Fr Leslie Walker)

23   Less than 2o miles from Steuart and 30 from Gillett.
24   Molliens-au-Bois.
25   Bombarded by 'the Paris Guns' or formally the "*Kaiser Wilhelm Geschütz*" or "Emperor William Guns.

The late spring and early summer months were dreary for Fr Steuart stationed at Rubempre, west of Albert and north of Amiens, less than five miles from Gillett at Behencourt. 1 May: 'A Cold, bleak day. Left Camp at 2 p.m. and marched to Rubempre, arriving a little after 8 p.m. Encamped in a field under canvas, where he witnessed: 'The village is full of French cavalry and artillery from the 10th Army, mostly from Italy'. His battalion went to Warloy on 4 May to dig trenches with 'Chinese coolies'.

His mood had changed by 15 May to amusement when invited to say Mass at the Chinese Labour camp, arguably one of the prime examples of the Universal Church:

> Went over to Robertson's Chinese Labour camp, with Fisher. Said Mass at 10. Served by 2 Chinamen, one of whom spoke to me for some time in Latin! Congregation of 30 with two European NCO's. Nearly all went to Communion after singing the Confiteor in Chinese. Other Chinese hymns and prayers chanted after Mass.

Latin had a useful part to play in bridging cultural and linguistic boundaries.

Unpredictable danger continued. Bombs were dropped at random, one landing in Rubempre village and killing a horse, in another incident they also killed a chaplain. The allure of these new weapons of war had taken its toll. Fr Baines, a Preston born priest of the Liverpool Archdiocese died on 31 May 1918 after injuries received a day earlier at Steenbecque:

> He was attached to the Divisional Artillery and was with a number

Fr Thomas Baines.

Headstone at Aine Communal Cemetery. Age 31. 152 Brigade RFA. KIA 31 May 1918.

of officers in a house when the Germans started bombing the place. Fr Baines went outside to see if he could see the aeroplane, and a bomb fell close to him badly shattering both legs and taking off his right hand. He was taken to a CCS and was attended by Fr O'Mara SJ and lived until 1 p.m. the next day and was conscious most of the time. I buried him at Aire were a large number of priests, officers and men attended his funeral.[26]

Regular fighting would soon restart and Fr Steuart nearly lost his life. 19 May: 'Mass at 8:30. Joined battalion between Harponville and Hedauville. Moved at night into line – in a bank at the junction of the Senlis & Bouzincourt roads. Raid on our left'. Next day he reported: 'Nothing doing. Casual shelling'. But at nightfall the situation rapidly deteriorated and as reported earlier, it was here that Fr Steuart received his third gas attack. His bravery almost made him blind and he was evacuated first to Amiens then Rouen and finally 'blighty' which he reached on 26 May by means of the Grandtully Castle.[27] He recorded the welcome afforded injured heroes: 'Tea, fruit etc at every station – cheering crowds in the streets! Am at the Second Western General Hospital, Whitworth Street, Manchester' and the next day was feeling 'much better'. His entries become less regular and more mundane until 21 June when he left for Queen Victoria's holiday home at Osborne House, Isle of Wight, now utilised for the recuperation of officers. He remained until 10 July until heading for his family home in Perthshire.

Fr Gillett's summer 1918 account gains importance through Fr Steuart's enforced absence. His activity in the period June and July reflected the general military situation in the area between Albert and St Quentin. This was largely a time for regrouping and stabilising before the Allied advances in August, accelerating in September. For Gillett it was a mixed episode. Normal priestly functions stimulated by the American's enthusiastic and public participation in Catholic services, were coupled with increasing visits to Paris, particularly shrines and churches. These were in sharp contrast to a personal and unfounded attack on his integrity which will unfold, and the accelerating sense of encouragement associated with the successful Allied advances. The juxtaposition between the mundanity of chaplaincy life at war with its dangers, despondencies with joys, and failures with successes, continued through to the end.

Gillett spent much of the first week in June cycling around 'putting up notices', celebrating Mass and generally living the life of a village priest. He enjoyed this rural distraction from the tough life of an inner-city parish. On 9 June his efforts were rewarded: 'Moved into wood at Molliens – a glorious cover in the hot weather':

> Feast of The Sacred Heart. Mass at Molliens – a great crowd from all around – many at Confessions and Holy Communion: in evening a great service with the

---

26   DAA Rawlinson to Bourne ref 78-2-30', 5 June 1918.
27   Grandtully Castle, Aberfeldy, Perthshire, which Steuart would have known well, his own home being close by.

French soldiers – soldiers create gusto, a good impression by their singing and devotion. Consecrations of England and France to the Sacred Heart. Outdoor Procession of the Blessed Sacrament in which our Tommies join heartily.

An increasing sense of security and normality now infused Gillett's entries, yet the military situation remained a cause for concern, particularly when on 12 June his 'boys' in the 11 Royal Fusiliers went 'over the top'. He visited them at Warloy on their return after five days battle.

Meanwhile for Fr Gillett, it was not British or French troops that now took centre-stage, but the arrival of the Americans who transformed his morale and work schedule. A refreshed and reinvigorated chaplain emerged as these energetic troops arrived. Disappointed by the poor response he received from the soldiers in the British units to whom he was deployed, he had conversely praised Irish and Lancashire troops for their devotion. He was not alone, for example Fr Francis Devas claimed that: 'Lancashire and Irish Catholic soldiers were not in the least ashamed of it being known that they were Catholics. That may seem a queer thing to say – and one which Irish people and Lancashire people may hardly understand. But outside these two holy places, the contempt of generations has left its mark on Catholics – especially Catholic young men – who have always found themselves in an insignificant minority'.[28]

The influx of American troops was therefore a refreshing spectacle providing both enthusiasm and numbers to satisfy his religious calling. Public expression of the Catholic religion once more demonstrated the breadth and reach of the Church and the chaplain's active part within it. It was not purely a reawakening of the religious life but at a human level too, in other words body and soul. Enthusiasm restored Gillett continued at an accelerating pace until demobilisation in 1919. 'In evening went to Pierregot and found it swarming with Yanks, who were apparently being hustled up to help'. On the next day after celebrating Mass he:

> Visited the Yanks and found out their chaplains. Confessions at Molliens again, later helped the American chaplains, five were going up to 11 p.m. – the boys were lined up in queues – the chaplains and I sat in a tent each – phew! Some Confessions – Never heard so many in 3 years with British troops.

23 June, Sunday: 'Mass at Molliens – Americans crowd in – In evening Benediction'. The soul having been addressed, two days on it was the body's turn: 'Idle day. Met Kilgannon and O'Donnell USA [chaplains] – in evening USA band gave us a treat in the wood – these doughboys some boys and no mistake'. Two days later after a chaplain's meeting the naivety of the newly arrived Americans was expressed: '2 Yank chaplains with us. Boche planes over us last night – Americans all up wanting to see them'.

28 JAL, F. Devas, 'Our Chaplains Experiences' in *Letter of Notices*, 33 (1915-16) 443.

Epilogue – Spring to Early Summer 1918

Fr Gillett's testimonies for June to August stand alone as Fr Steuart was in Britain from 25 May to 10 September, recuperating from the effects of gas. Even with one chaplain incapacitated it is possible to recognise that by mid-1918 there was a sense of relief that the German advance had been thwarted and that soon the tide would turn in Britain's favour. Nevertheless, it was too early to be over-optimistic; all the previous claims of a final British victory had been frustrated whilst the German Army remained a capable and increasingly desperate one. The cost in British lives was escalating at an exponential rate as open warfare garnered ever increasing casualties, including chaplains who accompanied the advances. Even so, the psychological uplift was unmistakable. With the defeat of Germany, Johnny would surely have a new master, but this was cold comfort for those who fell off the seesaw in the latter stages before victory was secured.

8

July–December 1918: 'End of Bloodshed and Strife, Everybody Going Mad With Delight'

Maybe they would but in July that was still merely an aspiration, the popular consensus of opinion in mid-1918 was that 1919 or later would signify the conclusion of the conflict. As it happened, the German effort imploded through: political and social unrest at home: starvation through the British blockade: the Allies resilience, determination and resources: and sheer war exhaustion. Military defeat would become inevitable as the summer moved into autumn but there was still a lot of fighting to be concluded until then. Even when hostilities were concluded in November 1918, formal peace was not achieved until mid-1919. Margery, so long suspended uncomfortably in mid-air, could by mid-summer 1918 see her seesaw slowly reaching equilibrium as the weight of the Allies took its toll. Progressively and determinedly this continued until Johnny Boche was left high, dry and friendless in November. The Armistice was a joyous and welcome affair for many, but for others even on the victor's side, it was a muted business: one full of loss, sadness, and uncertainty of the future. Many, trials still lay ahead.

As the summer unfolded German designs became increasingly frustrated. Although Kaiserschlacht had in many ways been a triumph for the German Army it had failed to fully deliver and was now going to reap the consequences. The arrival of American troops into the fray rekindled Ludendorff's worst nightmare. Furthermore, British and French resistance had remained stubborn and both armies became markedly more aggressive and professional. He knew the Americans were raw, but he also knew their resources were practicably inexhaustible. The one forlorn hope he now had lay in an attempt to seek advantage by exploiting situations of internal Allied friction. Quarrels between the Allies did arise, over munitions and particularly the deployment of troops. The desperate need for reinforcements for British and French soldiers became frustrated as the Americans engaged in building a new national army. They had made it abundantly clear that they would not bring an American army to war simply to plug gaps: even so this was hard to digest for allied commanders. Resolutely, General Pershing resisted their overtures and continued to build a new army, thereby establishing its own identity and that of his nation. They were determined to pursue their own objectives which included cementing a favourable post-war bargaining position. In the post-war world an American Empire would take its place in the *real*

176   Faith of Our Fathers

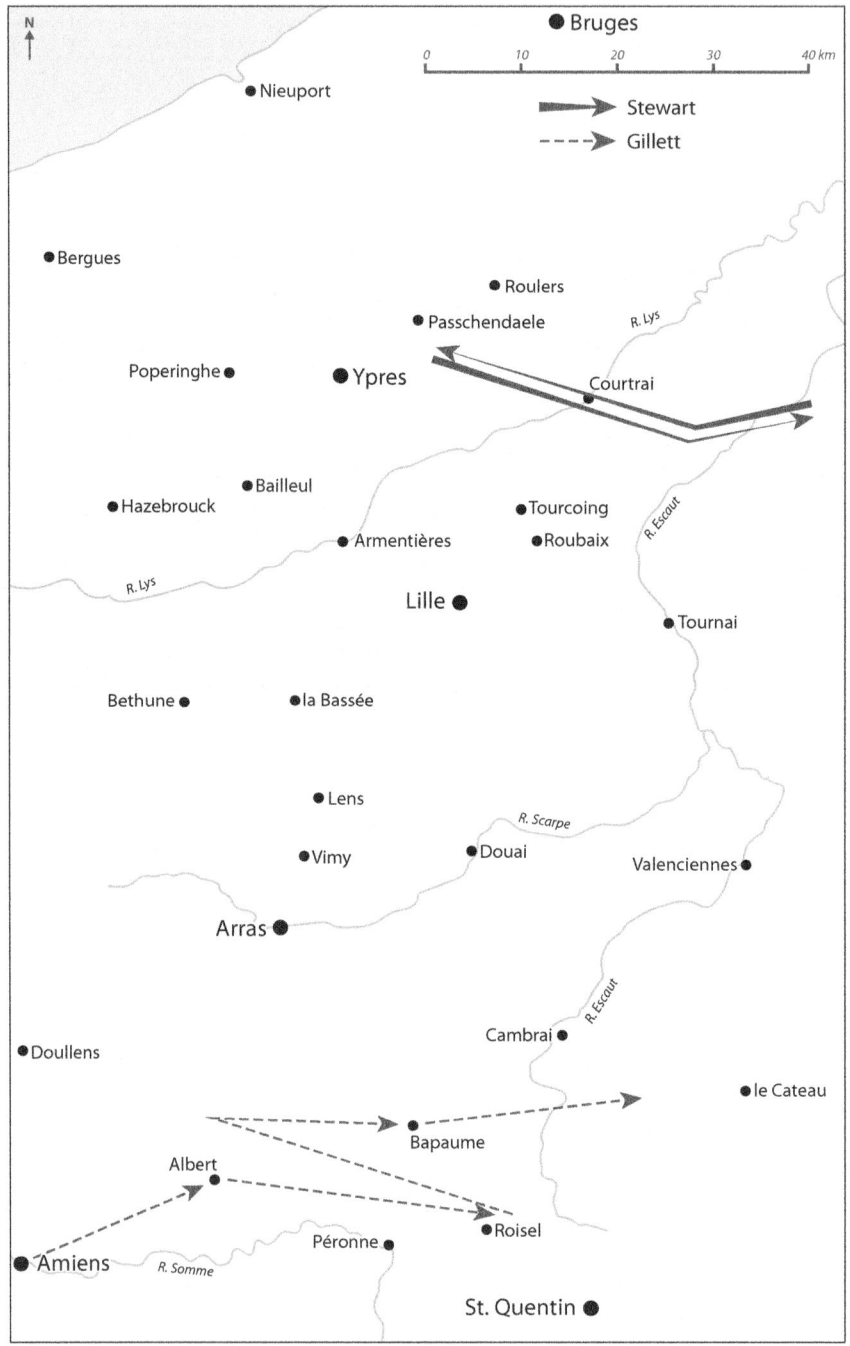

Map of Frs. Gillett and Steuart Late June to the Armistice November 1918.

politic of a new order, it could be argued that ultimately they became the new master of the seesaw. Nevertheless, as we will see, the Allies overcame their differences for the common good and thereby severed the straws that Ludendorff was clinging to.

Did HQ frictions have any practical influence on the fighting men? Not if our chaplains experiences are to go by. Soldiers [and chaplains] were far removed from their hierarchies and responded simply as people. As might be expected some soldiers welcomed the Americans enthusiasm and freshness hoping that their entry would signal a speedy end to hostilities; whilst others begrudged their late arrival and for those troops who had borne the misery of hard fighting of previous years a certain amount of resentment is understandable. This was the first meeting of the old and new worlds for many, but if the German High Command hoped to cause internal schisms, they were deluded. Little practical encouragement was received from the troops.

What can Catholic chaplains add to this part of the war story? Neither account suggests any friction. Fr Steuart seemed impervious to the Americans and rarely mentioned them, but he could not resist rank: 'Celebrated Mass for a congregation which included an American General'. His unfamiliarity with popular culture had shown earlier when he wrote on 1 October 1917: 'Doctor's place taken by an American Doughman [sic]'. There was no ambiguity from Fr Gillett who embraced 'these doughboys'. Fr Gillett's account suggests that the American inclusion was not only positive but massively so. He gives an insight into the boost he personally felt and to that of Allied morale. The French enthusiastic response on American Independence Day, 4 July 1918, is an exemplar: 'French planes about dropping bouquets amongst the American troops in our own wood, in honour of Independence Day. Americans make a great day of it; band out in evening and a boxing bout'. Gillett's enthusiasm was in part a response to the ebullient Catholic American's attitude to their religion, in stark contrast to his experiences with many British troops, but it was also a genuine love of: 'These Doughboys Some Boys and No Mistake'. Given the bloodiness and cruelty of war, Gillett's observations capture an altogether more humane and gracious outlook. Clearly *esprit de corps* was being established and a new sense of confidence was being restored. His observation, without judgement, that the Americans were learning the ropes of warfare where 'repatriation' of the enemy's goods were common currency, is interesting: 'Sat 6th July. Mass. USA troops had been up the line fighting at Ville – and returned this morning, carrying all sorts of souvenirs. Lunched with Curé of Molliens and the Curé of St Gratien who was formerly at Méaulte. Confessions in evening'.

The next day Fr Gillett experienced a truly American-free day. He played cricket. After the Armistice his relationship with Americans developed further and complimented his personal enthusiasm for life. Whether Fr Steuart disapproved of Americans was simply indifference is not clear. He was not naturally a sociable man and his lack of attachment to 'doughmen' may simply reflect his disposition towards 'foreigners' but there was no sign of hostility towards them, more disdain.[1]

1   See Appendix IX: A portrait of Fr Robert Steuart.

In July the shoots of military recovery could be sensed even if an outright victory was anything but assured. There were many hardships and casualties that lay in wait before the war was over. Entrenched self-interest and partisanship had dogged the Allies throughout, the resultant mistrust hampered full cooperation and minimised success. Over-riding national interests in favour of a common approach was elusive even four years into the war, and not the exclusive province of America. The in-fighting over strategic military aims between Haig and Robertson at Army HQ and Lloyd George in Westminster, and the British reluctance to accept French authority in the field has been well documented.[2] Therefore, General Foch's appointment as Commander-in-Chief of the Allied Forces in March 1918 was a decisive and much needed one. In time he won sufficient support to embark on a combined strategy to quell German attacking ambitions and to commence a steady advance. This began with combined operations at the second Battle of the Marne in July. General Foch oversaw necessary reforms to increase cooperation between members of the Alliance, recognising the need for united action not only between its members but also between branches of the forces. In the retaliatory response to the Spring Offensive later in the summer there is evidence of these improvements. Tanks, infantry, artillery and aircraft combined especially effectively in the Battle of Amiens in August 1918 with Canadian, Australian, British and French forces combining. The Americans carried out subsidiary military exercises to the south-east, but as Fr Gillett will testify, they were also involved in the main operations in the area of the Somme later in 1918.

The second Battle of the Marne on 15 July negated German expansion and created some stability. By the second Battle of Amiens on 8 August the Allies were on the offensive: '8th August was the climax of the war, and what happened subsequently was the natural sequel'.[3] There was now weight transference on the seesaw. Mc Williams and Steel describe in great detail the superbly professional approach to this battle, in particular the impressive diversionary tactics adopted to confuse the rumour mill prior to commencement of hostilities. Detailed and secret planning included creating diversionary and phoney communications traffic and crucially dispatched the Canadians complete with signallers to Ypres. It was a complicated ruse with 48 infantry battalions leaving Arras and Amiens heading north, before making an about turn south towards the Somme by nightfall.[4] When the battle started the German generals were taken completely by surprise and the seeds of uncertainty planted.

What was Fr Gillett doing in the midst of massive military preparations and subsequent action? On 3 July:

> At this time the troops were all around Warloy and forward – where a chaplain was always in attendance at the church for Mass and the evening devotions, so

---

2   For example N. Lloyd, *Passchendaele*, Chapter 1, 'Manoeuvres of War'.
3   James McWilliams and James Steel, *Amiens 1918: The Last Great* Battle (History Press, 2007) quoting Liddell Hart, p. 277.
4   For a full account read Part 1/2 'The Conjuror's Box', Op.cit.

troops always had convenience for duties. The details and transport of ASC were at Molliens and I visited them there.

Meanwhile his admiration for the Americans grew, particulalry for dentists. Toothache must have been a constant bother, having visited a French dentist at Boulogne in May 1917, and having been refused treatment by a CCS in 1918, it appeared that his problem was over: 'Visited American dentist in the wood and had some good work done'.

With Steuart convalescing until early September, Gillett continued his priestly work. On 12 July the Brigade, and Gillett with it, were on the move further west of Amiens to Bovelles. Before marching he visited all units: 'Confessions in Saisseval for Northants and 54 RAMC – not much encouragement'. Fr Fred Gillett was more relaxed and confident of the outcome of war, reporting on the Battle of Rheims on 19 July: 'Mass, visited Pissy and Clairy and in evening Confessions for Beds – only 5 turned up. News of our first success since first German oncoming on 21st March – news comes through of French success, 15,000 prisoners and 200 guns – thank God'! Gillett's physical and mental relief after so much toil and hardship was matched by the spiritual: 'Sun 21st July 1918. Mass at Saisseval – then at Floxicourt for East Surrey's in some little, wee chapel which was cram full – Buffs also came – Conferred them all – then Mass and Holy Communion: Evening service at Boyelles and Consecration to the Sacred Heart'.

This growing sense of achievement, fulfilment, and success in his mission was not to last long. This time the Catholic authorities to which he had given great service, respect, and obedience, appeared to collude to destroy this all too brief interlude of happiness. Many chaplains had unjust and unfair criticisms with which to contend. This episode demonstrates how the system of discipline and compliance which normally worked well, could go wrong. This case was conducted in a furtive fashion, even if the final result was the correct one. It bitterly disappointed and upset Fred Gillett, ironically, the Catholic authorities caused Fr Gillett more angst than the Army. His words in full:

> Mon 22nd July *Audi alter am partum* – a very heavy day for me – met by my Senior Chaplain and received a stunning communication. Mass in Chateau then off to Picquigny for chaplains meeting – Rawlinson coming and Smith [Gillett's SCF] – privately interviewed by Rawlinson and told I had been ordered home by my superiors!! Cycled back very sore. After three years of wicked war, to be asked back by fools in England, without enquiry of any sort, Bah! The irony of it all – *AUDI ALTERAM PARTEM*. Am very low and depressed'.

Audi alteram partem translates as 'hear the other side too'. It was a reasonable request and it was denied him, instead he was investigated without his knowledge or involvement and not afforded basic human rights. The intervention of an indiscernible reporting system was substituted to investigate an unsubstantiated allegation. In one respect he was lucky, many were not afforded such an investigation and were condemned on hearsay. Keatinge, by now *Episcopus Castrensis* in London, wrote to Rawlinson: 'The enclosed letter was sent by the Archbishop of Liverpool to Cardinal Bourne regarding Fr F Gillett. If it is true it is very serious. In a case like that I am afraid military discipline[5] may have to be used'.[6] There was no direct mention of the reason of the allegation against Gillett, and Gillett himself did not elaborate, but it followed a pattern that was almost certainly drink related. This is indicated in Rawlinson's response to Keatinge which states that: 'Frs. Meany and Keegan were found on the road in the same condition by another Catholic Officer'.[7] Rawlinson continued: 'I have started investigations with regard Rev F. Gillett'. Details of the enquiry are not on file, but clearly Rawlinson pursued his remit to root out a potential chaplaincy misdemeanour: 'The investigation I have made so far regarding Fr Gillett does not corroborate in any way with the report given to the Archbishop of Liverpool. It is of course easier to make a report of this sort than disprove it'.[8] *This is an important observation.* He then concluded his investigations: 'With regard to the accusations brought against Fr Gillett of the Liverpool Archdiocese, I have now carefully investigated the matter and found that *there is not a vestige of truth in any of them*. He has been doing good work with his Division for some considerable time'.[9]

Accused without his knowledge, astonishingly Gillett had been exculpated on 6 June 1918 *before* he was interviewed on 22 July, and sent home! The dates have been thoroughly checked yet the motivation for the disciplinary hearing and action remains incomprehensible. We don't have the contents of the interview but it seems that he was being punished for false allegations from which he had been exonerated! The chronology of events owes more to Bedlam than any rational process. There are two implausible explanations. First that his Archbishop had somehow withdrawn him prematurely. This is unlikely as the correspondence between these men in 1919 seemed cordial, and if he had a question mark over his behaviour would he have returned to Liverpool after demobilisation?[10] Secondly, that Bourne or Keatinge had withdrawn him for the same reason. This is also unlikely, what purpose could be served and would it be sensible to overrule Rawlinson for no apparent reason? It remains a mystery. Regardless, no significant damage was done. He did not return home and the whole matter seems to have fizzled out, carrying out his duties until demobilisation in September 1919.

---

5   Keatinge was out of touch or being disingenuous, in reality Courts Martial were to be resisted to avoid the scandal being made public, irrespective of the outcome. The accused were simply whisked away out of the Army.
6   DAA, 3231, Keatinge to Rawlinson, 6 April 1918.
7   DAA, 3231, Rawlinson to Keatinge, 8 April 1918.
8   Ibid., 20 April 1918. Author's italics to emphasise the truth of this comment.
9   DAA, 3231, Rawlinson to Bourne, 6 June 1918.
10 LAA 2 11V/G/26 Gillett to Whiteside correspondence, 19 July 1919.

This was a war not only of soul but also of body: including the body politic of Catholic aspiration. Rawlinson effectively accepted responsibility, interpreted then dealt with these dilemmas.[11] He was naturally empathetic and supportive of his men, thereby, conducting his first mission; but he also had to tip toe around and between both episcopal and military imperatives to fulfil his second mission. Intuitively he appreciated the bigger picture. Realising that the battleground of war would eventually be superseded by the battleground of peace, he astutely positioned his second mission for the time when Catholic aspirations, not to say survival, would replace military conflict.[12] Alas many feet were trodden on in the process, else quietly forgotten.

In any event Fr Fred Gillett was not from retiring stock. Three days later he had put matters behind him, replacing personal hurt with genuine care for the well-being of others:

> Mass – visited Cavillon to watch Divisional Steeplechase – what a glorious crowd – and beyond were men fighting and meeting their death – and the crowd here – who knew when orders would come and in turn they would grimly face the odds and with courage and grit. But today – make merry. Haig favours the meeting and Pershing – poor Haig he looks worn and anxious.

This is typically Fr Gillett, mixing soul and body, spiritual with material, and empathy for the plight of others. His consideration for war weary Haig suggests that his own worries had been jettisoned and were never mentioned again in his memoirs.

There was nothing of note until 6 August when he received an unexpected and perhaps compensatory bonus: 'Sent off for Army Rest Camp – lucky me'! He spent a happy few days there saying Mass and taking part in sports, Sunday was typical: 'Mass. About 20 present. In afternoon Belgian Sports – horse jumping – very fine – great mass of lovely creatures about. Nurses crowd up and we spend a great day'. He left Tréport camp temporarily to celebrate in Paris the anniversary of his ordination. His love affair with Paris was a permanent one: '12th August. Clear to Paris – Pilgrimage to Sacré Coeur to offer Mass for Foche and our cause'. The next day: 'Mass at Sacré Coeur – called on Knights of St Columba's – then to priests Club. In afternoon visited Notre Dame – in evening dined with American chaplains at Priests Club'. A further Mass for military success was celebrated at: 'Notre Dame Cathedral for Foch and our cause, then train at 9:15 a.m. for Tréport'. 17 August, despite 'a desperate days travelling', he arrived back at his unit: 'after a rather good time'.

Whilst he was away he missed the start of the Battle of Amiens on 8 August. This successful major battle is sometimes referred to as the start of 'the hundred day's

---

11 Rawlinson had limited real power with both the episcopacy and military but he did have influence, a good track record, and effective diplomatic skills. These were harnessed within a framework of common sense.
12 The concept of survival was not a far-fetched notion. The residue of persecution took many years to overcome.

offensive'. He saw the fruits on: 'Thurs 22nd August. 4 a.m. guns open up – attack reported and a success – orders to move up to wood and beyond Baizieux. On the move, the beginning of the end'. One can sense the pace of events quickening: '23rd August: '4 a.m. another barrage – visited Main Dressing Station at Franvillers. Fr Guinevan on the spot – then on to ADS on main Albert-Amiens road then on to Buiere (sic)[13] in search of Berks and on home'. The following day Gillett responded with his usual youthful enthusiasm: 'Still fighting and winning – cycled to Bresle and Lealvillers and back through Henencourt and Warloy – everybody now on the move and forward – hurroo!! Moving up to Heilly'. Next his reflective side to the fore:

> Sunday 25th. Mass in Bonnay, privately, heard Confessions of the 47th Division. Billeted in tents in a swamp – very little sleep, so got up early and did a cycle tour to Corbie and about. Poor Corbie, what a change since I last saw it in November 1916 – the Cathedral towers badly mauled – roof all done in and huge holes in the walls and round the houses and square blown to nothing. Australians all in Corbie.

Whilst the military pressed on, Fr Fred continued observing and making notes. 26 August he was at Dernancourt – Buire, immediately south-west of Albert: 'Boche reported to be retreating fast. 3rd Army in Bepaume – strolled along to Albert. In evening along the railway – now all blown up – this embankment had been used by the Boche guns as a strong defence line – here and there MGC lying dead by their guns and as yet not buried – Boche of course'. The next day Fred Gillett was reminded that the war had some distance to go and that he was far from being invincible:

> Visited Dernancourt and Meaulte, then on to Bray and from there side slipped to Etinehem, as the Boche guns opened up on a cross road and nearly did me in. From here walked on to Morlancourt and Ville home. Some trek – but what sights on the Bray – Meaulte road – men still lying unburied and of every description. Albert was by now a village with not a wall standing – every blessed place blown to bits – cemetery terribly shattered – Basilica merely a matter of debris.

He continued through: 'Ribemont, Mericourt, Freux, and Ville, which were all scenes of fighting earlier in the month. Church at Ribemont useable for Mass – but a huge shell hole behind the high altar – at Morlancourt and Treux churches practically destroyed'. The destruction of the built environment, usually but not exclusively religious, occupied his thoughts at the end of August. Nonetheless, he concluded the month in great spirits:

> Fricourt and Mametz merely names – it was here the July 1916 big push began – here were the old Boche prior to July 1916 – a wonderful semi-circle of positions,

---

13   Buire-sur-l'Ancre.

and all in their hands again in 1918, but now they are ours again and for good, for ever and ever. The advance is going on at a great pace.

Early September ushered in a relatively quieter phase for Gillett despite heavy shelling in the vicinity of Delville Wood and Combles. Then: 'Rumours Boche are going back fast. Trudged all over Delville Wood of 1916 fame. Division coming out for a few days rest to Trones and Bernafay Wood'. He did what he could to visit as many troops as possible which he refers to as: 'chased about all day after the units', noting as he did that: 'Dumps and fires ahead of us, signs of Boche retreating'. On 7 August he: 'Squared up with Brigadier for Mass tomorrow. Wonder will they see to orders being carried out'? He need not have worried on this occasion the Brigadier had actively promoted attendance: 'Sunday 8th. The Nativity of Our Lady. Masses in thanksgiving for recent successes – and for final victory – said Mass in hut at Combles, about 30 present. General Absolution and Holy Communion'. Thirty was not a large return given that the Brigadier had actively co-operated but it seems reasonable given the military situation and the paucity of Catholic troops in his units.

The weather was changing, not an unusual occurrence when military operations were planned. 10 September he was resigned: 'Slept in – stormy and wet – later tramped out in all the wet and slush on to the hills around Flers, where one gets a great view'. He braved the weather the next day to report: 'Mass in tent – visited a unit or two and tramped around the country, through Hardecourt, in 1916 occupied by the French troops – all sorts of French stuff about – of course no village left – all the 1916 fighting was carried on around here'. Two days later disappointed but fatalistic he: 'Fixed up Sunday Services, but find troops on the move, so useless'. Buoyantly he declared: 'News of American push at Verdun section'. On 16 September: 'Everybody moves – pass through Combles and Bouchavesnes and on to Moislains, where still some parts of buildings and parts of the church are above ground. Glorious day and the march quite a treat – poor Fusiliers fell into a booby trap and had some 20 lads wounded'.

Only 19 mile distant Fr John Fitzgibbon SJ was the next chaplain to die on 18 September just 50 days before the Armistice. Hailing from Castlerea, Co Roscommon, Fitzgibbon was 36 years old. He was killed by shrapnel at Attily whilst attending the wounded, including German prisoners whilst attached to 6 Division Field Hospital. His units were fighting at Holnon Wood at the Battle for Epehy.[14] He is

Fr John Fitzgibbon SJ. MC.

---

14 S. Bellis, Fr John Fitzgibbon in Damien Burke eds., *Irish Jesuits in the First World War*, (Messenger Dublin 2014).

buried nearby at Trefcon cemetery. He was awarded the Military Cross for a previous action.

In the intervening period since late May, Fr Steuart had been recuperating from the effects of gassing, unavoidably missing out in the reversal of fortunes at the Front. His activities at Osborne, Isle of Wight, and in Perthshire suggest a healthy recovery was made. Cycling, billiards, and fishing as well as socialising were habitual. Despite this he was keen to re-join his regiment. 21 July: 'Today, I received from the WO that I am appointed to the RAF Camp at Blandford. This is a great blow to me, as was confident of re-joining 12th HLI at once. At the same time I got a note from Rawlinson welcoming me back to France & promising me the 12th again'. Crossed lines were unavoidable and he was sent to Blandford Camp where there were only three Catholic officers. On 30 August after a round of frivolous pastimes he went on leave again to Scotland. His return to

Headstone at Trefcon Cemetery. Age 36. 6 Div RAMC. KIA 18 September 1918.

France was delayed until 10 September. His observations on returning were reminiscent of Fr Gillett's 'phoney war' at Boulogne: 'Went to Saint Martin's gas school at 9 a.m. Two very interesting lectures. Went to Cox's & lunching next door at a most excellent little café. Visiting the old basilica – it seemed somehow shrunken. Dined with Woodlock at Kelly's'. In his absence his servant Fisher had been reassigned to another officer: 'Rode to Divisional HQ with Cox. Found Fisher there. Can't make out whether or not he wants to come back to me'. It was probably not the best policy to cross Fr Steuart, only a week later he concluded that: 'Wrote to Col. Jones to tell him to keep Fisher, I have a new man Pte Brennan (57579) very willing and a good Catholic'.[15]

His sense of reality was restored when he moved to the Ypres sector to be with his battalion. On 17 September he noted: 'Three men killed and one seriously wounded in D Coy'. Irrevocably the tide was turning: 'On Tuesday night the 18th Lancashire Fusiliers took nearly 60 prisoners with very little loss'. Four days on he, 'picked a lot of blackberries' despite 'persistent shelling all round HQ'. His time in late September was spent visiting 2 companies of the Royal Scots and 'various oddments' including

---

15 Later Fisher wrote to Steuart appealing for money – his response is not recorded.

the Belgian battery. Things were changing dramatically as the breakout from Ypres commenced in earnest and it was of interest for him that the same battery laid down the first barrage on 28 September. He noted:

> Belgian barrage began at 2:30, ours at 5:30 a.m. Left ADS at 6 with Horne (senior C of E) & joined Schochet at Embankment RAP at Zillebeke. Many prisoners on route. Severe shelling all round RAP just got there in time. Set out at 10:30 to join battalion. Wandered right out of the road and eventually found HQ at Hedge Street Tunnels after encountering several barrages. Difficulty in establishing RAP. Finally found some shelter in abandoned Boche trench. Many severe shelling and bombing bouts during the night. Also very cold. Have advanced 6 miles.

Clearly the Ypres sector was having a harder time at the present than the Somme. The next day was one of personal sadness for Fr Robert. As his battalion moved off to Bulgar Wood he:

> Followed them. A good deal of shelling. Established in pill-boxes. Very wet, mosquito infested & somewhat damaged. Extremely violent shelling and very close. Cox killed instantaneously by a shell. Very much cut up about it as he was one of my best friends, a first-class soldier and a very brave man. RIP. Spent a good night. Mather seriously wounded.

The next day he witnessed more hostile action with a degree of progress:

> Moved off to re-join battalion. Zandvoorde and Ten Brielen taken, and we are now attacking Wervic. On the way met Sgt. O'Shea, very seriously wounded in the stomach. Gave him absolution and Extreme Unction. Fear he has a very small chance. Established one small RAP first in some huts and finally in three good pill-boxes between Ten Brielen and Wervic. A good many casualties & continuous shelling. We have penetrated into Wervic, but owing to intense machine – gun fire had to leave it again. Rather a large number of casualties. So many in the pill-box that I could not lie down and had to sit in a chair all night, did not sleep at all.

On 1 October he explained his hopes and the confusion of war:

> Relief to be at dusk and we are to be notified. Milligan and Bethune killed yesterday. No notification arrived so we set out and after miserable strayings & wanderings in rain and pitchy darkness, found a guide & eventually arrived at our destination – an abandoned Boche RE dump between Geluwe and Gheluvelt on the Ypres – Menin road. Slept 6 in a tent.

Steuart was unimpressed by military ineptitude:

> All breakfasted in bed! High Velocities started almost at dawn & kept up at short intervals all day. It was madness to put three battalions there. We were missed by a few yards again & again. Later in morning we were shifted to an open field half a mile away & set about building small shelters. Orders to move again to-night.

This duly followed but not with ease:

> Set off at 2:30 a.m. Pitch dark. Assembly point the very dump at the cross roads from which we moved this morning! It was heavily shelled just before and just afterwards. Marched down the Menin Road to Ypres, in at the Menin Gate and out of the Lille Gate & then to a rickety camp near Swan Chateau.

They were bombed at night but in the daylight hours enemy action was relatively unobtrusive. Not for long, two days later they were back in the line incurring Steuart's increasing criticism:

> Mon 7th October. Set off for line at 1:15 a.m. via Ypres, Potijze, Zonnebeke, and Becelaere. Crash shelling at Terhand cross roads, just as we came to them. We fell out until it was over but the 18th HQ got into part of it & the doctor (James) & the CSM were killed and three or four wounded. Our new HQ is very bad: under direct observation and with no cover at all. Shelling all night & missed by inches again and again throughout the night. One man, Pte Fewster of C Coy, had his right foot blown off. Very cold all night. HQ so exposed that we moved about 1,500 yards back to the rear of a small copse and dug ourselves in – or rather tried to – in a very draughty shelter.

It was unusual for chaplains to criticise the Army. Fr Steuart's involvement with these matters is more pronounced than any of the chaplains studied who were either ignorant or disinterested with military affairs. On the other hand, Fr Walker suggests that criticism was not only Steuart's domain, although his studies on canvas suggest that it is the officer class who were to be the recipients of his attention.

A rhyme accompanies the painting:

> Who daily to the trenches went
> Mid gases, shot and shell
> Yet ne'er a man e'er saw him there
> He did disguise so well
> Thus oft' exposed by night and day
> He very soon fell ill
> And home to blighty went his way
> With everyone's good will

The origins of the verse are obscure but carries the mood and style of the *'Wipers Times'* published at the Front. Contributors were soldiers and junior officers. Their humour was tolerated by higher authorities and considered good for morale, surprising given that the targets were habitually senior military and against a background of exacting discipline.

This depicts a scene at 'A Post at Le Touret with Richbourg in the distance' with a short narrative:

> *Officer in Command School of Instruction*: 'Hallo what's up?'
> *Worcester Officer*: 'Jolly useful things these engineering classes. My companies billeted over there. What, what!'

It is problematic to define with accuracy the motivation for these paintings and their comments. Perhaps they were just the artistic embellishment to soldiers own tales? It is clear that Fr Walker did not suffer fools gladly. Replying to a friend who thought that his time as a young Jesuit would be better spent on studying for exams, rather than his beloved woodwork for which he may be reprimanded he: 'Looking over his spectacles and peering through a mane of grey hair replied in a belligerent tone: Just let 'em try that's all'.[16]

Criticisms of the Army by Steuart may have been exacerbated by his anxiety for success. On 11 October he was happy to report: 'Hear that Cambrai and Le Cateau have been taken'. The next day he completed two years at the Front and amidst: 'Continuous shelling all around us. One man killed and nine wounded', he celebrated: 'Mass in the open in drizzling rain. Men from all units present'. 14 October brought a mixture of danger with a hint of gallows humour:

> Zero at 5:30 a.m. Advanced under barrage. Heavy mist soon rose which blotted everything out. HQ Coy with which were the MO & I, lost our way. A good deal of gas about. Emerged at last on the GHELUVELT – DADIZEELE road, where shelling soon became very hot. Callan and I were just opposite the door of a roadside house when a big shell burst right on the road & blew us through the doorway, Callan being hit by a small piece in the leg. Found our destination – "Detention House" – a pillbox – at last and got into it very gratefully. The day now brightened up and became very fine. Set off again about 4 p.m. and marched to bivouacs near Violin Farm just beyond Kezelberg. Since zero we have advanced 5 miles and taken a large number of prisoners. HQ established in a small wooden shanty which wouldn't keep out an umbrella!

Steuart was having a tough time as his units fought their way eastwards and his night's sleep was soon interrupted:

---

16 RCBF, Catholic Chaplaincy Papers, *Obituaries*, (no named publisher, 1958), p. 117.

'The Transit of Our Late GOC' – January 1916. (JAD, Paintings of Fr Leslie Walker)

The Advantage of a School for Officers – 29 December 1915.
(JAD, Paintings of Fr Leslie Walker)

All awakened at 2:30 a.m. by heavy shelling all around us. After a few rounds we had to get out of it at the double & spread out over the fields. Shelling went on persistently for a long time, always in much the same place, splinters flying around and all over us. During a lull we dashed back to our shack, snatched up our kits & off again just in time before shelling re-opened.

Whilst Gillett's units at this time were essentially consolidating, Steuart's were very much on the attack. After heavy shelling on 16 October he reported further advances: 'Off again at 5 p.m. for a new attack. Halted at 'Dark Houses' just beyond Moorseele (which was captured this morning). Set off again at 2 a.m. – a terrible march in rain & mud & pitch darkness. All objectives gained'. Fr Steuart was well suited to this type of activity and it is unsurprising that he revelled in military affairs: even in a supporting role he managed to create the impression of the officer-in-action rather than the chaplain equivalent. When demobbed in November 1919 he provided ample confirmation: 'I feel terribly out of it and dull. It has been a good time, the like of which I shall never see again'!

His units had crossed the Lys by 18 October establishing three bridgeheads. Victory was in the air, despite sometimes desperate albeit increasingly erratic opposition. The next day they: 'Marched over the Lys to Marcke about 4:30 p.m. Inhabitants are wild with joy to see us'. Despite sporadic machine gun fire, sniping, and some shelling, the emphasis of his accounts now shifted from the military to civilian. At Zwevegem:

> We came across a party of young Belgians who were shouting and romping across the fields. We soon found out what the matter was. They had found a dead German in the field, & after dancing round him, and (I understand) spitting on him, they tied a rope to his feet and dragged him off to a hole in the ground into which they flung him & covered him over. Beastly but I suppose they had had a lot to suffer from his like during the last 4 years.

30 October he:

> Buried at Keselberg one KRR man who had been dressed and labelled 'Tommy' by a Boche doctor and seven Germans who had been smashed up in a house by one of our heavies and were in a frightful condition of corruption. Of one man we could only find the lower part of his body. Some Belgians cut their boots off.

The next day both military success and civilian reprisals were noted: 'Attack by 104 Brigade and 2 Corps. Northwards along the Scheldt. Very successful. 104 brigade took nearly 200 prisoners. One of these attacked by a Belgian civilian and rather badly mauled'. On 3 November he was called in the evening to an old woman from Avelgham who had been gassed. 'Gave her Absolution, Viaticum and Extreme Unction'. It was a timely intervention as the woman, Enox-la-de Puret, died at 7 a.m. the next morning. Belgian Catholics were among those still benefitting from chaplain's efforts.

Gillett was meanwhile occupied in the Péronne area in September. His suitably re-established unit pushed slowly eastwards towards Péronne town. A great irony in Gillett's wartime experience was that despite shell, bullet, bomb, fatigue, disappointment, and self-sacrifice: it was a natural phenomenon which scared him most:

> Tues 17th September. Last night biggest storm in history – thunder, lightning, rain and I dunno what – tents all blown down and everything washed away – golly I was terrified – however, towards 6 a.m. the day got fine and turned out trumps, everybody searching for stuff – and everything hung out drying. I shall never forget it.

This natural incident was soon substituted by military action: 'Wed 18th. 4:45 barrage – attacking on a large scale – visited main dressing station and ADS, returning to camp about 4 p.m. After tea strolled out towards Péronne through Aillanes and Mont St Quentin where Australians effected a great piece of work. Good news through hurragh'! For Fred Gillett who enjoyed physical exercise this period became a chance for some simple joy: 'Visited ADS, quiet. In afternoon went on to meet Guinevan at 53 CCS and came back through Aizecourt-le-Haut. It is great – one can tramp anywhere and everywhere, across country and see old positions etc. etc. which Boche and the Allies have alternately occupied'. 21 October and his Division went over the top, he readied himself at the ADS in anticipation. There were no casualties reported and he gave Mass to 5 battle surplus soldiers and noted that: 'as a matter of fact many more were moved up to transport lines'. He then busied himself with the Transport Lines at Aizecourt-le-Bas and Tincourt, and watched them relay the telephone line through Moislains, 'very interesting'. He continued to service as many auxiliary units as possible including Wagon Lines and Brigades temporarily at rest. However, all was not going to plan for the military and September ended with caution: '27th Troops pushed up line hurriedly – Yanks are trapped at Roisel, less than 2 miles east of Tincourt'. Two days on: 'Visited Nurlu but everybody on the move – everything in a state of upset – troops pushing up the line to take part in the present fighting, which apparently is not going too successfully – miscarrying here and there'.

Then the usual oscillations in the state of events when on Monday 30 September: 'Strolled into Manancourt. Bulgars have given in!!! Unconditional surrender, this is the beginning of the end'. This was the fourth 'beginning of the end' claim by Fr Gillett and demonstrates that even such a stable and sensible man could be caught up in the euphoria and confusion of war. Official communications using DRLS or telephone were on their own prone to disruption, and in the absence of reliable news, local gossip generated scaremongering and panic. Misinformation was a significant contributor to swings in opinion and morale throughout the forces.

It is fair to say that Fr Gillett on the Somme had a very different October to Fr Steuart at Ypres, despite the fact that in relative terms the worst of the military violence was over for both men. Initially Gillett, after much confusion marched to Rainneville. This was certainly no gallop over open ground. In fact his unit had progressed only 30 miles and this due west and away from the German retreat. The military explanation for this arrangement is not clear and Gillett does not comment on what seems an illogical move. Possibly fatigue was a factor, consolidation and 'mopping up' another. In any event Fr Gillett had: 'Settled down by the church and had Mass regularly – a lovely church with little side chapel to Our Lady of Lourdes', and declared: 'Glorious news going around – end in sight. Hope of having finished with the line'. This suggests that his brigade would not be in the vanguard advancing towards Germany. By 4 October his optimism continued: 'Rumours of Turkey throwing up [sic]'. He continued his spiritual rounds of Mass and Confessions for his 53 Brigade, albeit with moderate response from the soldiers. In spite of this he consistently received succour and inspiration from civilians with whom he empathised. He recorded their plight throughout his time in France.[17] On 7 October 1916: 'One notices the number of old folks left in the villages, the young ones have been called up. And what workers the old people are; they seem to be forever occupied and apparently live on nothing, never a square good meal such as we are accustomed to'.

Strengthening the sense of impending ceasefire it is noticeable that Masses of remembrance were now being said for both dead soldiers and French civilians. Monday 14 October: 'Holy Mass – then on to Molliens for 'la féte des mortes' – after Mass all proceed to cemetery and each stands by the family grave whilst De Profundis is sung'. Fr Gillett was not outstanding at St Joseph's College Ushaw in the French language, but clearly the tuition must have been of a high order as he comfortably and regularly gave sermons, interpreted, and liaised with French civilians, clergy, and British troops. His biggest accolade came on the day that the Peace Treaty was signed at Versailles the 28 June 1919, when he preached in French and English at Notre Dame de Victoires in Paris to a mixed military and civilian congregation comprising French, British, and American supplicants. The Latin Mass was a useful common denominator amongst Catholics worldwide, but sermons or homilies were delivered in the local tongue offering a new challenge. Fr Steuart also knew French and was fluent in the German language despite rarely recording its usefulness except in a social context in 1919 or with prisoners of war as reported on 1 August 1917 at Ypres.[18]

By mid-October Fred Gillett was moving again by small stages, this time in a north-easterly direction. At Le Catelet, between Cambrai and St Quentin, he was fascinated by: 'Boche Line – the famous "Hindenburg", is all around this neighbourhood. The line is most interesting – all sorts of concrete dug outs and emplacements – dead Germans lying about'. The next day he managed to combine many of his interests together: physical exercise, religious history, empathy for the suffering, not forgetting fun and the overarching desire to say Mass:

> Trek again – through the outskirts of Le Catelet, on through Gouyy, Beaurevoir (from where Jean D'Arc escaped from prison) Ponchaux on to Avelu – Boche plentiful all over the fields and by the roads – evidence of their recent disasters.

---

17   Belgian civilians, except in the towns, had largely been evacuated in the Ypres zone.
18   JAL, Steuart Diaries, 1 August 1917.

The Division all train out in a ploughed field, under canvas but a wee farm house for a mess – some good fun together, rum galore and bridge, no end of fun. Camped about 10 minutes from Elincourt so tomorrow hope for Mass, as one can see the church and one hopes, it is usable.

The Nord-Aisne boundary provided a human moment: 'Sun 20th. Mass at Elincourt, where I met Fr Godric Keane of Salford, an elderly genial old man. Attended his Mass at 10 a.m. and heard Confessions – an excellent crowd. Rosary in evening at 5:30 and very well attended'. The 'genial old man' was aged 52 only 16 years his senior!

His interest in church buildings and their usage or state of repair continued:

Visited Maretz and found there the church had been mined and guarded and blown up just prior to being evacuated. In afternoon went to Premont, all knocked about – church a complete wreck, but on one of the pillars there hangs the pulpit crucifix untouched and which people refuse to move. Strolled to Serain where church was used by Boche as a hospital and so is not destroyed – but has no benches and very much knocked about inside; still altars are serviceable.

Confusion was rife, on 23 October as his unit marched to Le Cateau he added: 'Got to our supposed destination about midnight to find ourselves in the fields – what a mix up'. It had been a strange day, earlier he: 'Had to bury a 7th Buffs boy, who had been killed by a bomb which his mule had kicked and so lessened the fun. What a sight above the main road, horses lying all over the place, showing how the cavalry had got up and had skirmished'. This had become a period of reflection and fascination amidst the routine provision of services, with the usual intermittent interruptions: 'The Boche were firing at the top end of the road in which we were finding billets. Great attacks going on these days'.

On 24 October Fr Gillett again seized the historical opportunities at hand. The Battle of Le Cateau in August 1914 had been a defensive one with the French and British performing a 'fighting withdrawal', in reality a brave defeat with the loss of some 8,000 men:

Looked around Le Cateau of 1914 fame! Churches all badly damaged and houses all knocked about. Dead found in cellars. Streets here and there ruined and blown up – on entrance to Le Cateau, no end of horses lying about and several of our dead had been dumped there for burial. Looked around for a place for Mass on Sunday and struck lucky – found the Salle de Fétes untouched, used by our own Artillery Concert Party – so got the use of it for Sunday – hurroo!! – difficulty solved. Refugees returning now from the German lines, as Germans are unable any longer to keep hold of them owing to the rapidity of our pursuit.

In late October Fr Gillett and his troops were close to the finishing line, but not quite. On Wednesday 30 October he reminded us of the remaining dangers, the result of the devastation so far, and through no fault of his own, some of the less than successful aspects of his spiritual mission: 'Holy Mass – heavy bombing and shelling all last night – Benediction at the private chapel, the faithful few winning graces for the many indifferent – Le Cateau – phew! What a sight, ruin and troops'. Announcing the next day that: 'Austria and Turkey give in surely it must be the end soon'? Success continued and on 4 November east of Cambrai: 'Great battle for Mormal Forest – attended Corps Dressing Station all day, in Le Cateau 1500 passed through of all sorts, between 8 a.m. – 11 p.m.'.

Deaths so close to the Armistice are acutely poignant. On 31 October Fr Montagu SJ from Derry, attached to the 22 Brigade Royal Garrison Artillery, died from serious thigh wounds incurred three days earlier from shelling whilst walking between his billet and the local village church. Son of a Royal Navy Lieutenant Commander, he had four other brothers serving at war, his youngest Lieutenant A C Montague was killed when HMS Bulwark was sunk. Fr Walter is buried at Awoingt Cemetery.

Cruel fate also awaited Fr John A Watters. He was in France only four months when he fell sick in the pandemic influenza outbreak of late 1918/19. Hospitalised at a CCS on 31 October he died a week later, aged 26. Described as a 'gifted and amiable brother' by the Bishop of Plymouth, little else is known about him other than being born in Mayo and attached to the 115 Infantry Brigade HQ. He is also buried near Fr Montagu at Awoingt south east of Cambrai, some 12 miles from Fr Gillett at Le Cateau.

On the same day as Fr Watters death, Fr Gillett's compassion was aroused by the plight of refugees:

> Refugees trooping back – in all sorts of conditions and with what little goods they could gather. And what a scene as they 'look' for their homes, left by them in good condition, but now destroyed by the recent fighting. How sad it all is – poor folks deprived, robbed indeed of home and belongings – what is going to become of them?

This was to be the last action in this zone. Next day he coyly announced: 'Rosary 5:30 p.m. Everybody on tip toe of excitement, peace whispers going around – yah at last'! The day before the Armistice, Sunday 10 November 1918, a sense of fait accompli existed: 'Mass in 'Spare Parts' theatre – crowded out – at 3 p.m. and 6 p.m. Rosary – Poincaré to visit Le Cateau – hung about to see him but didn't turn up – car broke down'. When the great day arrived it is worth quoting Fr Gillett verbatim:

> Mon 11th November 1918. Holy Mass – at 11 a.m. precisely CEASE FIRE ordered – ARMISTICE concluded, cessation of hostilities. Thank God. At 8:30 p.m. Rosary in our chapel, today Vicaire of Cateau takes over. End of bloodshed and strife. Lights up now as long as we like – only drawback is we are in a desolate hole and can get nothing for a celebration – rotten and everybody going mad with delight.
>
> RUM ISSUE!!

Fr Walter Montagu SJ.

Headstone at Awoingt. Age 32. 22 Brigade RFA. KIA 30 October 1918.

Awoingt British Military Cemetery Frs. Watters and Montagu.

For Fr Steuart the last few days of the war revealed that his fighting unit 12 HLI was nearly exhausted. They had marched east of Courtrai towards Brussels. On Saturday 9 November:

> Marched off at midday. Arrived at billets near Tieghem. Here we heard that the 41st Division & the French have already crossed the Sheldt, that the Boche is in full retreat and that Genl. Foch has given them till midday on Monday to accept the terms of the armistice. Also (but unconfirmed) that the Kaiser and Kronprinz had abdicated and the revolution was spreading in Germany.

The next day they continued: 'Marched off about 9 a.m. and crossed the Scheldt on footbridges. Marched to billets in Sulsique. The roads have been mined in many places but the RE have located the unblown ones and made them harmless. Very cold night, slept on the tiled floor'. Steuart's account of the ceasefire is produced verbatim so that both men's accounts can be compared:

> Mon 11th November. Marched off at 9 a.m. and billeted at Leynstraat at about 1:30 p.m. Crowds cheering us all along the road. News of conclusion of Armistice reached us on the march. It's almost impossible to realize that the war is over. I hope I shan't have to return to civil life too soon. I also can't help feeling disappointed that I haven't been able to get a decoration – mostly real hard luck, I really believe. Kaiser and Kronprinz have bolted to Holland. All Germany is in revolution, very much on the Bolshevik model. Expect we shall hear some miscellaneous scrapping to do yet when we get into Germany. Am sleeping in Mess with CO and Jonas'.

This concluded both chaplains war in combat. The subsequent release allowed both men to express their inner feelings. For Gillett it was a time of celebration, observation, and frequent services and Sacraments. For Steuart it was a time of frustration and a genuine sense of grievance that he had not been formally recognised with military honours for his efforts. The Armistice to the end of the year appeared to be an interlude of suspended animation. Each man will be observed in turn.

Fr Gillett:

> Tues 12th November. Mass of thanksgiving at Pommereuil for 55th Brigade. Rosary in Le Cateau at 5:30 p.m. Take a last look at German cemetery at Le Cateau, laid out in 1914 and in which many of the 1914 heroes were buried – a huge cemetery which has been well cared for – half reserved for the Boche and the other half for the Allies. English and French names very conspicuous.

Next day he celebrated: 'Mass at 6 a.m. Moved to Serain – everybody in high spirits – War and its horrors over and no longer any fear. Flags sported in every direction – French and British colours seen everywhere'. At Serain the local Curé had returned from war and responsibility for the civilians returned to him, but not before Fr Gillett had: '[got] things a bit in order – church clean and serviceable – though no benches'. He continued to say Mass and Confessions regularly although it is not clear whether they were for soldiers, civilians, or a mix. In all probability it was the latter with an emphasis on soldiers. A week later he reported that Mass attendance was excellent, yet for the Rosary it was only poor: 'everybody lying down'. The reasons emerged the next day when the troops' latest chores were explained: 'Troops occupied now collecting ammunition and generally clearing up the battlefield', or more probably: 'football which is played morning, noon and night nowadays'.

Men had enjoyed participating in football, boxing, athletics and other sports before the war. Fr Gillett has shown these activities were actively promoted and became more organised throughout the war, although the true purpose behind these apparently mundane pastimes may have escaped him. The arrangement of two unlikely bedfellows, camaraderie and aggression, received official sanction from the allied authorities:

> Popular manly games … were approved forms of military training … they trained the mind as well as the body and as team sports they encouraged discipline and reliance, facilitated the development of physical strength and stamina, and also possesses a strategic element which required mental skill to quickly adapt to a changing environment … not only for the playing field but also the battlefield.[19]

Gillett's testimony confirmed these trends and behaviours and soon he will describe the social scene he observed in liberated Paris.

Things continued in a light vein but he was already planning spiritual services for the soldiers. On 24 November he advertised a Lourdes trip for February, which will be discussed, concluding that it was a: 'Glorious trip we had and how it will live long in the memories of all of us'. 'Idling about' was a regular feature followed by the Divisional Review which he described as: 'a very fine – slow march past, a great show'. On 4 December: 'King visits the area – and walks amongst us – great excitement. In afternoon great footer match Beds 4 v Royal Engineers 2'. Civilians were again the centre of his account: 'Mass at Serain – moved to Caullery in teeming rain – plenty of houses left – but church blown up – villagers all put in cellar just previous to evacuation and left there until released by the English – whilst in cellar, church is blown to atoms – luckily house not affected only windows'. Interesting stories began to emerge after the German defeat: 'Selvigny, here Curé watched the wiring of his Church and cut the fuse wire at night – in the Chateau too one of our fliers who had lost his bearings was sheltered for three years'. On 14 November: 'Visited Esnes, where Joan of

---

19 Thierry Terret and J A Mangan, *Sport, Militarism and the Great War: Martial Manliness and Armageddon* (London Routledge 2017), p. 20.

Arc was imprisoned, then Harcourt and Ligny.[20] Church destroyed at Esnes. Lovely church at Ligny, but certain amount of stuff taken from it and tabernacle door broken'.

Desecration and looting were not uncommon throughout the war angering chaplains. Fr Rockliff reported gratuitous damage to a convent:

> A large convent of the Sisters of Charity through which I wandered, every door in every room had been pulled out and the contents up-turned on the floor. It is the same in the sacristy, a perfect litter of vestments and altar linen covering the floor. An ornamental hood at the back torn off and missing. There are empty chalice cases … the outer brass doors of the tabernacle had been wrenched and twisted off its hinges … men played the harmonium and roaming around with absolute freedom.[21]

Another remarked: '… the locks were all smashed off, the chalices stolen, the vestments all trampled on'.[22] As early as 1 October 1915 Fr Drinkwater commented: 'Walked to Noyelles and made enquiries about the church there but the Curé lives in Annequin now. They say the church has been looted twice now by the troops'.[23]

Malicious damage, theft, and callous irreverence were made more upsetting because these attacks were by British troops. The quantity of defacement that chaplains observed and recorded does not support allegations of endemic anti-Catholicism in the British Army, yet remained upsetting and embarrassing for chaplains. Who were the culprits and why? Was sectarianism, so prevalent at home reappearing at war, or were there other motivations for such defacement towards Catholic religious articles such as: general mischief, iconoclasm, theft masquerading as the spoils of war, fatigue, or some local and unknown provocation? The truth has been lost in time but the reality was that for some, their stances towards religion revealed at worse abhorrence and loathing, or at best apathy and ignorance. Attempts to rationalise these acts of vandalism must recognise the hideous and brutal experiences these men had lived through. Constructing a worldview of their own in which they had been turned into and now operated as killers, cannot be ignored. The process was dehumanising in a war of intensely cruelty and violence.[24]

---

20 Ligny-en-Cambrésis.
21 DAA, Rockliff to Rawlinson, 25 September, (no year given but probably 1916). This is an abridged but not isolated version.
22 DAA, 3238, anonymous chaplain to Keatinge, 7 April 1915.
23 BAA, Drinkwater Diaries, 1 October 1915.
24 The war has been sanitized. The Albert First World War Museum, at the northern side of the Albert Basilica, reveals the hand-made weapons that each side made for trench raids. They were constructed to cause massive damage and were widely employed by both sides before grenades became in regular supply. The juxtaposition of Christian morality and barbarism is a contentious one.

Time was hanging heavy for Fr Gillett, but he revived with Christ's birthday approaching. On Christmas Eve: 'Confession in Walincourt. Midnight Mass in Walincourt and though rotten wet, cold night, not at all a bad turn up. Communions good and people come from neighbouring billets'. Then on Christmas Day 1918:

> 2nd and 3rd Mass at Ligny where I now act as Curé for the inhabitants who have returned in good numbers. High Mass. Some excellent congregational singing – the common of the Mass. Gloria, Credo, Sanctus, Agnus Dei, sung by all and very good. Spoke a few words in French which quite suited them. Rosary and Benediction at 3 p.m. At 7:30 mess dinner and most sober I've ever seen in France – officers idea of Christmas is a binge!

There were more idle days and 'beastly weather' until Fr Gillett saw the end of a momentous year with beautiful singing by Curé de Messe at the services and: 'Dinner at 7:30 in Ligny with ADC HQ – glorious time – saw New Year in then to bed in Curés house'.

From mid-November Fr Steuart was temporarily housed in 'wretched billets' in Ingoyghem, east of Courtrai now known as Kortrijk. Soon he marched out to Harelbeke north east of Courtrai where his spirits rose, albeit with caveats: 'Good mess. I have a bedroom in the house of a Doctor Predhorn: good room but the windows all smashed'. He was now able to settle down to more regular priestly duties particularly 9, 12 and 18 HLI's, Royal Scots and 104 Brigade RFA, and enjoy a celebration. On 15 November: 'Had our Armistice Dinner at the Royal Scots Mess. Very successful. Thirty present and most of them very happy by the end of the evening'.

Steuart's time was for the present taken up with dinners, routine work, and concern over not receiving official military recognition. For many of the clergy the award system was either modestly received, or for some was mildly amusing and of little real interest.[25] Steuart was, on the other hand, a man who put great store in the reward system completely consistent with his ethics. Grounded in military tradition as a Stonyhurst Officer Cadet, not to mention his familial status from his Jacobean roots, his concerns were plausible. In social terms recognition was also coveted, on 7 August 1919 he visited friends in Farnborough and simply noted that: 'Nita and Dan to dinner. He showed me his VC'. Whatever the underlying reasons for his disappointment he felt unjustly treated and recorded this repeatedly in his diary *ad nauseam*.

On 25 November he took time to visit fellow Society of Jesus brethren in Courtrai, but was pre-occupied over a failed recommendation: 'Fr Dolan [SCF] told me that he had recommended both me and Sheridan for the MC. He was asked why he

---

25 Medals were rarely mentioned by chaplains in all the available records. Fr Steuart was an extreme case whose antithesis was Fr Fitzgibbon who seemed to be humbled and embarrassed at gaining his MC. The *Kilkenny People* of 3 March 1918 wrongly accredited Fr Fitzgibbons as receiving the VC instead of the MC: a hasty note to Fr Nolan his Provincial corrected this and his tone suggested deep shyness even about the MC.

recommended me, & he said he didn't know of any specific act of gallantry but that I had been more in the trenches & in action than any other chaplain he knew. Sheridan has got his, but mine has fallen through'. On 28 November he was on the march again to Ypres town. Despite the relative comfort of his new billets the nagging issue of recognition resurfaced:

> A miserable rainy day. Billeted in the Ramparts: very strong and warm. Found out that I have been recommended for some decoration (I don't know what) by the Battalion. The Adjutant, this morning in the Mess, asked me my full name & the dates of my absence on sick leave, & on the form on which he took down these particulars. I just caught a glimpse of the words 'For Gallantry or …' – we shall see!

Steuart's disappointment at lack of recognition came to prominence after the Armistice. This was a time when thoughts went to rewarding those whose contribution may have been in support roles rather than for gallantry. With time on his hands the sense of injustice gnawed at him, on 15 December he continued: 'Ceremonial parade by the Divisional General for presentation of medals. One man (a Royal Scot) got the Croix de Guerre "for good work in the Orderly Room!!!!" Then on Saturday 25 January: 'It seems that Dolan [SCF] has got both the Military Cross and the Croix de Guerre. Apparently I am a wash out!' On 26 February 1919: 'Houston tells me that his recommendation of me for an MC has been reduced by a Brigade to a mention! I have certainly had pretty rough luck throughout'.[26] He was finally rewarded on 23 August 1919: 'I find I have been mentioned in dispatches. I am afraid I don't feel excited about it. I am excited to this extent that I am annoyingly reminded by this that I have had four recommendations, each by some ridiculous & unforeseen accident has failed'.

Was his search for recognition vanity and somewhat irrelevant for a man on a more important mission, that is, to save souls? This would be an understandable but harsh assessment. There is no doubt he was a fine priest even if he did veer towards the officer first and chaplain second. In his diary he pasted the newspaper cutting announcing his MID from '*The Times*' of 5 July 1919, suggesting that despite an element of rebuff in being given a minor honour, he still inwardly cherished it. The distribution of war medals can be arbitrary and despite the accuracy and worthiness of many cases, some receive medals they barely deserve, whilst others perform acts of extreme bravery without any recognition. Fr Steuart's actions of the 20 May 1918 could well have fallen into this latter category. His gripes make unpleasant reading but he was a human being with a sense of grievance.

The mechanism for awarding honours or not, was in any case devalued after being reduced to an allotment basis. On 22 February 1919, Fr Fitzmaurice SJ was recommended for an MC by Lieutenant-Colonel J D Scott Commanding 2 Battalion

---

26 Ibid., 26 February 1919.

Royal Irish Regiment for: 'Continual gallantry and devotion to duty at all times, and especially in every action in which the Battalion has taken part, from and including the 2nd Battle of Ypres 1915'. The Public Record Office contains the correspondence and the reply on 3 March: 'It is regretted that it is impossible to include the attached recommendation, unless as one of the 49th brigade allotment. The number of Officer Honours put at the disposal of the Division was exceedingly small and may not be exceeded'. This raises serious questions about the efficacy of the honours system and may explain Steuart's dilemma. Although many Catholic chaplains did receive honours including several Military Crosses, none received the Victoria Cross. The biographer of the renowned Irish Jesuit chaplain Fr Willie Doyle claims that Doyle was recommended for the VC at Frenzenberg but: '... the triple disqualification of being an Irishman, a Catholic, and a Jesuit, proved insuperable'.[27]

Rawlinson was later to recognise the frailties of the military rewards system and on 29 February 1919 wrote to all chaplains still serving:

> There are some who have been through three, or even four years in the front line, whose splendid work has never been recognised by any Military Honour. Although I am aware that there were none who sought honours less, still I regret that they have never received this special recognition of the excellence of their work and their hazardous duties.

Steuart was not alone, another non-rewarded Jesuit CF Fr Bernard Page from Preston, did not seek honours but merely asked that when demobbed could he return with his army unit 1 Battalion Loyal North Lancashire's. On 5 March 1919 Rawlinson replied: 'I understand your desire and will do my very best for you ... you certainly deserve anything you can get after your long service without ribbons or honours. I only wish it where otherwise but it's outside my hands'.

Fr Steuart remained irritable throughout late 1918. Marching to a camp of Nissen huts at Millam, 10 miles north of St Omer he objected to damp bed linen and : 'The woman of the house at our Battalion HQ is a terrible nuisance, and full of grievances & shrill recriminations'. Was Fr Steuart, as he would later claim, really missing the action now that the fighting had stopped? Things improved at Millam where he busied himself by journeying to St Omer and Calais for Mess provisions. This seemed to please him but on 7 December his annoyance resumed: 'Bryson brought back from leave. He & Ptes. Hannah & Queen get the Croix de Guerre' and again two days later: 'Schochet [American doctor] told me that he had put me in for an MC for Sept 28th show but that the CO had said he would not send it in till later. I wonder if I am in for two things'.

Fr Robert Steuart led a routine existence throughout December. On Christmas day he reported: 'Midnight Mass pretty well attended. Mass again at 9 a.m. & at

---

27 O'Rahilly, *Father William Doyle SJ*, p. 330.

11:30 at 311 PoW Camp. Heard nearly 80 prisoners Confessions'. Amidst 'fearful weather', the year ended with a: 'Battalion dinner. Most successful. A tremendous lot of drink going about. The guardroom overflowing. Battalion Mess opened'. He failed to mention that he was the Mess victualler!

Epilogue – Mid-Summer to Autumn 1918

This momentous year witnessed a near military defeat for the Allies on the Western Front in spring and early summer. By mid-summer to early-winter the complete opposite was the case. Germany collapsed under the weight of continual military reverses underwritten by the gravity of economic, social, psychological, and political pressures. The Armistice was a public declaration that the Allies were the new masters of the seesaw.

The increasingly mobile and open nature of war had created a steep rise in casualties. Catholic chaplains responded to the turmoil the best they could. Both Gillett and Steuart were good examples of their efforts, criss-crossing each other to accompany their soldiers. Chronicling the frantic activity of 1918, interspersed with periods of routine, these two determined men typified Catholic chaplains in general. Their spiritual efforts were continual but have been minimised to allow pastoral and secular day-to-day activities to be explored.[28]

The war had cost all combatants fortunes in men and matériel but now that the Armistice was signed, and the guns had cooled down, what was to happen to the remaining troops on both sides? And what would become of civilians? Would a peace be signed or would the terms meted out by France in particular, create a German backlash, perhaps one with a military dimension? Were the domestic political situations especially those on the losing side, stable? What of the Bolshevik threat? How long would troops remain in khaki and what tasks would they perform? What would chaplains do now that the French Curés were back from fighting?

In 1919 Gillett would remain in France and Steuart later entrain to Cologne in occupied Germany permitting their personalities to blossom in peace. Both men will contribute their experiences and in doing so throw light on the real day-to-day situations in France and Germany. Continuing to support the needs of Catholics at large they also had opportunity to slacken off their clerical collars and engage in social commentary and social action.

28 Bellis, 'Catholic Chaplains', Chapters 3 and 4.

9

1919: 'Sic Transit Gloria Khaki!' – 'Ave Atque Vale!'

Frs. Gillett and Steuart responded to the end of their war as Catholic clergy might do – in Latin! But what did they experience in 1919 before demobilisation? With the war seemingly won if not yet formally concluded, what were their roles and anxieties? Did the background of social, political, and military unrest both at home and in the occupied territories permeate their remaining months in khaki? How would they express their feelings as survivors in a new world? Despite developing quite a taste for France, its people, and the Americans, Fr Gillett was rather glad to leave the ranks of the uniformed, 'Sic Transit Gloria Khaki' is his manipulation of the Latin 'Sic Transit Gloria Mundi' in other words: 'Thus passes the glory of the Army'. Fr Steuart's farewell 'Ave Atque Vale' or simply 'Hail, Hearty, and Farewell' disguises the fact that he did not wish to return to civilian life. Both did return to former times, but examining their 1919 experiences in France and Germany respectively, adds an extra layer to our knowledge of chaplains revealing part of the prevailing zeitgeist in these countries and whilst revealing much of the character distinctions between the two men. This period beyond November 1918 has been hitherto neglected by chaplaincy historians.

Society was changing before the war and did so irrevocably during it. The war had thrown the classes together and challenged pre-existing societal perceptions: a social revolution may have been out of the question but long overdue reform was urgently needed. On the tails of victory, more enlightened political and religious leaders were conscious of the need for a more equitable society. Furthermore, they would be goaded into change by a population who were becoming aware not only of the gross injustices with the present and preceding régimes, but also of their own capabilities. A modernising reconstruction programme embracing the new realities was required. Improvements slowly emerged that were fairer, if not pluralist or radical enough for many.

The Catholic Church was in the forefront of linking social and political reform with religious revival. Archbishop Whiteside of Liverpool talked of reconstruction in 1916 and by 1919 he developed these ideas further. He wrote: 'Reconstruction is bound to come; reconstruction in the relations of nation to nation; reconstruction in the relations of man to man; and particularly in the relations of capital and labour; and reconstruction even in religion'.[1] This neatly combined Pope Leo X111's encyclical Novum Reverum of 1891, in essence a treatise on labour-capital relationships and the keystone of Catholic social teaching, with the sentiments of American President Woodrow Wilson's plans for a League of Nations. The Catholic strategy, not to mention the loyal impulses of its congregations, was one of cooperation with the lawfully elected government and secular fealty to the King, retaining the Pope's jurisdiction on spiritual matters. In doing so a degree of self-development in line with its own social and religious policies without interference was the expectation. Generally the outcome was in line with these objectives as Catholicism grew apace until the 1960s. These advancements were for the future – but what of the immediate post-armistice era?

What country would the victorious troops return to? Unemployment, strikes, lock-outs, challenges to their traditional roles not to say livelihoods through the rise in women's suffrage and particularly the role of women now that the men were returning, rise of organised labour, the growth of state interventionism, and the impending threat of civil war in Ireland, notwithstanding the economic and psychological consequences of the war awaited their return. Hardly the spoils of victory and returnees, many of whom were physically or mentally disabled, might be forgiven if they ruminated if indeed Britain was the victorious nation. Social and economic reform, particularly decent housing was urgently needed. Alas, the promise of homes 'fit for heroes' remained a pipedream, even if the Addison Act later in 1919 created future growth in the housing market through local council participation.

In the international sphere leaders also presided over an uncertain future as Britain surveyed the new world landscape. Military and political minds dreaded the possibility, no matter how unlikely, that the Bolshevik revolution might impact on Britain and ushered troops to Russia to support the 'Whites'. In reality this was nothing more than a half-hearted adventure and was soon curtailed, but it demonstrated the establishment's anxiety at the time. Fr Steuart was well placed to observe the validity of these fears in Germany in 1919. Could the revolution gaining a foothold in Germany spread throughout Europe, thereby threatening not only British domestic but also Imperial interests? Would the German institutions reject peace terms, and if so would there be a military reaction? And what of French reconstruction which at its core contained an understandably strong desire for Germany to pay harsh reparations, could this destabilise Europe in general?

---

1   LAA. His work is detailed in the 1919 *Ecclesiastical Education Fund Pastoral* and is a remarkable document which senses and distils Rerum Novarum within the desire for a 'Britain fit for heroes'. The tone is distinctly favourable to improved conditions and a 'living wage' but is also balanced by the rights of capital, 'a fair day's work for a fair day's pay'. This exactly replicates the underpinnings of the Pope's document and it is possible to see the moderating effects which influenced Catholic participation in trade unions in future years. This Catholic interpretation was encouraged by Archbishop Whiteside.

All of these domestic and strategic scenarios were conducted against the background of demobilising an army of efficient armed killers; some of whom were soon to be involved in bloodshed in a part of Britain which had fought side by side with these same men. Ireland would suffer making Redmond's assessment of British fair play naïve, incompetent, or worse. Not only the Irish but Arabs and Indians would also soon find out that 'fair play' was at the behest of singular English expediency; now that the war was over, independence from Britain would have to be fought for tooth and nail, ensuring that the seeds of injustice and betrayal were sown deep within the Empire's hitherto, loyal subjects.

In the aftermath of the cessation of hostilities, the British at home experienced a heady mix of insecurity and triumphalism which developed into a mood of solemn reflection. Public and conspicuous Remembrance Services and prayers for fallen comrades, complemented private commemoration and grief borne out by friends, neighbours and relatives. Not only conventional religion was sought to try and find peace and some form of comprehension, there was also a sharp rise in spiritualism which appealed to those disenfranchised from orthodox religions or whose moral certainties were no longer satisfied. Despite this generally uncertain aura, Catholicism in Britain enjoyed a period of continuing expansion and revival until the mid to late century. Both our diarists experienced this period of steady progress when they returned home, Fr Gillett taking advantage of new opportunities in the newly formed Diocese of Lancaster in 1924, whilst Fr Steuart was appointed Superior of the Society of Jesus at Mount Street in 1926.

The British Army in France commenced a phased withdrawal. It was a gargantuan logistical feat, and planned in part to allow those demobilised to be assimilated at home. In the meantime, and despite unfairness in the process, those remaining were tasked to help clear the battlefields of human, animal, and material waste. Horses were sold off or shot, cemeteries constructed, the dead interred or re-interred and identified as far as possible, and old comrades remembered. It is conveniently forgotten that this vast undertaking would not have been possible without Chinese contracted labour, skilled and unskilled, numbering 140,000 in total. By April 1919 the British still employed 80,000 Chinese, the French 35,000, reducing to 50,000 and 25,000 respectively by the summer. 200,000 German PoW's too had a contribution to make.[2]

In Germany the newly formed Army of the Rhine's tasks were to ensure compliance with the Armistice demands and later those of the Peace Treaty, and to provide some order to the civilian population if required. Although the once mighty German Army was still a potential threat, serious German military resurgence was thought unlikely.[3] Guerrilla warfare, however, remained a concern on the ground as Fr Steuart will

---

2   Olusoga, *The World's War*, p. 403.
3   In 1920, German forces entered the Ruhr to confront left-wing strikers. Legitimate or otherwise, the French Army responded, thrusting deeper into Germany which acted as a forceful if temporary deterrent.

demonstrate. Until May, both men were in France where Gillett was to remain and they continued to practise their priestly duties to men and women of all nationalities, combatants and non-combatants.

It is not clear when Fr Fred Gillett fell in love with Paris but by 1919 he was well-smitten. He continued to visit with increasing regularity, frequently with American Army Catholics, and his unrestrained joy allows an insight into the French celebrations in the capital city. His devotion to the Virgin Mary shone through his whole war-time experience, and now revelling in liberation euphoria he wanted to share his devotion with as many troops as possible, culminating in a pilgrimage to Lourdes for British troops. Gillett's natural ebullience found expression but always within a deep and genuine love of his Faith and vocation. Fr Steuart transferred to Germany in May. He observed a range of political and military situations and offered his own analyses. He seemed at home with the military circumstances that befell him, even if he became somewhat disoriented by a difficult moral dilemma with a fellow Catholic officer. His interests in 'high culture' meant frequent visits to the opera where his knowledge of languages proved a personal benefit, granting he was not averse to 'low culture' with cinema, boxing, and horse racing being common indulgences. Fr Steuart was innately more circumspect than his fellow diarist and took his military ambitions seriously, perhaps disproportionately so. Not a man of the people, even so he fulfilled his religious duties diligently. Both men's conduct were shaped and driven by the margins of their upbringing and social class, and were further underpinned in Fr Steuart's life by strong military associations, and in Fr Gilletts by the plight of the poor.

Fr Gillett in France

Until 24 May he was based near Ligny, south East of Cambrai until assuming responsibilities for a prisoner of war camp in Méaulte just south of Albert. In Ligny his life was a daily routine of celebrating Mass and the Sacraments throughout the neighbouring villages of Caullery, Clery, Villers-Outreaux, Esnes, and Selvigny. Fr Gillett was a sociable man absorbed by people's day-to-day lives, particularly the local clergy and their encounters under occupation. On Friday 10 January: 'Mass. Had long chat with Curé of Selvigny in course of the morning – Curé of Walincourt was put in gaol for not saluting a Boche. Not at all infrequent for Boche to shoot down the streets to intimidate'. At Selvigny on Sunday 19 January his continuing disillusionment concerning army cooperation in facilitating Mass attendance resurfaced: 'Mass in Selvigny to 54 Brigade – but no one turns up – only 12 fellows – notice not properly announced'. By now he had learned to deal with this type of frustration preferring a more meaningful use of his energies as this example of remembrance, joy, and certainly relief demonstrates: 'The church is full of colour, French and British flags all over it – in cemetery of the church some of our 1914 men are buried and a little monument to them'. Remembrance and joy will resonate in the weeks to come permeating his last few months on the continent.

On 15 January the Curé at Ligny returned. Fred remarked: 'Alors fini maintenant a Ligny' but he was not 'fini' in the surrounding area. Nevertheless, he did have more time to explore and enjoy the company of fellow chaplains, in particular an old friend Fr Bernard McMahon [sic] a Dubliner with 17 Manchester's.[4] On 24 January he rode his 'byke' [sic] and had a 'glorious spin' and the next day: 'Watched Beds 1 v RFA 0 – Mingay – a Blackpool goalie, kept goal for RFA'.[5] The next day he visited Lesdain and: 'Caught them at Vespers there but what a sight – an unfurnished and much knocked about Church – 12 people and as cold as the proverbial hell! [sic] How the Curé lives I dunno'! On 2 February in his usual unassuming way he recorded that he had: 'Got horseflesh for dinner today – not an uncommon diet during period of occupation, the folks tell me'.

Fr Gillett's proudest accomplishment was taking troops to Lourdes. It is worth retelling almost in its entirety, witnessing the geographical, practical, and religious detail which neatly crystallizes Fr Gillett's personality and beliefs:

Lourdes Trip

> **Sat 8 February 1919.** No Mass – on the road to station at 4:30 a.m. – very treacherous, slippery – beastly cold. Hung about long enough for train to come in (Caudry) – at 6:30 on the way – but so cold we all froze in the carriage. Through Cambrai of the 1917 battle grounds to Amiens where we arrive late – got away from Amiens 4:30 p.m. but late again in arriving at Paris and so missed our 8:30 train and had to put up in Paris – in station subway specially arranged for our British soldiers under the YMCA. Had all my kit pinched here.
>
> **Sun 9.** All up by 9 a.m. and then off in a bundle to Sacré Coeur where I said Mass for them and showed them around the Great Basilica. Then walked them around the Champs Elysees to the Madeleine, then in for lunch and after lunch did the churches with them – Notre Dame Cathedral, Sainte Chapelle, the Court Chapel now disused, Hotel de Ville, St Germain, where a bomb or rather a shell from 'Long Tom' fell on the Good Friday of 1918. At Notre Dame de Victoire and then tea and gathered our belongings for the train.

---

4 Gillett spells his name incorrectly as McMahon, should be MacMahon. This is a regular occurrence in chaplaincy records and indicative of the confusion within 'official statistics'. Fr F McMahon with 142 Field Ambulance did exist.

5 Harry Mingay made over 150 appearances for Blackpool, some few miles from Lytham, Gillett's home.

Mon 10. Entrained at Quai d'Orsay Station 8:20 last night and travelled at night through Orleans, Poitiers, Angouléme, Bourdeaux and Pau. Here we changed and in an hour's time steamed into Lourdes. What a glorious entry – just as we got into Lourdes the Grotto comes into view, apparently at the foot of the Pyrenees. A gradely tea at 5 o'clock – a hurried run to the Grotto – dinner at 7 p.m. then Rosary etc. at the Grotto. Matins and Lauds going on in Basilica. At 11 p.m. to bed and not before our time.

Tues 11. Mass at Grotto by Special Privilege, by one of the chaplains. I said Mass in Crypt at Sacred Heart Altar. Attend High Mass at 10 a.m. in Rosary Chapel. What a crowd of people, British soldiers given a place of honour, 1 Archbishop and 5 Bishops all present. After Mass Procession at Grotto. At 2 p.m. Vespers and Sermon – then to Grotto to undrape the banners of Alsace and Lorraine. In evening Rosary at the Grotto and Flambaux Procession ending up in the Rosary Chapel with ringing of the Credo.

Wed 12. Mass in Basilica at High Altar, after Mass went to see the Panarama of Lourdes – gorgeous. Then made the Stations. In afternoon went up to the Pic du Jes. In evening Benediction at the orphanage. Then dinner and final visit to Grotto where Rosary is said for benefactors and a hymn sung, then we all turn in for the night.

Thurs 13. Mass in Fr Nevins Chapel.[6] Visited Bernadette's House where she lived after the apparitions began. In evening Benediction at Poor Clare's' Convent. Dinner – Rosary at Grotto then bed.

Fri 14. Mass – visited shop and bought up souvenirs – visited Bernadette's brother who lies dying. In afternoon Stations. Then turned in, flu coming on, but the party goes to some Convent for Benediction to return for dinner and then Rosary at the Grotto.

Sat 15. Mass said at the Grotto – morning free for everybody; most of them buying up everything. In evening Benediction at Carmelite Convent.

Sun 16. Mass in Fr Nevin's Chapel. At 10:30 entraining for home again – called in at Bernadette's Convent, where she went after apparitions were known and prepared for First Holy Communion. A stay of 4 hours at Pau, where we had a look round and at 5 p.m. we're on our way to Paris.

---

6   Fr J J Nevin SJ IRL who took over Lourdes Soldiers Mission after losing a limb at the Front.

Mon 17. Got to Paris about 9 a.m. – and got breakfast at American YMCA then saw our lads fixed up – arranged meeting time for tomorrow at 8:15. Went off to meet Fr McMahon at the hotel Windsor – where we spent the night.

Tues 18. Left Paris at 8:15 through Chantilly – Creil – Compeigne – over the old battlefields of 1918, Noyon -Chauny – Tergnier – Jussy – St Quentin – Busigny and finally Caudry where we detrained to get to our several billets. What a glorious trip we had and how it will live long in the memories of all of us.

Wed 19. Mass at Caullery – then knocked around to tell my friends of our glorious trip.

Fr Gillett was matter of fact when the next day he simply noted that his friend: 'McMahon demobbed'.

The following days were spent 'trudging' or 'toddling around' but still recording the plight of others: 'Noticed French working on the fields with spades – no ploughs left them'. The highlight of March 1919 was: 'The Annunciation. Mass. Procession in honour of Our Lady, Cambrai town all decorated'. The heavy snows of March had ended when he took leave 19 April to 20 May which he spent between London and Liverpool, as usual he did not complete his diary on furlough. The 20 May was a significant day as his identical twin brother Harry sailed for France as Chaplain to the Forces. Both brothers had schooled, trained, been ordained, and worked together and now it was Harry's turn to do his bit for King and country. Fred's feelings were of brotherly love as they both entrained to Amiens were Fred saw Harry off, granting that Harry's late entry into the war would have not gone without witty comment!

Four days after his brother arrived, Fred visited Harry at his CCS in Bouzincourt which he described as: 'a most desolate spot'. It was hard to imagine on a glorious July day in 2013.

Harry was described by his brother as a 'lucky

Fr Gillett at Marian Shrine Lourdes 1926. (Lancaster Diocese Lourdes Records in Talbot Library Preston)

Bouzincourt Memorial, 8 July 2013.

dog' when demobilised on 9 June, leaving 10 days later. He was in France for little more than a month which does not make a deal of sense but did allow the continuation of parallel experiences, of sorts, to be maintained. This continued in peacetime as both celebrants returned to Liverpool parishes before joining the newly formed Lancaster Diocese in 1924. Harry's Lancaster Diocesan Obituary claimed that: 'He would, with twinkling eyes, count the ending of the war as a speedy response to his own landing in France'. But was Fred the man who should have been demobilised rather than Harry? The same obituary claimed that: 'He was demobilised so quickly because of a mix up in Army circles with his brother Fr Fred. They had served near each other and had many stories about the resultant confusion'. This account seems plausible as they were working within a few miles of each other and by all accounts their likeness made them indistinguishable. Fr Fred's recorded knowledge of the Army's organisational capabilities had been, with justification, less than complimentary.

Whatever the reason it allowed Fr Fred to enjoy his free time in France, but first the PoW camps at Méaulte became Fr Fred Gillett's responsibility allowing him to hone his minimal German linguistic skills. He celebrated Mass on 9 June which the: 'Boche attend voluntarily – a good crowd. Crowds of visitors to Allies v Boche footer game in evening and after them the escorts have a match'.

Despite the relaxed relationships with the German PoW's, scars on the local community were all too obvious and painful. Gillett noted previously the devastation to civilian property and now turned to the numerous battered churches in this area. On 13 June he said Mass and then: 'visited Curé at Ville – has a wee little corner of a wee hut for a wee chapel – on Sunday says Mass in a portion of the old presbytery of which only 4 walls stand. What a sight; just a few people round the altar erected amongst the debris and dirt'. Fr Gillett's simple and genuine empathy for buildings and people in France was no doubt a continuation of his sentiments acquired in the bleak poverty of the Liverpool slums. Sunday 22 June: 'Mass at Morlancourt and Meaulte, attended Blessed Sacrament Procession at Ville – what a sad night – but how wonderful the courage and heart of the people in a village where not a house stood complete'.

Many chaplains noted the destruction and Fr Walker painted it.

Neuve Chapelle Jan 1916. (JAD, Paintings of Fr Leslie Walker)

Neuve Chapelle, 20 July 2013.

Richebourg St Vaast, 10 January 1916. (JAD, Paintings of Fr Leslie Walker)

Richebourg St Vaast, 19 July 2013.

1919: 'Sic Transit Gloria Khaki!' – 'Ave Atque Vale!'   213

Vielle Chapelle, December 1915. (JAD, Paintings of Fr Leslie Walker)

Catholic chaplains openly and frequently displayed concern and dismay for the military destruction or misuse of churches. Fr O'Connor of 16 HLI brought the matter up with Rawlinson.[7] Rawlinson, whose policy to retain military cooperation at the highest level in France has been established, replied in consistent and expected fashion to the latest query: 'I need hardly point out that it would not do to interfere with military operations, and if it is considered necessary to use the church in this way we can hardly object, and if we did, we should only be turned down'.[8] Other clerics were more imaginative and attempted to understand the psychology of the German approach to violation of religious buildings. Fr Fitzmaurice SJ interrogated a captured German officer on the subject who replied: 'If you will insist on placing your guns, in or near churches, what do you expect from us, to throw jam at them?'[9] Fr Walker painted devastated churches proving that it was definitely not jam that was being thrown, by either side. When referring to another painting, that of Vielle Chapelle he remarked that: 'The enemy occupied the church in October 1914. They were driven out three days later by British troops. The church, in the tower of which machine guns

7   DAA, 3235 O'Connor to Rawlinson, 4 June 1916.
8   DAA, 3235, Rawlinson to O'Connor, 11 June 1916.
9   JAL, Fr Fitzmaurice, 'Our Chaplains Experiences', in *Letters and Notices*, 33 (1915-16), p. 157.

had been placed, was destroyed by British shell fire'.[10] Churches were regrettably military locations of value being used for observation, sniping, accommodation, or tending the wounded. Both sides found it necessary to destroy or use these vantage points as a matter of expediency, not malice, despite suggestions that the German destruction to buildings when retreating owes more to vindictiveness than rationality.

Fr Walker's paintings illustrate his interests in the war but he was also a pragmatist keen to rebuild French churches post-war. He wrote to Rawlinson with a detailed plan on how he proposed to bring a scheme into fruition: '… a collection of sketches of the ruined churches of France and Belgium should be made with a view to publishing them, the profits accruing to go toward the restoration and rebuilding of same'. At the end of the letter he wrote: 'I mentioned this matter in a private conversation with the Bishop of Arras, who at once offered to place all available information at my disposal'.[11] It is not known if Walker succeeded but it is ironic that having confiscated Catholic churches, the secular French authorities were encumbered with the legal responsibility for their repair after the war.[12]

Before Fr Gillett started to appreciate the relaxed nature of his new situation, it is worth noting how his everyday routine was both very self-demanding and fulfilling. Much of his time was spent celebrating Mass and analysis of the diaries of Frs Steuart, Drinkwater, and Gillett throughout their service with the Army, reveals that Fr Steuart said Mass on 211 occasions, Fr Drinkwater on 278 occasions and Fr Gillett a staggering 698 times which equate to 1.4, 1.6 and 4.5 times per week during their commission. Fr Gillett's commitment to the fallen was also evident, on the 25 June: 'Trudged to Bouzincourt and Aveluy to visit cemeteries and read 'recommital services' for Fr O'Sullivan's grave in Bouzincourt 'communal' cemetery'. He never recorded meeting Fr D V O'Sullivan but he often met Fr John O'Sullivan a fellow Ushaw alumni.

He continued to say Mass on every possible occasion, nevertheless, 25 June marked a new, if fleeting phase in his life. He declared: 'On my way to Paris on 1 a.m. train from Albert'. Paris held many treasures including countless churches and sites of devotion, not ignoring the joyous expression of a population freed at last from war. In Paris, Fred was free from the military, free to express his Catholic ideals without the incumbency of military and secular restraint, and free to fraternise with those people who shared his principles: the Catholic Americans and the people of Paris. It was a joyous and once in a lifetime opportunity of which this canny Lancastrian took full advantage. On 26 June he said Mass in the Madeleine in Paris 'Then "did Paris" – motored around to Bois de Boulogne – put up at Hotel Gibraltar, an American YMCA hostel', and on the next day he was honoured at the: 'Fête de Sacré Coeur

10   JAL, Paintings of Fr Walker SJ.
11   DAA, 3235, Walker to Rawlinson, 18 March 1919.
12   Today that is still the case. A visit to Chartres Cathedral in July 2015 demonstrated that the renovation was part funded by the French Government with commercial partners and the European Union. A tourist attraction but also an active Catholic church.

– Mass at Montmatre – attended High Mass at 10 – and got place of honour in the Sanctuary – Vespers at 3 and Procession of the Blessed Sacrament and the Blessing of Paris. What a huge concourse of people – wonderful! It was now time to return to the PoW camp at Meaulte for the present but not before he celebrated victory at: 'Mass in Notre Dame de Victoires'. When he arrived back on 28 June, driven by a 'party of Yanks' he recorded with obvious glee: **'PEACE SIGNED AT VERSAILLES** at 3 p.m.'. After a day or two celebrating Mass and visiting cemeteries, he resumed his new 'career'. On Tuesday 1 July: 'Mass – Wet day – Took American's on a Cook's Tour over Somme battlefields – Fricourt – Mametz – away on the left Combles – Bepaume – Le Sars – Albert and home'. The next day: 'Mass – motored with the Yanks to Paris – through Proyart and Rosieres and Montdidier – St Just –Clermont, Creil and Chantilly, a glorious run'. Two days later was a time of relaxation, with Mass at Madeleine and strolling around Paris, he had anticipated the next day's events. 4 July: 'American Independence Day! – American Review in Place de la Concorde – in afternoon went to stadium and saw feast of games – boxing, running, jumping, baseball and goodness knows what. In evening an American variety – excellent'. Afterwards it was again: 'Mass at Madeleine, then home by train for Sunday duty'.

Apart from services for the PoW's, duty centred on battlefield commemoration and cemetery recommital services. Between 8 and 12 July he had:

> Tramped to cemeteries over the battlefields between Becordel and Morlancourt. Visited cemeteries at Martinsart – Mesnil – Hamel – Thiepval and Pozieres – tramped over the old battlefields of 1916. Cemeteries again at Uille Road (Authuille Road, Thiepval) then across country to Regina Trench and Courcelette – what a wilderness. Then cemeteries at Crucifix Corner – Authuille – Blighty Wood – Paisley Avenue and Thiepval.

He interleaved these tasks with daily football and with a good reputation as a sportsman in seminary was probably an asset to the teams he elected to join. Whilst his diaries are ambiguous with respect to his playing involvement, it is unlikely that Fred watched idly from the sidelines. He was comfortable with soldiers, skilled at football and cricket in many positions, he came from a city with a developing footballing passion and heritage, and even though it may have been frowned upon by some officers not wanting to encourage fraternising with the ranks, some Catholic chaplains opted for association rather than segregation. Confirmation exists in the form of medical reports concerning Fr John Holiday who after being de-mobilised reported to the Northumberland War Hospital with a knee injury: 'The officer received an injury to his left knee when playing football in France'.[13] Holiday was 36 at the time and had been attached to 58 Infantry Brigade [Northern].

13   PRO, WO 374/34134.

Fr Gillett soon returned to Paris for events he would remember for the rest of his life. On Sunday 13 July after celebrating Mass at Méaulte and Morlancourt, he went:

> To Paris with Hobbs by the 6 p.m. – got to Paris 11 p.m. and tramped all night along the Procession route. People up all night many sleeping in the places they had taken up for the Procession. What life all night though, how cheerful the crowd and never unseemly.

The big day arrived:

> Mon 14th July 1919. France's Day – Mass at St Augustine's – then to review the Procession. Got a lovely spot in the Place de Concorde and saw the whole show. Magnificent. Nothing more or less! On the move till well into the morning. The whole city up all night.

The activities continued if at a more sedate pace: 'Tues 15th. Mass at Madeleine – saw a delightful wedding service. Madeleine never empties all day, continual stream of visitors all day long passing in and out'. Next day he visited Versailles south of Paris with: 'Dr Coombes and his wife, saw the wonderful Palace and Chamber of Mirrors where peace was signed and went all day through the ground; visited the Trianon Palaces'. Mass in Madeleine followed the day after before returning to the PoW camps at Méaulte.

After 'sleeping in and having a lazy day' on 18 July, he was again alternating between Méaulte and Paris. 20 July: 'Toured Paris again with the Yanks. Passed through Combles -Bouchavesnes – Moislains – Fricourt – Mesnil – Bertrancourt, Bony where we visited the American cemetery – then inspected the famous Hindenberg Tunnel – on then to St Quentin – Ham – Compeigne and at last Paris at midnight'. The following day after Mass at Madeleine he visited: 'Chapel of Sisters of Mercy in Rue de Bac where Our Lady appeared. Met an old Mount Carmel girl – Porteous – doing a turn at the Olympia, so went in evening – excellent!' The next day was a curious mix of history and slapstick: 'After Mass – visited Royalist Cemetery just near the hotel – in afternoon went to a cinema show – Charlie Chaplin, the same rage as England. 11:15 returning to Meaulte by train'.

He enjoyed the lighter aspects of his current time in France but never forgot that he was first and foremost a priest. He took his responsibilities diligently, detaching himself when required and designating remembrance as his highest priority. Between 28 and 30 July he visited Grove Town cemetery near Méaulte, and empathised with: 'Lots of poor Irish buried here after July 16 stunt – brought from line and evidently were in a CCS here and died from wounds, most were wounded at Guillemont and round there'. In afternoon he visited cemeteries at Senlis and Hedauville and continued the next day at Mailly-Maillet, Colincamps, Auchonvillers and Englebelmer where he found it: 'Rather curious to see Crucifixes in Englebelmer Church and one at Hargicourt Cemetery near Bony untouched when all else around pulverised'. Cemeteries at Becordel, Mametz, and Montauban followed the next day.

Mailly-Maillet Church – 19 July 2013. (Notice bullets holes remaining from the First World War.)

Engelbelmer Church, 2 May 2013.

The routine altered slightly at the beginning of August when from his camp: '3 Boche escape – great excitement – poor guards out all night on useless job'. At midnight on Sunday 3 August, Fred Gillett was: 'on my way to Paris with Mac for the Bank Holiday. Finished up with a car ride through the Bois de Boulogne – a glorious day on the way home at 11:45'. His war work was tapering to an end. On 18 August he entrained at Albert for the Paris-Boulogne Express for a short return to Liverpool to conduct a wedding at St Carmel. He was back in Méaulte by 23 August, a mere six day's absence.

Fr Gillett was, even at this late stage, frustrated again by the Army's disorganisation. His hopes were dashed when he arrived in Amiens: 'to secure (at last) the long promised transport for chaplains' and found that it was: 'a broken down motor byke'. Whether he left in disgust, or tried to have it repaired has gone unrecorded. The 'long awaited transport for chaplains' was not mentioned again. It had little effect as on Wednesday 17 September after saying Mass in Candas: 'On return find 'Demob' order in – HURRAH'!! After preparing for home and leaving his portable altar for Méaulte Church on the 19th he was: 'Away at 6:30. Leave Boulogne at 5 p.m. after forging my papers. Folkestone at 7:45 p.m. London at 10 p.m. at the end of my army service'.

That was Fr Fred Gillett's final thoughtful act in France for his fellow Catholics of all races and social compositions. It was also his final act as a Chaplain to the Forces.

SIC TRANSIT GLORIA KHAKI

Portable Altar – Interior. (UCA)

Portable Altar – Exterior. (UCA)

Fr Steuart in France

It is no surprise that Fr Steuart's diary notes, 3 January: 'Major Houston told me that he had put me in again for an MC for the 28th. September show. I am becoming quite bewildered and don't know what I am going to get out of all this in the end'! Shrugging off his frustration he now turned his attention to remembrance and the Somme. On Wednesday 8 January he:

> Left for Albert. Visited Aveluy Wood, taking several photographs of graves, old dug-outs etc. After lunch went straight to Bray, distance about 6 miles, carrying the crosses by turns. Took photographs of a number of derelict Whippet tanks by the roadside, most of them marked "Erobert v.d. 2 Armee'. Bray is pretty badly battered but Albert is in the condition of Ypres.

On Monday 13 January he: 'Went to Signals School & fetched our purchases – crockery, cutlery, gramophone etc'. These articles were for the Mess but are reminiscent of the criticisms meted out to a small number of Jesuit priests: 'As transport is difficult the chaplain should be warned not to bring excessive kit. That seems to be the chief objection to a chaplain, most arrive with bed, library, gramophone etc'.[14] His life revolved around routine canteen duties, socialising, and religious services until 29 January when the military man inside became alive:

> Wakened by Sumner at 5:30 a.m. & told that Battalion was moving off at 7. 30 – whole Brigade. Told that Calais was in insurrection. Chinks & Portugooses [sic] joining in. We were to be ready to fight as soon as we detrained. Lewis guns with cased ammunition & field dressings served out. To our amazement we were taken through Fontinette Station on to Dunkirk. One of the Area Commandant's staff (Capt Fervillaud) afterwards told me that one engine driver was one of the ROD[15] sympathisers with the strikers and has taken us on to Dunkirk on purpose. We were in cattle-trucks and the cold was intense. We were kept in a siding for over 2 hours, and then returned slowly to Calais, arriving about 7 p.m. Marched to No 6 Leave Camp West. MO and I found good quarters in the camp hospital. Dinner in a sort of Officers Club in the camp.

---

14 DAA, 3234, Fr Hessenhauer to Rawlinson, 9 June 1916 complaining about Fr Shaw SJ in particular and Jesuits in general, but there is no evidence other than his observations to support this contention. Some Jesuits were in any case from poor backgrounds.
15 Railway Operating Division.

The excitement intensified on the next day:

> At 10 a.m. whole division moved out to mutineer's camp. The 105 surrounded them on 3 sides & the 104 went in front. Hands up all round: the 4 ring leaders arrested and handcuffed: the rest, some 10,000 (mostly ASC & RGA) marched out peacefully enough and were shipped off to their units. Went into the town in the afternoon: had tea at the Sauvage.

Are these accounts reliable? They were undoubtedly genuinely reported events, if a little dramatic: having tea at the Sauvage takes the intensity out of the account. Fr Steuart's capacity to romanticise was often evident but increased almost to the point of the grotesque after the war, when the triumphalist atmosphere was conducive to either derring-do storytelling, or sickly and misleading sentimentality:

> It was a misty morning, and the white fog mystified the sounds from the just-awakened camps around us ... Shouts and whistles and a thousand confused rumours of a busy camp reached us, and in the distance a mellow baritone voice was singing "The Roses of Picardy". With these familiar sounds of everyday life ringing in his ears and the bite of the sharp morning air on his face, in full strength and youth, he died.[16]

This account was purportedly of a soldier executed at dawn. His diary only mentions one such event which has been discussed. The original is surely more poignant and representative than this trite version.

Returning to events in Calais, as he confined his observations to his private diary it is probable that Fr Steuart simply got carried away with the occasion. It could be argued that the truth of this mutiny was kept secret which given the times is entirely plausible, indeed the National Archives informs that in 1918 there were small-scale mutinies in Calais and Folkestone, but has little detail.[17] There had been similar incidents in the war. On Christmas Day 1917: 'The British sent troops to the 'Chink' camp to put down what they described as a mutiny. Nine Chinese men were wounded when the troops opened fire, and two were killed'.[18] In any event in 1919 the whole matter faded away but there was still drama the next day: 'Tonight a Royal Marine Labour Corps man fired a revolver into one of our tents. Killing one man and wounded another'.

The main value of Steuart's accounts are that they exposed the tangible tensions created by de-mobilisation frustration. In the early stages those most needed at home

---

16 JAL, *The Month 1923* (Spring/Summer).
17 <www.nationalarchives.gov.uk/pathways/firstworldwar/spotlights/demobilisation.htm> (Accessed 22 March 2017).
18 Olusoga, *The World's War*, p. 311.

with jobs awaiting them gained priority release. Some Territorials, for example 10 Battalion [Scots] Kings Liverpool Regiment, were predominantly middle-class: shipping clerks, insurance agents, solicitors, and local administrators among them, and volunteered under the expectation that they would return to their former jobs 'after the duration'.[19] The mutiny described by Steuart was in the early phases of demobilisation which meant that many men who had fought for the longest time were the last to go. Tensions were understandable. Regular soldiers were not as usually affected; they had established tours of duty enshrined in Kings Regulations. Others such as miners were desperately needed at home and they too returned. Conscript and non-British soldiers bore the brunt of delays, supporting Steuart's eyewitness account of the Portuguese and Chinese reaction to continued detainment. In any event the government revised its strategy in January 1919 to defuse further trouble. The new arrangement was based on age, how long in service and how many battle wounds and honours. It is not clear if that was extended to other soldiers of the Empire or Labour Corps, but there were cases of Commonwealth soldiers rampaging in British ports whilst their transport home was delayed throughout 1919.

Amidst the shenanigans, Fr Carey SJ from Limerick, whilst serving the needs of soldiers awaiting demobilisation, became a victim of the influenza pandemic. Fr Daniel Roche SJ informed the Principal Chaplain that: 'Fr Timothy Carey SJ was brought in here on Sunday last [Calais] suffering from an acute attack of influenza. I saw him immediately he was admitted. He was so ill on Monday that I gave him all the Last Sacraments. Though everything possible has been done for him his case is now regarded as hopeless. p.s. Fr Carey died later at 12:30 p.m. RIP'.[20]

Fr Carey was closely connected with the Catholic Club at Audruicq which he managed. His funeral in early 1919 was civic in nature, benefitting not only from the stable condition which allowed a proper funeral service but also from his close association between himself, the Army, and the civilian population, with whom he had forged close links during the war. He is uniquely buried in a civilian plot in the graveyard attached to the church:[21]

Fr Timothy Carey SJ.

19   H. McCartney, *Citizen Soldiers*.
20   DAA, 3235, D Roche SJ at Calais to Rawlinson, 27 February 1919.
21   Possibly because of his close connections with the villagers or because his death was post-armistice. The only CWGC graves at Adruicq are Second World War airmen.

At Adruicq Churchyard in a civilian grave. Age 41. Audruicq Catholic Club. Died 27 February 1919 Influenza.

Colonel Gordon (a non-Catholic) and five other officers of the Garrison themselves bore the coffin on their shoulders from the gun-carriage to the Sanctuary and then from the Sanctuary to the grave. The approaches to the church were lined with troops ... farewell volleys were fired and the Last Post sounded ... The large church [Audruicq] was crowded to the doors, one aisle being filled with British soldiers, the other with French civilians. Outside the Church surged a vast crowd of soldiers and civilians anxious to pay their respects of affection and respect. The Very Reverend B S Rawlinson OSB, Senior Roman Catholic Chaplain in France pronounced the Absolutions and officiated at the grave.[22]

Two days after the 30 January insurrection and the restoration of order, he received his leave warrant and: 'Carrying both my pack and my suitcase. [I] Lunched at the Tête d' Or'. He embarked in heavy drizzle, spending the night of 3 February at the Sauvage in Calais. In thick fog his boat journey the next morning was 'dead slow' arriving at Folkestone at midday. On arriving in London he immediately applied for a leave extension. After visiting relatives in Ryde he entrained to Perth arriving late on 10 February. His time on leave was uneventful but on his return fifteen days later

22 DAA, Ephemera, not accredited or dated but shortly post-war.

he committed to join the British Army on the Rhine. His fluency in German would be an asset for both his social and working life. Whilst awaiting reassignment to Germany he based himself in Poperinge, Hooge, and Ypres town, ministering to the Royal Scots, various Machine Gun Companies, and the Lancashire Fusiliers. Steuart now indulged in two 'sports', boxing and cock-fighting. 1 March he reported: 'Wells was knocked out last night in the 5th round by Joe Beckett' but the next day his curiosity back-fired at Hooge: 'Went to see a cock-fight in a barn just beside the camp. I only saw one fight and was pretty disgusted by what I saw. I can't understand where the 'sport' comes in'.

At this quiet time he involved himself increasingly in Mess duties and socialising. 15 March: 'Had tea at 18th HLI Mess & borrowed a piper from them for tonight. The dinner a great success, though I am afraid nearly everyone – the Brigadier included, was "hinging" before the end! Had reels after dinner & a farewell speech from the Brigadier, who goes to a new Brigade on Monday'. The sense of battle-hardened units slowly disintegrating through demobilisation saddened Steuart who desperately wanted the HLI to stand together, as it always had done, and retire as complete battalions. The expansion of Army involvement in Russia and Germany now surfaced to temporarily distract him: 'Cobb, the doc, left us today for the Army of Occupation on the Rhine. News came that 10 of our officers are to join the 1st Scottish Rifles at Rouen. It may be either Germany or Russia after that'. The uncertainties for Steuart were a mix of caution and optimism, but Germany was his preference.

Accounts of his routine work are interspersed with reports of the demobilisation of various officers, the whole slowly crumbling. As ever a complete contrast offered itself to him on Sunday 30 March:

> Not more than half a dozen at Mass. Ronald, MacMillan, J Gray, Gordon, & Oliphant demobbed. Warning order came to stand-to on account of rumours of some (undefined) disturbance at Dunkirk. The whole Division is to form one Battalion of about 350 men!) commanded by Col Dawson RFA, & the 106 Brigade A Company commanded by Col Furber'.

The next day he reported: 'No further news of Dunkirk stunt', and the following day any hope of flickering excitement was extinguished: 'Dunkirk stunt finally off. Had tea at Téte d'Or'. On 4 April: 'Heard (from the Chaplain's Weekly) that I am for the Army of Occupation till the end of July. [Erroneous]. Our Brigade goes to Dunkirk for demobilisation'. During the next few days he visited old haunts around Ypres then wrote to Rawlinson: 'asking leave to go home with cadre'. In spite of not receiving clearance when his unit arrived at Dunkirk on 16 April for repatriation, he took a chance and accompanied them. He was surely relieved when: 'After dinner, wire came from GHQ, "Instruct Chaplain to the HLI, RHJ Steuart to accompany Unit to Glasgow"!!!'.

19 April Steuart and his Brigade sailed for Tilbury on a Russian ship the SS Mogileff. He clearly enjoyed the journey and his military associations. Next day: 'Loaded up &

left by train at 8 p.m. Cheering and shouting & singing at all the stations till it was dark. Tea at Peterborough. Very wakeful night'. The next day: 'Arrived at Ripon about 7 a.m. – nearly 12 hours for a four hour run! Marched to No 17 North Camp where we had an excellent breakfast. Went to "Tantalizing Tommy" at the Garrison Theatre with CO, Campbell, McKenzie and QM Amusing but pretty broad at times'. 23 April: 'On the CO's suggestion I am going to take leave tomorrow pending instructions from the WO'. This he duly did and returned to France on 5 May. Some two days later: 'I am to join the Army of the Rhine, travelling tonight on the 10:15 "Cologne Express". Very glad as I greatly dreaded an Area Chaplaincy in France'. The reasons for dreading France are not clear, probably the lure of a fresh country whose language he was familiar with and the prospect of military involvement appealed. However, it will emerge that he was to be disillusioned, being attached to a corps was a very different experience to that of a regular regiment. While he headed east on an adapted Red Cross train the 'Arctic' to Cologne, Fr Gillett remained in France.

Fr Steuart in Germany

Fr Robert Steuart's reports from Germany were dissimilar to Fr Fred Gillett's in France, each characterised by the contrasting cultural, political, social, economic, and psychological states between Germany and France, and their own differences in personality. Steuart was generally comfortable with the military, relishing the opportunity to become involved and never shy from committing his military stratagems to his diary. He thrived, as Gillett had done, in extracting as much pleasure from the cultural environment he found at hand, even if both men sometimes had differing social aspirations. Exploring the Rhine countryside, attending opera's and discovering golf were among his pastimes. He observed and reported on his 'analysis' of the German religious psyche, commented on the political and military possibilities, and still found time to involve himself in other pursuits such as boxing and gambling. He enjoyed comparing the cost and value of goods and services and sharpened his Mess purchasing capabilities by taking advantage of the failing German currency, for both private and Army benefit.

8 May 1919 he arrived at Cologne. Reporting to the APC he was attached to V1 Corps Mechanical Transport Company. As we will see this would not be a happy marriage. Soon he had found a billet: '… in the Mess itself. [With] a very nice old couple Schlösser, a retired merchant service skipper'. 11 May he described an approximate pattern for his life in Germany: 'Mass at 9:30 at the Church Mechteren Strasse. I had to sing & did it very badly. Went to the 'Gotterdammerning' at the opera with Carter. "Mai Bole" with the Schlössers at night'. Next day he introduced the first murmurings of attachment discontent: 'The men of the MT Coy have gone on strike owing to delay in demobilisation, but have promised to hold on till Wednesday'. That day he walked across the Hohenzollem Bridge to Deutz, and although the strike did not transpire, the seeds were sown for future conflict with men he had little respect or liking for.

Gradually he introduced himself to the officers, celebrated Masses, and continued to explore: 'On 18th went with Carter [shared batman] to a sort of Earl's Court place near zoo. Afterwards went with him to *"Die Lustige Witive"*. Very good'. His diary three days later showed the variety of units he was serving and his intrigue of military strategy. The desire to be with divisional troops re-emerged: 'Visited Cyclists, Vet, Evac. Coy, "M" Anti-Aircraft Battery & Corps School. Vague rumours of an advance into Germany. If it comes off I will apply for an infantry battalion'. A mere fortnight after arriving, he formulated his opinion of the military situation in earnest:

> Thurs 22nd May 1919. There are strong rumours – or rather evidences – that we may have to advance and occupy more German territory. Apparently there are grounds for thinking that the Boche will try the effect of refusal to sign the Peace, in that case we advance, but as our strength is overwhelming they care for nothing in the way of fighting beyond, perhaps, a sort of guerrilla warfare.

Was this Mess talk or a calculated analysis based on fact, or simply a desire to amuse himself as a military and political strategist? Whatever the reason it is unlikely that Steuart was living in a world of fantasy and probable that there was some grain of truth in his analysis shedding light on the actual situation on the ground. He was not privy to senior officer information but would have had an ear for Mess gossip, his imagination and aspiration would do the rest.

His first observation of the socio-political situation in Germany was made on the 24 May: 'No trams at first this morning owing to a strike at the Power Station'. This in itself is not the hallmark of societal disintegration, but neither does it suggest a populace at ease. The situation was echoed in Britain experiencing its worse strike record in history. Steuart testified on four separate occasions to arrangements on leave being thwarted by rail strikes. As early as 6 February he bemoaned: 'Railway strike. Meant to go to Ryde to-day but no trains'. Political concerns could not deter his new found pastimes and he was soon socialising again, playing tennis and visiting the opera: 'Went with Carter to Tennis Club in afternoon and to "Nachthalter" ("The Moth") at the Reichshalten Theatre. Very good. I take over the Mess today'. The Mess had been, and remained, an important function for Steuart providing him both an opportunity to be useful, and providing access into at least junior officer society although he may have preferred a more senior cadre. Nonetheless, he benefitted from their company, 7 Feb: 'Capt Williams, an APM called at the Mess after dinner. In private life he is a big-game collector in Africa'. Dinner followed a classical concert at the Gurzenich Hall where he attended: 'A Requiem by Brahms vocal & Beethoven Symphony in C minor No 5 Opus 67. The symphony was magnificent but the Requiem, rather tedious'.

The late May weather in Cologne was hot. Resourcefully, Steuart decided to borrow a motor-cycle and when the: 'Byke broke down on one cylinder, I got a passing signaller to put it right'. This enabled him to ride out the next day: '… all through the town and across the river'. The next day he showed even greater resource: 'Motored with Major in evening to a spot some 15 kilos across the Rhine, where we got out & walked across country an hour to Biesfeld where we met the motor again. Bought some eggs (50pf. each i.e. about 12/2d.) & butter (6mk. A pound i.e. about 2/.)'. He constantly referred to the cost and value of items, influenced no doubt by his Mess duties. After a sung Mass on 1 June he: 'entrained to Bonn on the "*Rheinuferbahn*" in the afternoon. Very hot. Women standing up the whole way & not a Boche offering them a seat'. He was not a lover of bad manners.

Resonances of Fr Gillett's difficulties now appeared: 'Went to Műngersdorf in afternoon [for Mass] but no one turned up. I heard from Gwyn, of the Cyclists, that my notice was not put in orders after all'. Simple routine was soon usurped by a serious moral dilemma, when in mid-June Fr Steuart was confronted by the threat of suicide by a fellow Catholic officer. Shortly that threat became reality. Three areas of concern arise, they are: first the religious dimension as suicide in the Catholic Faith is the most heinous of sins: secondly, his dismissal of what was clearly a desperate plea for help from this officer: and thirdly his part in the cover up. His narrative follows and the issues generated will be analysed. It is worth bearing in mind, however, the differences between 1919 and today in attitude and the knowledge of mental issues and how to respond to them. For instance the Catholic authorities today may well judge the victim to be mentally unwell and unable to make a proper conscious decision to take his own life, therefore not committing suicide. The background of Steuart, characterised by the traditional male values of his class and era or the 'stiff upper-lip', was also a factor. But equally, if not more importantly, was priestly training. As established, their formal education was excellent but not the slightest attention was given to the emotional development of these young and sheltered novices, or of their personal inter-relationships with their congregations. Modern generations will quickly identify this omission as the Achilles heel of the Catholic project, but such thinking was anachronistic in a society with a very different value system. Steuart lacked the experience to deal with people.

The short period from 13 June when the danger was first alerted, to 17 June the date of the subsequent burial, will appear in full. Finally the Court Martial on 22 June will be quoted. 13 June: 'Went for motor ride with Hody, to the Königsforst on the other side of the Rhine and walked in the wood for an hour. He is frightfully nervous and depressed & told me of his previous temptations to suicide. He goes on a month's leave on Sunday & is not likely to come back'. The next day: 'Went to Bockleműnd for the "7" AA's. Only one, a Preston man named Walton, to Confession. Had tea afterwards with the Pfarrer. Alone with Hody after dinner. He talked again about his (imaginary) miseries & about the moral aspects of suicide'. Sunday 15 June:

> On coming back from the 9:15 Mass I find that Hody has tried to kill himself with morphine & has been taken to hospital. Went to see him. He is unconscious & they are giving him oxygen & artificial respiration. It was evidently deliberate, as he left his will & letters etc. & in a long letter to Gooddy tells him categorically what he has done & asks him to "camouflage" it to his relations as

an accidental overdose. He died this evening at 6 o'clock. I was able to give him conditional absolution. Gooddy is almost off his head

16 June, Steuart bought Hody a wreath on 'behalf of the Mess' and on Tuesday 17: 'Hody buried at Südfriedhof. Military Honours'. Military matters intervened and this matter does not appear again until 22 June: 'Court of Inquiry into Hody's death at 10:30 in the 36 CCS, I gave evidence in to his state of mind. *The object of the court is, of course, to make out his death was accidental*'.[23]

Was Steuart a superficial man with little sensitivity or empathy for a fellow officer? Was his response at best feeble or at worse negligent? Was he being ironic and quietly lampooning the Army or blindly protecting them? Consistent with his officer ambitions his loyalty towards the British Army in general, the officer cadre, the good name of the regiment, and that of Hody's family were potent internal forces; there could be no question of lampooning the establishment to which he owed allegiance. Steuart's acquiescence in the cover up with the military in this sad affair is a classic example of officer first and priest second. But did he have an alternative? Would he object to a trial which may have been morally questionable but was conducted legally and within the due jurisdiction of a Court of Inquiry: and even if he objected to whom would he appeal? With little space or intention to manoeuvre in this formal process, he nevertheless, made a number of errors of judgement with which he was not competent to deal. But given his own character it is difficult to see how he would do things differently should the occasion arise again. His was an unqualified assessment without psychological knowledge and competence, a merely amateur judgement reflecting his lack of engagement with people in general. His ethics were questionable as was his lack of genuine compassion, but given his situation a definitive assessment remains open to speculation, perhaps he was simply overwhelmed by the whole incident? In any case he was 'small fry' in the Army and his presence at court, although advantageous to have the clergy on one's side, was not fundamental to the outcome.

If, as an officer he 'did his bit', as a chaplain his response can only be regarded as weak and uncaring before the suicide, and not much better after it. He failed in his pastoral care dismissing his 'miseries' as unconsequential and ignoring a potential suicide threat. Steuart did provide the minimum, but crucial spiritual service necessary after death, when he ministered conditional absolution or the remote remission of sin and its consequences. This charitable assessment by the priest can be offered when he believes that the deceased would satisfy the requirements of Confession had death not already taken place; the state of his mind prior to suicide would have been the determining factor. It would be normal, and particularly so of a fellow officer, to say prayers at the cemetery and say Mass for the departed. The fact that he did neither suggests Steuart wanted to bury the incident with the unfortunate Hody, reaffirming Steuart's inclination towards military imperatives over religious. Laid to rest with

23 Author's italics.

Military Honours completed the illusion. Today this incident seems unsavoury and chock full of hypocrisy, but is this criticism historically sound and fair? It is for the reader to judge, as Antony Beever, when trying to unravel the myriad of motivations in the Spanish Civil War noted: 'A definitive answer is beyond the power of any historian'.[24]

On the same day as Hody's burial 17 June, Fr Steuart offered an insight into the mood on the ground reporting renewed British Army preparations. In this phase he was very much an officer first and priest second: 'Today is "J-3" Day. All getting ready for an advance in case the Germans do not sign the Peace'. He continued on Monday 23 June: 'The time limit for the Peace Terms is 7 p.m. to-night. The news came in the afternoon that the German Government has accepted them unconditionally'. Later that day, from high politics to polite society etiquette: 'Had tea at the V1 Corps Club'.

Fr Steuart frequently alternated between quasi-war correspondence and increasing irritation caused by some of his fellow military. Tuesday 24 June: 'News that the Germans have sunk their own fleet at Scapa Flow, a breach of the armistice terms which is punishable by death'. This dramatic military news was overshadowed by the annoyance of others, his comments were scathing:

> I am rapidly coming to feel that I can't stand this Mess much longer. It is not merely their rowdyism, all very bad form that feeds me up. They seem to have one idea of pleasure only, and that is getting blind, helpless drunk. They have no control at all over their men, and the batmen are simply intolerable. What is wanted is a strong OC who will put the fear of the Lord into them. Here the bounders who have had all the soft jobs in the war with no more risk than say, the inhabitants of Poperinge, are now disgracing the British Army in the eyes of the Germans – as I know from what I heard said. I wish Rawlinson could have found a Battalion for me instead of these mechanics, water tank navvies & grocers.

The rhetoric he employed suggested that his failure to gain recognition, at the expense of lesser folk, was anything but dormant. His disgust at their rowdy behaviour was exacerbated by being associated with 'bounders who had all the soft jobs', further compounded by their previous occupations of: 'mechanics, water tank navvies and grocers'. These men, he believed, were inferior types compared to divisional troops and particularly officers of his previous acquaintance. By recommending a strong Commanding Officer 'who will put the fear of the Lord into them', he signified they type of man of which he approved. His intolerance towards the wider strata of society failed to recognise that these men had also been unrecognised, despite being integral parts of the war machine, the majority without the perks and pay of chaplains not to mention the respect of their patrons.

---

24 Antony Beever, *The Battle for Spain: The Spanish Civil War 1936-39* (London: Phoenix, 2006), p. xxxi.

Fr Steuart was unravelling and as he did so, he became less and less likeable, however, this current wave of condemnation soon passed and despite his loathing of men getting 'blind hopelessly drunk' he bought the Mess a new supply of beer directly from the brewery on the 26 June. Now that the threat of real or perceived military action had rescinded, frivolity was restored. He attended: "The Dollar Princess" (in German) at the Reichshalten Theatre. Very pretty music and quite a lot of English phrases in the play'. As ever both the casual and quasi-serious were reported:

> 28th Mass at 7:15. Went to clothing store & got cap and handkerchiefs for Carter & two ties for myself. I wanted boots but they had none of my size. The German Plenipotentiaries passed through Cologne station about 11 yesterday morning. News came tonight that the Peace had been signed between 3 & 4 p.m. this afternoon. There was no mafficking that I could see and apparently things are to go on in the occupied area much as before until the Peace is ratified by the various Governments. This may take three weeks or a month.

Whilst Fr Gillett was enjoying the spoils of the Allied victory in France and combining this with visits to cemeteries, both were denied Fr Steuart. However, the defeated nation was not as devoid of entertainment as might be supposed. Together with opera and cinema, he enjoyed the Cologne horse races and on 12 July: 'Went to second day of meeting. Spotted three winners and four of five places. Won altogether about 100 Mks'.

Steuart's relaxation was regularly combined with seriousness. The next day he expounded a critique of German Catholics, paradoxically containing elements of a certain Protestant analysis of Catholicism:

> The curious contradictions between the unscrupulousness, savagery, & treachery of the Germans at war and their religiousness and piety at home, (the Catholics at any rate) puzzled me for a long time. Either religion was somehow (impossibility!) at fault or we are mistaken about them. Yet neither can be true. It has just struck me what the real solution is. I was led to it by the experience of the way in which Mass is always accompanied by congregational singing, prayers & meditations read aloud, the recitation of endless Hail Mary's & Our Fathers &c. I believe the truth to be that people are drilled to worship, just as the troops are drilled to their duties. It is militarism in another dress, in much the same way as their apparent devotion to music is also. The spirit of militarism – corporate action, survived and sustained not by the individual but autocratic authority for a national ideal of denunciation – has infected even their religious life. Performance of their religious duties has been drilled and beaten into them by the authority whose myriad 'verbotens' regulated all the rest of their lives, so that, speaking brutally, the personal element has as little scope in this department as it has in the military sphere. Their religiousness is not, however, a show: it is a uniform.

This was not a complimentary assessment of his co-religionists but typical of popular German stereotyping which still endures. Had the brutality of war prompted such an analysis?

By mid-July he was feeling 'seedy with a curious noise in my ears'. His priestly duties were mixed with materialist opportunism, taking advantage of the raging inflation in Germany: 'On 16th bought a pair of Zeiss field glasses. They cost 375 Marks i.e. £17-5-0 at pre-war rates, but actually five guineas at the present rate of exchange (72 Marks odd to the pound)'. A bout of activity followed bridge and cricket matches. 25 July: 'Went out at the night with the DAPM Williams after deserters. Raided the Rosenhof and got 2 civilians, 1 nigger and a soldier who is to be the ringleader of the gang. Raided three houses afterwards & got two more soldiers in what is, apparently, an unlicensed brothel!'. This was hardly a spiritual matter indicating that Steuart had overstepped the mark for the activities of a Catholic chaplain. He was now resolutely more officer than priest, at least within his own ego.

After Mass on the 27 July he joined his company on the Rhine: 'Nearly all the whole Company and nearly all the officers except Gunning and myself went for a river trip. They were back about 7:30, Jock being more offensively drunk than I have ever seen him before – and that is saying a good deal'. His rancour was assuaged when on 3 August he departed on leave. On this particular occasion it appeared that Fr Steuart, whose life style when permitted was at least comfortable, would now be a little more extravagant. On Monday 4 August: 'Arrived London about 1:30. It is a Bank Holiday. Went to "Joy Bells" at the Hippodrome. Very good. Saw George Robey for the first time. Stayed at the Rubens'. Next day: 'Bought a pair of boots – 57/6d'! On Wednesday 6 August: 'Went to Farnborough arriving about 11 a.m. Lunched at Tumbledown'. The weather was: 'Ferociously hot. Nita and Dan to dinner. He showed me his VC'. On Friday 7 August he went to Ryde in the morning and then set off north for Perth where he played golf declaring that he was: 'Surprised to find that I am not at all bad'. More golf and golf-croquet followed,[25] interspersed with purchases of blue serge material and copious amounts of high tea. He left for London on 17 August arriving in time for midday Mass at Westminster Cathedral, spending the night at Rubens Hotel opposite Buckingham Palace, before proceeding to Cologne. Fr Steuart chronicled his leave fastidiously, frequently mentioning family, their children, and his siblings in the religious life. Sport replaced tree-felling of previous breaks as he became more indulgent on leave. Undoubtedly this particular leave period was important to his mental recuperation from war, for despite concealing his emotions he had been showing increasing signs of withdrawal and irritability.

Refreshed, he seemed to consciously decide to enjoy himself more. Arriving at Cologne on 19 August: 'about 3 p.m. just in time to see Mac and Webb off on leave. Webb has left no Mess funds and 2 bottles of whisky! Went to torchlight Tattoo in Stadtwald Park. A splendid show'. After 'mouching about' he bought: 'Ten tickets in the

---

25   Original name for croquet.

West York's Sweep, to be drawn on Monday'. On 22 August he ventured out: 'Motor biked for the afternoon. Some trouble with its engine which a very obliging dispatch rider put right for me'. His complimentary remarks soon gave way to annoyance. Next day: 'Confessions at 5 p.m. I find I have been mentioned in dispatches. I am afraid I don't feel excited about it. I am excited to this extent that I am annoyingly reminded by this that I have had four recommendations, each by some ridiculous & unforeseen accident has failed'. Lack of recognition was surely the weightiest drag chain on his emotions, but the 'persistent drunkard Jock Simmons' was a close second: 'He is little better than a drunken rough, however decent he can be when he is sober, and a perpetual source of worry and annoyance to the Mess. He was dead drunk again to-night'.[26] Fr Steuart was relieved when: 'The best news I have heard for some time is that Jock Simmons leaves this Company for good on Monday. He is going to India'. Curiously, Jock Simmons caused more heartache to Steuart than the entire German military.

His nemesis left on 25 August. Suitably liberated, Steuart pursued socio-political comment. On Wednesday 27 August: 'Great liveliness in the Schildergasse & Hohestrasse where the military and civil police were breaking up attempted meetings of discharged Boche soldiers. They were demanding the resignation of the (civil) Chief Constable & had already tried to force in their nominee, a shoe-maker!' His dismissive attitude towards a mere shoemaker may be rude, yet the picture he painted of the break-up of law and order with disillusioned soldiers forming a soviet style local government by force, was a helpful social and political observation. Steuart was acknowledging the anxieties felt by many at home. It may have been exaggerated propaganda but the Army was preparing for possible intervention if their political masters sought fit. In the event, this was his last example of political or military nervousness suggesting that his concerns, or his ability to realistically assess them, had been inflated. All the same he depicted the zeitgeist on the ground before peace was finally achieved.

Steuart continued to pursue enjoyment and trivialities, but not always fruitfully. Visits to the zoo and waxworks, the latter which Steuart described as a 'fearful washout', were followed by social lamentation. 5 September: 'Dempsey and Carter and their wives to dinner. I took a lot of trouble to have a really nice dinner – fish, chicken, ices, peaches & grapes, Champagne, liqueurs etc. – but it was a failure. The wives were dull and looked bored'. Next day he had recovered his self-confidence going to the cinema in which one of his pugilist heroes Bombardier Wells appeared. By contrast he was still actively celebrating the Sacraments and on 7 September visited Cologne Cathedral: '… to hear the famous Fr Dionyius, a Franciscan preacher. Very fine'.

Early September was 'frightfully hot'. He passed the time by motor-biking to: 'Bocklemünd and other places' and then to: 'A concert at Deutches Theatre. Very good. Backhaus played a lot of Brahms & Chopin. There was a really first class violinist

26 A newspaper cutting is pasted in his diary.

Barker, and an excellent tenor, Morgan'. Next: 'Carmen at the opera. Good, but the Toreador had one of those wobbling, uncertain voices that rather spoilt it'. A Rhine trip to Roland-Eek[27] above Bonn coincided with a change in the weather which he described as: 'rather dull and cold coming back'. The "Tales of Hoffman" on 18 September were 'excellent' and he then: '... dined with fellow chaplain MacMahon [sic]. First had Champagne with a stabbed peach at the Köhler'.[28] Confusion over identity is revealed once more. Gillett had confused Mc for Mac and now it was Steuart in reverse Mac instead of Mc! He was talking about Fr Francis Thomas McMahon, a Southampton born priest of St Peter's church Winchester in the Portsmouth Diocese. Stationed with 142 Field Ambulance Army of the Rhine he was demobbed on 21 October 1919.[29] Theatre again on 23 September: 'Went to "Damaged Goods" (Les Avaries of Brieux) at the Deutches Theatre with MacMahon and Brown. A very strong play & amazingly frank, all about siphylis [sic]! I can't imagine it played in England'.

General Joffre arrived in Cologne on 26 September and offered a photo opportunity which Fr Steuart seized: 'Saw him very close and took a snap of him'. After more theatre at the Köhler he played golf with an officer called Lambeth: 'Both of us very poor. Went with him to the opera, "Der Fliegende Hollander", very good indeed'. A railway strike in England was noted then he visited: 'The Horse Show at Merheim Kalk. Not up to much. Prizes given out by Genl. Haldene, V1 Corps Commander'. "Madame Butterfly" at the Opera which was: 'Very good, and the staging excellent. Sir W Robertson a few places from me. House so crowded that the entrance were full of people standing', was succeeded by the "Jesters" concert party'. On 3 October he: 'Went to "Hindle Wakes" at the Deutches Theatre with Mann. A pointless play'. The play is set in a fictional northern mill town and in many ways anticipated the 1960s kitchen sink dramas. Class, social commentary, sexuality permissiveness, particularly the leading lady's frivolous attitude to casual sex, would surely have tested the broad mindedness and tolerance of most clergymen in 1919. The combination of topics in one show was alien to a man from Steuart's background, making his review "a pointless play" muted and predictable. After Mass on 5 October he: 'Went to Rodenkirchen with Mann before midday and played 36 holes. Erratic but better form'. Undeterred the next day he: 'Bought a set of golf clubs at the NACB'. Then: 'Went alone to "Die Walküre". Magnificent'. To complement his clubs he ordered two golf bags from a saddler in Venloer Strasse. In spite of this his form did not improve: 'Played a foursome with Mann, Potter and Wallace. In bad form'. 12 October he reported that: 'MacMahon [sic] just got news of his immediate demobilisation', which actually took place eleven days later. He was proud to: 'Put up my fourth chevron' signifying three

---

27 Unable to locate.
28 Confusion over identity is revealed once more. Gillett had confused Mc for Mac and now it was Steuart in reverse Mac instead of Mc! He was talking about Fr Francis Thomas McMahon, a Southampton born priest of St Peter's church Winchester in the Portsmouth Diocese. Stationed with 142 Field Ambulance Army of the Rhine he was demobbed on 21 October 1919.
29 PRO, WO 374/45086.

years military service, on 13 October 1919. Three days on his golf bags arrived: '… which I had made by a master saddler. Very well made. The price – 42 marks'.

The jollities were soon to stop. On 20 October he heard that: 'Official notice that the V1 Corps will be broken up on the 31st of this month. Don't know what will become of me, demob I presume'. After golf the next day he sought clarification from Fr Sheehan SCF MC but could only deduce that: 'He knows no more about what is going on than I do'. Pugilism then took centre stage, on 22 October:

> Went to Boxing match at Lunar Park with Mac. One Boche, Fritz Jungweiss, lightweight champion of German Navy, knocked out Pte. C. Green, Remount Depot, in 3rd round. Green wasn't really fit but Jungweiss is a dangerous man. He was challenged by Cpl McBrearty, a Caithness man also of the Remounts, who has the reputation of being a man killer. Hope I shall see the fight. The last bout, an extra, between a Cologne and an Aachen man, was the funniest I have ever seen. Every time C hit A, A went down!

Personal issues now intervened. He heard from that his aunt Gerty was 'very ill'. Saturday 25 October he received a wire: 'Gerty dying. Can you come'? He was immediately granted Special Leave. Just before leaving he heard: 'Gertrude sinking'. His journey did not go smoothly:

> Mon 27th. Accident during night, coupling broke. Delayed by an hour and a half. Very rough passage: took over two hours to cross. Arrived Victoria 3:15. Left Waterloo 3:55 arriving Portsmouth 6:30. Arrived at Ryde about 7:45. Gerty died this morning at 10:20. A great grief to me that I couldn't have seen her alive. She looked so peaceful and happy. Said Mass for her. Malcolm & Q arrived about 4 in the afternoon. I am sleeping in a room in Wilkes' house. Found letters of condolence from Frank & Connie, but no mention of coming to the funeral!

He was uncharacteristically emotional at the burial of his devoted aunt whom he visited on most furloughs: 'Wed 29th. Funeral at 11. I was celebrant at Mass & at the cemetery. Canon Morgan deacon, and Ronald sub-deacon. John bore up very well, but I had moments of breakdown'. This side of Fr Steuart's personality occasionally emerged and showed an altogether more gentle spirit, alas they were mere glimpses.

After a few days break in London he returned to Cologne on 4 November but it was now packing up time. Next day he: 'Called on Sheehan and found that my demobilisation papers have come! Am to go on the 11th. Heartily sorry, now I know the time has come'. Then: 'Shopping & packing up. Sold clubs to Potter'. On 8 November: 'Sold British warm to Gooddy & automatic pistol to Anderson'.[30] His last Mass as

---

30 This pistol was not mentioned elsewhere suggesting that it was a recently acquired item, possibly for sporting use on his return.

chaplain was celebrated the next day, Sunday, for 124 Field Ambulance at Ubierring. Monday, after packing and saying farewell he: 'Got my demob papers at barracks in Ulrichgasse. Have to proceed to Kinross'.

Fr Steuart had conducted himself honourably as both army officer and priest throughout the war, and although the tensions between the two positions are palpable he did not let his spiritual duties suffer. He was, however, prone to irritability, for example on commencing his journey home:

> Tues 11th November. Started at 11 a.m. from Bonner Tor station. The train consists of cattle-trucks and two passenger coaches with broken windows. A perfect scandal, especially as a lot of returning Boche prisoners passed us in a perfectly good corridor train. No means of heating, just hard frost & snow. Sheer misery. Took 4 hours to reach Dűren 20 miles away! Sharing a "carriage" (!) with Capt. McLean (Cyclists) & Lte. Heaven (RASC) & Hollingsworth (Devon's). Fixed my waterproof sheet over some of the broken windows, & Heaven had 3 blankets which we shared. Also we had nearly 2 bottles of whisky. But it was a miserable night with no food until 7:30 p.m.

Having served so faithfully his anguish was understandable, but his grumbling and cantankerous nature compare unfavourably to Gillett, whose simpler background had fashioned a humbler personality much closer to the Christian ideal.

His trials and bad humour continued: 'Wed 12th. Still chugging along through Belgium. Stopped at a remote siding and had lunch about 12:30 – bully and pickles again at [left blank] near Armentieres and had dinner – Bully and pickles – at 9 p.m.'. The next day: 'Arrived Calais around 2 a.m. and had to load our own kits on to the lorry'! He recalled being at No 8 Camp: 'where the mutineers were in February of this year', and: 'about 4 a.m. had some sort of scratch meal'. This mundane existence was soon to be replaced by his relish at assuming a military responsibility, which in truth was more administrative and supervisory than martial, but he embraced the opportunity, raising his spirits. When asked to lead a draft to Kinross, he responded: 'After lunch spent the whole day in front of the fire as it was snowing hard. Reported again at 6 p.m., & got instructions. Accepted to oblige a Major who was not going that way'. Notwithstanding the purely honorary title of Captain he delighted in his new authority: 'Fri 14th Paraded at 8:45. Marched my 10 men to the docks. Left Calais about 11. Passed President Poincaré in mid channel. Arrived Dover about 12:45, and didn't leave until after 3 p.m.'. The next day he: 'Arrived Edinburgh about 7:30, and Kinross about 9:30. Got my draft to the Camp and then went to the office where I was demobbed myself'.

This was the end of Fr Steuart's military involvement. He was a man who had a legitimate place within both the clerical and military establishments but his frustration that he was not recognised by either, was profound. Recognition for chaplains was wholeheartedly given by soldiers and civilians but Fr Steuart, without the experience and warmth of the common man or woman, was reliant on the establishment for kudos, the establishment did not respond. His real purpose dictated by his mission was spiritual, despite this he mourned:

> My (with effect from Nov 17) service has been exactly three years, one month & two days. As soon as the process was over, I realised I was a civilian again with just a courtesy right to wear uniform for one month more if I chose. I feel terribly out of it and dull. It has been a good time, the like of which I shall never see again!

Ave Atque Vale!

Some comrades in his regiment did not completely abandon him and it was with joy that Doctor Campbell of the HLI offered him overnight accommodation to attend the regimental dinner. He returned home, packed and left Perth for Wishaw via Glasgow on 20 November, where he had a 'very pleasant night'. The dinner was next evening at 8 at St Enoch's Glasgow where he made a speech to 50 people presided over by Major Houston.

Now it was time to return to religious life. Entraining for St Pancras to visit the Society of Jesus, he occupied room number 19 in Mount Street, home of the English Order. Later he would become the Superior of his fellow Jesuits, thereby, finally receiving the recognition he longed for.

Epilogue – 1919

Frs Gillett and Steuart shared the same religion, mission, and endeavour. In line with the social complexity of Catholicism and its universal role, their credentials spanned the breadth of accessible social strata within the Army. Such diverse personalities and idiosyncrasies represent the gamut of Catholic endeavour; many more populated the spaces in-between. Their spiritual efforts and methodologies were the same, yet for much else they were distinguished from one another by their distinctive personalities. An intimate comprehension of these men evolved through reading, transcribing, and re-reading their personal chronicles. Handling the actual manuscripts, written in pencil or smudged fountain pen ink, brought parts of their work and their lives into being. Visiting the churches and cemeteries they wrote about enhanced the developing relationships between the author of this book and the authors of these diaries. Spending time in the geographic locations where they were born, lived, studied and practised added to the sense of 'walking in their shoes'. The total project has been an enthralling and engaging experience. Paradoxically, distance was also created through the realisation that even the best efforts of the researcher are mere snapshots of these men who existed and recorded in extraordinary circumstances and for a finite period; not to mention the confines of their personal diarist techniques. Undoubtedly both operated within their own human frameworks at war, and what little evidence there is suggests a consistency carried on throughout their lives. Alas, it was not possible to meet and talk with them, although someone who did meet Fr Gillett in his later life testifies to his amiability and gregariousness, hence supporting his consistency of behaviour throughout the war.[31]

The surviving sporadic and fragmented data on individual chaplains has been drawn together and explored through the lives of two men, and contextualised within the war and British society in general. Most Catholic chaplains performed due diligence if not heroics for their fellow co-religionists and now have representation, the vast majority slipping under the spotlight but typified by Gillett and Steuart. Famous chaplains need no further introduction, and the few infamous chaplains at the extremes have been deliberately relegated to the margins. The intention has not been to glamorize the best or sensationalise the worst, but redress the imbalance of history within the context of the overall Catholic mission thereby establishing a sense of proportionality. Despite this, predictably, and discouragingly, celebrity interest retains popular appeal.[32] This study has resisted this trend recognising that the contributions of many minorities in the Great War suffer from historian's amnesia; this version of historiography restores the memory loss of a fine circle of men to whom their fellow co-religionists, and indeed any neutral, can feel especially proud.

31 Brian Plumb Liverpool Archdiocese Archivist in a conversation at the Salford Archives with author 2013.
32 For example, the continual obsession with Willie Doyle. Any search for Catholic chaplains will unearth a mass of published and potential projects for Fr Doyle.

Appendix I

Statistical Dilemmas

This appendix will not appeal to those who, given unreasonably tight deadlines, grasp at official or at least previously published statistics without interrogation; any resultant errors are then replicated and driven even harder into the shrine of historical 'facts'. Gathering reliable statistics of Catholic chaplains is problematic. Many variables and gaps in our knowledge exist. Despite a number of years applied to clarifying the situation, my conclusion is that there will never be wholly trusted statistics, but it is possible to get closer than before. Statistics should be treated with caution and used for illustrative aids rather than academic sureties. A brief but by no means comprehensive explanation why these statistics are so difficult to verify follows:

- Those who use official lists, such as the Army Lists, gain a good approximation of who was on the payroll. Alas precision suffers when, for example, names are difficult to establish, such as MacArthy and McArthy, O'Connell and Connell, Kelly T E and Kelly T V and Kellie T E. [In the text Frs Gillett and Steuart prove the point by misspelling friends names – McMahon and MacMahon – both getting them continually wrong]. Sometimes a chaplain will use his religious name such as Aloysius Gribbin, or his secular name Joseph Gribbin. Usually they are correctly listed but not always, duplication and omission can occur, so which one's can we trust? Further problems arise when a chaplain signs a 1 year contract and resigns within, or at renewal. As the figures for the year run from autumn to autumn in the next reporting year, then they may fall in the gap between. To compound these statistical problems, the Army class all chaplains as belonging to the Army Chaplains Department. This means they do not allocate a fighting unit or theatre of war. This makes the task of identifying a chaplain by his military unit impossible by this means. When one theatre of war, such as the Western front, is the dedicated place of study the problems are exacerbated.
- Catholic Directories are a useful source. Alas they are not 100% reliable when reporting CFs and particularly matching dates between when they left the parish and when on active service, accuracy also depends on correct reporting and collating between parishes and diocese. They remain a limited but useful source

for diocesan priests. Irish versions are elusive in England but can be accessed in the National Library of Ireland in Dublin.
- The Society of Jesus does provide up-to-date and reliable sources for their chaplains' involvement as CFs. Both the English and Irish Provinces are separate entities with the same high standards. Unfortunately other religious orders did not follow suit.[1]
- The Rawlinson Papers in the Benedictine Downside Abbey does have large amounts of data. As these are the individual papers for all chaplains (incomplete) then it is very time-consuming reading each one and transcribing snippets of data into a database. Many do not mention their unit or location for military reasons, and frequent changes are not always recorded or make sense. Fragmentary but genuine and priceless evidence, without this archive any in-depth assessment of Catholic chaplains is impossible, but the data needs to be complimented by other sources and not used piecemeal.
- Priests as unmarried men, very rarely corresponded externally to friends or family, thus denying a possible avenue of research material.
- Many were simply cast-off from their religious homes as missionaries and did not leave evidence of correspondence with their diocese or order. Most dioceses did not capture random correspondence between priests. If capture was initiated, subsequent bishops either rid themselves of the paperwork, or failed to allocate resources for their safekeeping and retrieval, perhaps not understanding the value of historical documents; a strange response from a Church which prides itself on its roots. It is thanks to outstanding individual archivists, often amateurs, who filled at least some of the gaps.

Despite these research limitations, historians continue to quote and re-quote statistics as accurate historical facts, even outside the particular and limited study of Catholic chaplains. Just a few examples will suffice:

> On British casualties:
> Keegan does not quote British casualties but claims 'a million British Empire's dead'.[2]
> Gordon using figures based on 'the Official History' quotes 564,080 British and Dominion Casualties, which excludes: 319,824 missing or taken prisoner, 1,837,613 wounded, and 3,496,333 sick or injured, or 6,217,905 in total.[3] Impressive but can such precision ever be 100% accurate?
> Strachan assiduously avoids quoting figures about casualties, probably the correct course of action.

---

1   Some of the smaller Orders were not contacted or have dispersed.
2   John Keegan, *The First World War* (Hutchinson 1999), p. 451.
3   Iain Gordon, *Lifeline*, p. 159.

These examples show the variation is statistic reporting. Keegan's employs a general and non-cited statistic. Gordon offers a precise breakdown but a wide interpretation of categories within the term casualty. Strachan resists the temptation to report presumably through lack of genuine evidence. These historians have access to greater sources of material than do those examining Catholic chaplaincy, and yet vary in their figures, definitions, and willingness to regurgitate statistics *ad nauseum*.

A similar situation exists with men executed:
Beckett claims that: 'a total of 361 men were executed during the war of whom 291 were serving with British regiments.'[4] Yet the British government claimed 306 men had been 'shot at dawn'[5] when pardons were granted in 2006. The questions are who do we believe, whom can we trust and whose definitions do we use?

The same differences and more apply to chaplaincy statistics.[6] This study used statistics sparingly and only after reflection, recognising that despite exhaustive research there are simply too many variables to be certain of the reliability of figures, furthermore, over-reliance on statistical data can produce rather skewed and careless history. The one indicator of 700 Catholic chaplains on the Western Front is my own, and is based on all of the above sources, but as chaplains still occasionally appear from an obtuse source (usually from external enquiries) then approximations are the best that can be reliably achieved. It's a decision for the researcher: to legitimise unsubstantiated figures or to reduce reliance on statistics and instead to suggest intelligent interpretations based on the available evidence. It should be remembered that Rawlinson in GHQ, the Principal Chaplain responsible for all Catholic chaplains on the Western Front and the only man who could have the data, was never able to produce precise numbers, such was the mutability of war. Statistics have only been used on occasions when they have been substantiated, or when employed in areas of interest rather than historic fact.

Another area of historical misrepresentation relates to 'war stories'. Suffice it to say that many accounts, some in print and referred to as reliable sources, fall very far short of that description, tending towards imagination rather than fact. Memory, euphoria, sentimentalism, vanity, deception and a range of other possible motives demean the true history of a fine body of men who deserve better. Treat these accounts with care and apply to them academic criteria and common sense, they soon unravel to expose themselves as at best careless or lazy, at worse deceitful.

4　Ian Beckett, *The First World War: The Essential Guide to Sources in the UK National Archives*, (PRO), p. 145.
5　Des Brown, Minister of Defence, *The Guardian*, 9 November 2006.
6　The author recognises the challenges facing the researcher. At this juncture a comparison of chaplaincy statistics will serve no purpose. Rather in the main thesis, when statistical data is quoted, it will be questioned at that time.

Appendix II

Chaplains KIA and Buried on Western Front

Name	Order/Dioc	Origin/Seminary	Buried
Baines Thomas	LIV	Preston, Ushaw	Aire Communal Cemetery
Burdess Mathew	HEX	Sunderland, Ushaw/Rome	Villers Faucon
Carey Timothy	SJ IRL	Cork, Milltown Park	Audruicq
Collins Herbert	WSM	Middlesex/Oscott	Cabaret-Rouge Souchez
Clarke Stephen	IRL	Kilmore Co Cavan	Tyne Cot Panel 160
Doyle Denis	SJ IRL	Kimberley SA/St Bueno	Dive Copse
Doyle Willie	SJ IRL	Clongownes/Dublin	Tyne Cot Panel 160
Fitzgibbon John	SJ IRL	Clongownes/Roscommon	Trefcon
Gordon Michael	SCO	Glasgow	Coxyde
Grobel Peter	SAL	Middlesex/Valladolid	Boulogne Eastern
Guthrie David	OSB	France/Qarr	Varennes
Gwynn John	SJ IRL	Galway, Milltown/Louvain	Bethune Town
Knapp Francis	ODC	Sussex	Dozinghem
Leeson James	LIV	Liverpool, Upholland	Pont de Jour Athies
Looby Patrick	LIV	Cahir, Waterford/Paris	Poelcapelle
McDonnell John	SAL	Clare, Lisbon	Beuvry Communal
Montagu Walter	SJ	Port Stewart, Stonyhurst	Awoingt
Monteith Robert	SJ	Carstairs, Stonyhurst	Ribecourt
O'Sullivan Donal	IRL	Killarney	Bouzincourt
Shine James	PLY	Ballylaffin Cahir/Waterford	Boulogne Eastern
Watters J.	PLY	Mayo	Awoingt
Whitefoord Charles	SWB	Ludlow, Oxford	Bagneu, Gezaincourt

Appendix III

How CFs with British Army Died on Western Front

Chaplains Name	Religious Diocese	How Died	Military Unit
English/Scottish			
Burdess Mathew	Hex	Booby Trap Bomb	Gloucester's
Baines Thomas L	Liv	Aerial Bomb	RFA
Leeson James	Liv	Shell	Royal Fusiliers
Monteith Robert	Liv/SJ	Shell	RFA
Grobel Peter	Sal	Pneumonia	DAPC Boulogne
Whitefoord Charles	Sby	Shell	London
Collins Herbert J	Wsm	Shell	Black Watch
Gordon Michael P	Glasgow	Shell	Inniskillings
Guthrie David M	OSB	Shell	East Lancashire
Carey Timothy	SJ	Influenza	Adruicq Catholic Club
Montagu Walter P	SJ	Shell	RGA
Irish via England			
Looby Patrick	Liv	Shell	Northumberland Fusiliers
McDonnell John J	Sal	Shell	55 Div MGC
Shine James	Ply	Shell	Middlesex
Watters	Ply	Influenza	unknown
Irish/South Africa			
Doyle Denis	SJ	Shell	Leinster's
Irish			
Clarke Stephen	Cavan	Shell	Lancashire Fusiliers
Doyle William	SJ	Shell	Royal Dublin Fusiliers
Fitzgibbon John	SJ	Shell	RAMC
Gwynn John	SJ	Shell	Irish Guards

Chaplains Name	Religious Diocese	How Died	Military Unit
Knapp Francis S	ODC	Shell	Irish Guards
O'Sullivan Donnell V	Kerry	Shell	Irish Rifles
Died at or on way home			
Bertini M	OSB	Pneumonia	RAMC
McIlvaine John	SCO	Drowned	Notts and Derby
McAuliffe C	OFM	Heart condition	Base Hospital Rouen

Appendix IV

Catholic Chaplains Died in Other Theatres of War

Name	Religious Diocese	Origin	Details
Prendergast Mathew	Hex	Lismore, Waterford	KIA 16/9/18 Cairo War Cemetery
Finn William	Mbr	Yorkshire	V Beach Gallipoli
McGinty Henry C.	Liv	Liverpool	Pneumonia 8/11/18 Giavara Military Cemetery
Strickland J.	SJ	Ireland	Pleurisy 15/7/17 Addolorata Cemetery Malta
Bergin Michael	SJ	Roscrea, Ireland	Shell Australian 51 Div, Renninghelst, Belgium
O'Meehan I.J.	OFM	Ennis, Ireland	Accidently shot, 19/12/19 Mesopotamia
O'Dea Laurence	CAP	Kilkenny	Illness aged 66 4/11/1917, Crawley Cemetery
Kavanagh Bernard	CSR	Limerick	21/12/17 Jerusalem War Cemetery
Watson Charles	CSSR	Belgium	22/7/18, Sunstroke, Basra, Mesopotamia,

Appendix V

Pre-War Missions of CF's KIA

England	Ireland	Irish/English	Scotland	Irish/South African
Baines Thomas	Carey Timothy	Looby Patrick	Gordon Michael Patrick	Doyle Denis
Burdess Mathew	Clarke Stephen	McDonell John Joseph	Monteith Robert	
Collins Herbert J.	Doyle William	Shine James		
Grobel Peter	Fitzgibbon John	Watters		
Guthrie David M.	Gwynn John			
Leeson James	Knapp Francis (Simon)			
Whitefoord Charles	Montagu WP			
	O'Sullivan Donal Vincent			

Appendix VI

Chaplaincy Organisation

ARMY CHAPLAINS DEPARTMENT.

Approval has recently been given by the War Office to certain changes in the Organisation and War Establishment of Army Chaplains for duty with the Army in France.

Organisation.—It has been decided to introduce one system of organisation for all Chaplains and the present organisation of the Church of England has been adopted. To effect this Chaplains of all denominations, other than Church of England, will be grouped into one for purposes of administration.

This organisation is shown in Appendix A, and the posts lately created are underlined.

The suffixes "C. of E." or "Non C. of E." will in future be used by Senior Divisional Chaplains. The suffixes need not be adopted by Senior Chaplains of Armies, Corps or Bases as the titles conferred on these Chaplains provide the necessary distinction between the two branches of the Chaplains' Department in France.

The functions of the Senior Chaplains of Corps and Divisions are to minister to the Corps and Divisional Troops.

They will also act in an advisory capacity to co-ordinate the work of their subordinates within their Corps or Division in accordance with any special instructions that may be issued by the Deputy Chaplain General or Principal Chaplain.

The Senior Chaplain of a Corps or Division is not an *administrative* appointment.

Establishment.—In addition to the appointments and posts as shown in Appendix A, Chaplains have been allotted to Divisions on the following basis:—

(a) In the case of English Divisions (viz., all British Divisions at present in France except those enumerated under b, c, and d):
- 9 Church of England,
- 4 Roman Catholic, and
- 4 Presbyterian or Nonconformist.

(b) In the case of Scottish Divisions (viz., 9th, 15th, and 51st):
- 9 Presbyterian,
- 4 Church of England, and
- 4 Roman Catholic.

(c) In the case of the 16th (Irish) Division:
- 9 Roman Catholic,
- 4 Church of England, and
- 4 Presbyterian or Nonconformist.

(d) In the case of the 38th (Welsh) Division:
- 9 Nonconformist or Presbyterian,
- 4 Church of England, and
- 4 Roman Catholic.

Although the above establishment per division is laid down, nevertheless the precise manner of allotment need not be adopted in practice, but the Chaplains of each Denomination may be allotted and varied under instructions issued from this Office.

There is also a small reserve pool of Chaplains for both C. of E. and Non C. of E. Denominations to meet emergency needs, and to allot for work in hospitals, bases, etc.

G. H. FOWKE, Lieutenant-General.
Adjutant-General, British Armies in France.

GENERAL HEADQUARTERS,
19th December, 1916.

Copies to all Units except Overseas Contingents.

Appendix VII

Burial Directives

INSTRUCTIONS REGARDING BURIALS.

A.G. 3212(O).

1. These instructions are not intended to supersede those issued to Chaplains for burials in ordinary trench warfare, or the regular procedure for rendering burial returns on Army Form W.3814.
2. *Responsibility.*—Each unit is normally responsible for taking the bodies of its own dead to the place appointed.

Burials will normally be undertaken by Divisions.

3. *Personnel.*—(i.) Each Corps has a Corps Burial Officer who works with the representative of the Director of Graves Registration and Enquiries.

(ii.) Burial parties will be found whenever possible from units not engaged in the actual operations.

Each Division should earmark a party, about 100 strong, with a due proportion of Officers, Chaplains and N.C.O.s, who should be instructed in their duties beforehand.

(iii.) Armies will earmark Labour Companies from which parties may be detailed and allotted to Corps as required. The Corps Burial Officer will get in touch with the units selected.

4. *Material required.*—(i.) Tin labels, or discs, at least 6 inches in diameter, painted in conspicuous colours. These will be stamped with the serial number of the grave and the number of the Corps.

(ii.) Wire rods, at least 4 feet 6 inches long, on which the tin labels will be hung, and which will be fixed in the ground at the head of each grave.

(iii.) Stout labels bearing the same number as the tin label over the grave, for attachment to each packet of effects.

(iv.) Ration bags and sandbags for packing effects.

(v.) Improvised stretchers.

(vi.) These materials will be issued by Corps to Divisions, who will be responsible that each tin label not returned is accounted for on a roll. (See reverse.)

5. *Sites for Burials.*—(i.) When existing cemeteries cannot be used, sites suitable for eventual acquisition by the French Government should be chosen with a view to convenience of transport, by light railway or otherwise, and should be at least 100 metres distant from groups of houses or ruins and from any spring or well, and near a road.

(ii.) As many bodies as possible should be buried in each cemetery. The larger the number of bodies buried in the same place, the smaller the probability of subsequent disinterment. Cemeteries should be arranged in rows, each row designated by a letter.

(iii.) All units concerned must be told the location of the cemetery selected.

6. *System of Burial.*—(i.) The Corps Burial Officer will be responsible that the burials are carried out in accordance with these instructions.

(ii.) Officers in charge of Burial Parties will divide their parties into " bearer sections " provided with stretchers for collecting the dead, and " sandbag parties." The duty of the latter will be:—

(a) To remove boots, greatcoat, equipment, and place them on one side for salvage.

(b) To collect all personal effects and the RED identity disc, and place them in a ration bag or pocket (cut off the man's tunic), and tie them up. The GREEN identity disc will be left on the body and buried with it.

(c) To sort ration bags into sandbags as laid down in para. 7 (iv.).

(d) To lower bodies and fill in the graves.

7. Burial Parties must observe the following routine:—

(i.) Remove nothing from the dead until the body is ready to place in the grave.

(ii.) Bury dead of different nationalities separately.

(iii.) Bury officers with men, except General Officers whose bodies will be disposed of as directed.

(iv.) Mark each grave (whether containing one or more bodies) with a wire rod and disc; the label referred to in para. 4 (iii.) will be tied to the single packet of effects or to the sandbags of packets of effects (according to whether one or more bodies are buried in the grave).

8. *Disposal of Records and Effects.*—(i.) The officer in charge of a burial party will make out a nominal roll, of which a specimen is given on reverse.

Names will be entered in block letters in the order in which the bodies are buried.

In addition to signing and dating the roll, the officer will add his rank, name, and unit in block letters.

The sandbags and rolls will be sent to the Corps Burial Officer, who will make four copies of the rolls.

(ii.) The Corps Burial Officer will send:—

(a) The original rolls in the sandbags containing effects to G.H.Q., 3rd Echelon, and obtain receipts from the R.T.O., of which the original will be forwarded to G.H.Q., 3rd Echelon, by registered post, and a copy to Corps Headquarters "A."

(b) The copies of the rolls to Corps Headquarters "A," who will dispose of them as follows:—

1. One copy to 3rd Echelon, G.H.Q.
2. One copy to D.G.R. and E., War Office, Winchester House, St. James's Square, London, S.W.
3. One copy to D.A.D.G.R. and E. of the Army.
4. One copy will be filed at Corps Headquarters for record.

(iii.) (a) The rolls and effects of Allied dead should be disposed of as follows:—

French.—Monsieur le Directeur du Service des Tombes, Mission Militaire Française, Attachée à l'Armée Britannique, G.H.Q.

American.—Adjutant-General, Headquarters, A.E.F.

Portuguese.—Officer Commanding, Portuguese Headquarters, S.P.O. 10.

Belgian.—To Monsieur le Chef de la Mission Belge, G.H.Q.

(b) Those of Enemy dead should be sent to D.A.A.G., Prisoners of War Section, Le Havre.

GENERAL HEADQUARTERS,
22nd July, 1918.

G. H. FOWKE,
Adjutant-General.

Appendix VIII

Example of Letters to Families of the Deceased

Fr Keating SJ's first letter:

> Shortly after he entered the hospital I was by his bedside, but could do nothing at the time as he was not quite himself. A day or two later I was able to hear his Confession and administer Extreme Unction: I judged it more prudent to defer Viaticum for the time. Meanwhile he seemed to be progressing favourably and was put down on the list for England. However, about two days before his death a sudden change took place and he relapsed into unconsciousness, in which state he remained till the end. He received Viaticum nearly four days previously and I gave him his last blessing and plenary indulgence before he lost consciousness. Thank God he was well prepared to go. The nurses and myself had grown fond of him: he was so patient and uncomplaining and cheerful also. Whenever, I asked him how he was, the reply was: – "I'm doing bravely today". He was buried by me… and I was able to say Mass for the repose of his soul the morning after his death. During his illness both nurses and Doctors gave him every attention and nothing was omitted that could add to his comfort. You have my deepest sympathy, dear Mrs Halfpenny in your great loss. Your husband was a good, pious man and I am sure that God has shown him mercy. He died well and he died in a good cause. May he rest in peace, and may God give you all consolation in your sorrow.

16 August 1916 he replied to Mrs Halfpenny:

> Your letter with enclosure reached me safely. Your good husband was not in a condition to make any lengthy or connected remarks while under my care: his state was too lethargic to admit of that. So I heard nothing from him about yourself and the children. I am very sorry that this was so: otherwise a message would have given you much comfort. But his thoughts would surely have been of you and yours. Next week I hope to be able to say 4 Masses for the repose of his soul. I thank you from my heart for your good prayers in my behalf, I need them. We are very busy just now. Sincerely yours in Jesus Christ.

Appendix IX

A Portrait of Fr Robert Steuart SJ

Born Reigate, Surrey, 1874. Educated at St. Bueno's and Stonyhurst. Died 1948. His family home was Tulliepowrie House, Strathtay, near Dunkeld, Perth, Scotland. Fr Robert Steuart's obituary defines him as: 'He combined simplicity with dignity and hardihood with a fastidiousness at times verging him on the intolerant, especially when in his older years he saw that that kind of life, which he judged to be good, was doomed to disappear.' Later: 'His inherited and acquired 'culture' made him 'interesting' to all. He wished tacitly to civilise: he was 'a man of the world' yet not 'worldly': he maintained his deep personal reserve; and although his patience was heavily taxed (this was always true) he did not try to penetrate unasked into the defences of another'.[1]

Fr Steuart enjoyed a relatively urbane life away from the Front, but only in so much as a gentleman of his day might reasonably expect. By contrast there were limitations imposed on him by his background: he could not be expected to have a beer in an estaminet with common soldiers for example. He was not alone here Fr. Hessenhauer wrote of another Jesuit: 'I am finding it rather difficult to push Fr Shaw he is terribly afraid of private soldiers'.[2] Be that as it may, Fr Steuart's relationships with lower ranks, even with fellow Jesuit chaplains, were insular.[3]

Fr Steuart's diaries reveal his faults and strengths. He was true to his type, a good priest and a brave one; but he was delusional, haughty, sad, and at times lonely. He was not a likeable man and in many ways exemplified the decay of the values to which he was enslaved. This was brought into sharp relief by the war and the unfortunate fact that his training, upbringing, and social skills, were simply not wanted by the Army at the level he was anticipating. He was a chaplain and, therefore, a Captain class 4. He may have been suitable in a senior domestic role dealing with that echelon of Catholic society with which he was familiar, but this was not the situation at war, he was, as '*Information and Hints*' had advised all Catholic chaplains [you are]: '... a Captain

---

1   JAL *Obituaries*, pp. 125-9.
2   DAA, 3234, Hessenhauer to Rawlinson, 11 July 1916.
3   JAL, Steuart Diaries, 1 December 1916: 'Passed Wolverston riding, going in the opp. direction through Millencourt. Didn't speak'. Wolverston was a fellow SJ from London.

Robert H. I. Steuart SJ. (JAL Obituary)

in rank, and as such you are only "small fry" in the Army'. Fr Steuart never grasped this even to the end of the war. He could not escape the values he had acquired in peacetime, as his obituary implies: 'Privilege connected to it [life] carried a certain obligation',[4] an obligation he no doubt felt but was powerless to act on.

Fr Robert Steuart is a difficult man to understand and his obituary does not help in this matter attesting to: '… his attention alike to University personages and to the poor of the Oxford slums'.[5] This was 1923 and he may have changed but it seems highly improbable given his apparently staunch and apparent impermeable nature. The same obituary gets closer to explaining Steuart's difficulties: 'He had not been parish priest so far: possibly the war had left his touch a little hesitating'.[6] In the final analysis he did not have the preparation for his role as Army chaplain because he had not been prepared for secular priesthood. He was increasingly anachronistic and would have been better utilised in another role commensurate with his advantages. He was another victim of the war but assuredly an unknowing one.

Underneath the stern exterior he did show glimpses of real humanity, such as attending the soldier shot at dawn and his aunt's funeral, alas such warmth was soon extinguished. He was simply a man of his time from a certain narrow, but not uncommon social perspective; but he was a good and honest priest and worthy chaplain.

4   Ibid, p. 128.
5   Ibid, p. 128.
6   Ibid, p. 130.

Appendix X

A Portrait of Fr Fred Gillett

Born in Lytham in 1882, his identical twin brother Harry and he both went to Ushaw and were ordained by Bishop Whiteside at St. Peter's Church, Lytham, Lancashire, in 1906. Both became CFs and on their return from the Western Front worked in Liverpool before the formation of the new Lancashire Diocese in 1924. Harry was a CF for about 4 weeks, Fred 46 months. Fred died in 1969, his brother in 1958. Fred and Harry were the names used by both priests throughout their live

Fr Gillett was an active and sociable man. For relaxation he enjoyed sports at war as he had done at Ushaw. Football mainly, but also cricket, rugby, and athletics in general. He made his time count in France and Belgium by embracing the physical aspects of life: walking, marching, and riding a bicycle, horse, and possibly in 1919 a dilapidated motorcycle. These activities which he relished allowed him to explore the countryside and especially historical and religious places. He loved and respected the French rural peasantry for their toil, frugality, and endurance. Drawing parallels with the 'Tommy' he frequently showed compassion towards their mutual sufferings and torment. His circle of chaplains was wide and tended to be diocesan but not exclusively so. He reunited with alumni from Ushaw seminary: Frs. McBrearty, Pickering and Harker, either at chaplaincy meetings or by accident. His socialising before the Armistice was limited to entertainment or sports on offer and perhaps sharing an occasional meal or drink, or religious service.

There was a private side to Fr Gillett who wrote in a minimal manner about emotional or personal aspects of his life, even about his mother's illness and death. He mentioned his twin brother Harry only when he enlisted in late 1918, and again when Harry was demobbed shortly after. When he said Mass for 'dear father' it was a rarity. He wrote very

Fr Harry Gillett – Identical Twin of Fr Fred Gillett. (Obituary in *Lancaster Diocese Directory* 1959)

little about anyone else, his was a priest's life punctuated by loneliness. On leave he mentioned Liverpool his adopted home, but little else. He liked the occasional drink or 'clerical tea' but such releases were few and far between and conducted in the appropriate manner, granting that he had an extended Christmas celebration in 1916 leaving his diary blank for three days.

To conclude, Fred Gillett was a solid, reliable, unassuming, affable chaplain and priest. As a man he was personable and showed great compassion for those less well off. His pragmatic qualities mark him as a man true to himself and his vocation. He was treated very indifferently by his own Catholic authorities during the war but was recognised later and made a Canon. Despite suffering a long-term illness which recurred in 1956, he returned to active priesthood after his retirement. He died on 1st February 1969. *The Longridge News*, a non-denominational publication summed up Fr Fred: 'He was very human and approachable to everyone he met. His walks around the parish were prompted by halts for a chat at the various farms he was passing, and he was ready to talk to anyone at all from children to adults and from farmer to local landowner'.[1] Fr Fred Gillett was an extraordinary, ordinary man, and his diary and subsequent study 'in his shoes' provided a great insight into not only the man, but the role of a chaplain on the Western Front.

1   *Lancaster Catholic Directory* 1970, p. 127.

Appendix XI

The Hymn Faith of Our Fathers

Faith of Our Fathers! Living still
In spite of dungeon fire and sword
Oh how our hearts beat high with joy
When e'er we hear that glorious word

> *Faith of Our Fathers! Holy Faith!*
> *We will be true to thee till death*
> *Faith of Our Fathers! Holy Faith!*
> *We will be true to thee till death*

Our Fathers chained in prisons dark
Were still in heart and conscience free
How sweet would be their children's fate
If they like them, could die for thee

Faith of Our Fathers! Mary's prayers
Shall keep our country fast to thee [Irish Version]
Shall win our country back to thee [English Version]

Common
And through the truth that comes from God
Oh we shall prosper to be free [Irish/Philadelphia Versions]
England shall then indeed be free [English Version]
Our Land shall then indeed be free [New York Version]

Faith of Our Fathers! We will love
Both friend and foe in all our strife
And preach there too, as love knows how
By kindly words and virtuous life

This hymn develops into a rich stream of emotion as it flows from bleak persecution to hope and forgiveness. The first verse evokes the persecution of Catholics in both England and Ireland. The next continues the theme which has resonances of 'Muscular Christianity' connecting historical sacrifice with the war. Verse three allows a national emphasis to be inserted. In the English case it is the well-trodden path of conversion of England to Catholicism. The Irish version has both a political and religious meaning vis-à-vis Ireland achieving political self-determination, and retaining its religious independence from Protestant persecution. It is the fervour which accompanied the singing that gives meaning to either of the explanations of verse three, and helps explain how Catholics in general felt and expressed themselves from, as some saw it, the yoke of heresy and persecution. Verse 4 assumes the core Christian values of love and forgiveness.

Bibliography and Sources

PRIMARY SOURCES

(Please note that requests for the information below are specific and generally do not require, or possess, a catalogue number. Where they do exist they are quoted.)

Archival Sources Diocesan
Archdiocesan Archives Birmingham – Fr John Sharp
    Fr #Drinkwater's Personal War Diaries
Archdiocesan Archives Dublin – Noelle Dowling
    Archbishop Walsh Papers
Archdiocesan Archives Liverpool – Dr Meg Whittle and Brian Plumb
    Archbishop Whiteside Papers. Many are found under EBC. Full index is available.
Diocesan Archives Nottingham
    Frs Tonge and Richmond Papers
    Ad Limina Reports
Diocesan Archives Salford – Fr Lannon
    Bishop Casartelli Papers
    Fr Gillett's Personal War Diaries*

*N.B. there are copyright issues which have not been resolved, which is why the author copied from the originals in pencil and then transferred to a Word document. The digitised form has been presented to the Archive and Fr Lannon should be consulted for permissions.

Archival Sources Religious Order
Benedictine Downside Abbey – Fr Rawlinson Papers. Nos. 3231-3235 refer to boxes containing individual chaplaincy correspondence, others are labelled ephemera, and bishops correspondences. As they are in the process of being digitised the current categorisations may no longer be valid. However, they all reside together in a suite of boxes which are alphabetically arranged by chaplain.
Cistercian Abbey Archive, Roscrea, Tipperary – Fr O'Herlihy Papers.

Jesuit Archives Dublin – Fr Gill's Personal War Diaries and other chaplains' files. The files are marked CH/with the relevant number relating to each chaplain. An index is provided.
Mungret, Belvidere, and Clongowne College, Publications, Papers and Syllabi.
Jesuit Archives London – Fr Steuart's Personal War Diaries, Fr Walker's Personal War Paintings – Various Jesuit Magazines and Obituaries

Archival Sources Educational
Diocesan Seminary College, Ushaw – College Educational Diaries and Syllabi
Jesuit College, Stonyhurst – The Stonyhurst War Record 1925, College Magazines and Syllabi

Archival Sources Other
Amport House Royal Army Chaplaincy Department Amport – Catholic Chaplaincy Papers
Army Bishops House Aldershot – Catholic Chaplaincy Papers
National Army Museum London – Fr Gwyn's Letters
National Archives – Public Record Office, Kew – War Records ranges WO 339 and 374

Newspapers
Catholic Herald
Catholic Times and Catholic Opinion
Clonmel Chronicle and Waterford Advertiser
Freemans Journal
Kilkenny People
Munster Advertiser
Liverpool Catholic Herald
Liverpool Daily Post
Tipperary Nationalist
Tipperary People
Tablet
Universe

Magazines and Periodicals
The Catholic Fireside: The Popular Illustrated Monthly
Catholic Family Annual and Almanac – Archdiocese of Liverpool
Catholic Union Gazette
The Month, Jesuit English Provincial Periodical, [quarterly]
The Ushaw College Magazine,
The Stonyhurst War Record
The Stonyhurst College Magazine
The Stonyhurst Association Newsletter

The Clongownian, [Clongownes College Magazine]
The Belvedarian [Belvedere College Magazine]
Punch

Directories
The Lancaster Catholic Directory
Catholic Directories for England and Wales (annual)
Catholic Directories for Ireland (annual)

Hymnals
Unknown author, *The Parochial Hymn Book: Words and Melodies*, (Burns and Oates 1883)
J. Hacker, *Catholic Hymnal*, (Buffalo, 1902)
Sisters of Notre Dame, *Sunday School Hymn Book*, (Philadelphia Press, 1888)

Encyclicals and Papal Bull
Pius X., *The Doctrines of the Modernists*, (London: Burns and Oates, undated)
Leo X111, *The Workers Charter – Rerum Novarum*, (London: Catholic Truth Society 1958, 1891 original)
Benedict XV, *Ad Beatissimi Apostolorum* (Appealing for Peace) November 1, 1914, accessed on 6th June 2015 at http://www.papalencyclicals.net

Libraries
British Library – Colindale, North London
Kilkenny Library – Damien Brett
Thurles Library, Tipperary
Talbot Catholic Library – Preston [now closed]
Universities of Liverpool, Preston, and Lancaster

SECONDARY SOURCES

Books
Aan de Wiel, Jerome, *The Catholic Church in Ireland: 1914-1918: War and Politics*, (Dublin: Irish Academic Press, 2003)
Adelman, Paul, *Great Britain and the Irish Question, 1800-1922*, (London, Hodder and Stoughton, 2001)
Atkinson, Rita, Atkinson, Richard, Smith, Edward, and Bem, Daryl, *Introduction to Psychology*, 11th edition, (Forth Worth: Harcourt, Brace, Jovanovich College Publishers, 1993),
Beck, George A., ed., *The English Catholics: 1850-1950*, (Glasgow: Burns and Oates, 1950).

Beckett, Ian F. W., *The First World War: The Essential Guide to Sources in the UK National Archives*, (Richmond: Public Record Office Publishing, 2002)

Becker, Annette, *War and Faith: The Religious Imagination in France 1914-1930*, (Oxford: Berg, 1998)

Beever, Antony – *The Battle for Spain – The Spanish Civil War 1936-39* – (Phoenix London 2006), pxxxi.

Belchem, John, *Irish, Catholic, and Scouse: the History of the Liverpool Irish 1800-1939*, (Liverpool: Liverpool University Press, 2007)

Bloch, Marc, *The Historian's Craft*, (Manchester: Manchester University Press, 2012)

Bowman, Timothy, *Irish Regiments in the Great War: Discipline and Morale*, (Manchester: Manchester University Press, 2003)

Boyce, David George, *Nationalism in Ireland*, 3rd edition, (Dublin: Routledge, 1991)

Buchanan, Tom, and Conway, Martin, *Political Catholicism in Europe 1918-1945*, (Oxford: Clarendon, 1996)

Burke, Damien, ed., *Irish Jesuit Chaplains in the First World War*, (Dublin: Messenger 2014)

Bush, Jonathan, *Papists and Prejudice: Popular Anti-Catholicism and Anglo-Irish Conflict in the North East of England, 1845-70*, (Cambridge: Cambridge Scholars Publishers, 2013)

Cannadine, David, *Making History Now and Then: Discoveries, Controversies and Explorations*, (Basingstoke: Palgrave – Macmillan, 2008)

Catholic Truth Society, *Compendium: Catechism of the Catholic Church*, (London: Catholic Truth Society, 2006)

Catholic Truth Society, *A Catechism of Christian Doctrine*, (London: Catholic Truth Society, 2013)

Catholic Truth Society, *The Penny Catechism of the Catholic Church*, (London: Catholic Truth Society, 1912)

Cecil, Hugh, and Liddle, Peter, *Facing Armageddon: The First World War Experience*, (London: Lee Cooper 1996)

Corrigan, Gordon, *Mud, Blood, and Popycock: Britain in the Great War*, (London: Cassell, 2004)

Crerar, Duff, *Padres in No Man's Land*, (Montreal: McGill Queens University Press, 1995)

Cubitt, Geoffrey, *History and Memory*, (Manchester: Manchester University Press, 2007)

Curtis, Liz Perry, *Apes and Angels: The Irishman in Victorian Caricature*, (Newton Abbot: David and Charles Publishing, 1971)

Curtis, Liz Perry, *Nothing but the Same Old Story: The Roots of Anti-Irish Racism*, (London: Information on Ireland Publishing, 1984)

Denman, Terence, *Irelands Unknown Soldiers: The 16th (Irish) Division in the Great War*, (Dublin: Irish Academic Press, 1992)

Dooley, Thomas P., *Irishmen or English Soldiers*, (Liverpool: Liverpool University Press, 1995)

Doyle, Peter, *Mitres and Missions in Lancashire: The Roman Catholic Diocese of Liverpool 1850-2000*, (Liverpool: Bluecoat Publishing, 2005)
De Groot, Gerard J., *Blighty: British Society in the Era of the Great War*, (Michigan: Longman, 1996)
De Groot, Gerard J., *The First World War*, (Basingstoke: Palgrave, 2001)
Dungan, Myles, *Irish Voices from the Great War*, (Dublin: Irish Academic Press, 1995)
Dungan, Myles, *They Shall Grow Not Old: Irish Soldiers in the Great War*, (Dublin: Four Courts Press, 1997)
Eriksen, Thomas Hylland, *Ethnicity and Nationalism: Anthropological Perspectives*, (Chicago: Pluto Publishing, 1993)
Evans, Martin Marix, *Over The Top: Great Battles of the First World War*, (London: Acturus, 2004)
Ferriter, Diarmaid, *The Transformation of Ireland 1900-200*, (London: Profile, 2004)
Fielding, Steven, *Class and Ethnicity: Irish Catholics in England 1880-1925*, (Maidenhead: Open University Press, 1992)
Fitzpatrick, David, *Ireland and the First World War*, (Dublin: Trinity History Workshop Publishing, 1986)
Fitzpatrick, David, *Politics and Irish Life 1913-1921: Provincial Experience of War and Revolution*, (Cork: Cork University Press, 1998)
Fuller, J. G., *Troop Morale and Popular Culture in the British and Dominion Armies 1914-18*, (Oxford: Clarendon, 1990)
Gilbert, Martin, *The First World War*, (London: Weidenfeld and Nicholson, 1994)
Gordon, Iain, *Lifeline: A British Casualty Clearing Station on the Western Front 1918*, (Stroud: The History Press, 2013)
Grayson, Richard, S., *Belfast Boys: How Unionists and Nationalists Fought and Died Together in the First World War*, (London: Continuum, 2009)
Graves, Robert, *Goodbye To All That*, (London: Jonathan Cape, 1929)
Gregory, Adrian, and Paseta, Senia, *Ireland and the Great War: A War to Unite Us All*, (Manchester: Manchester University Press, 2002)
Gwynn, Denis, *A Hundred Years of Catholic Emancipation*, (London: Longmans, 1929)
Hales, Edward, *The Catholic Church in the Modern World – A Survey from the French Revolution to the Present*, (New York: Image, 1960)
Hâsek, Jaroslav, *the Good Soldier Švejk – And His Fortunes in The World War*, (William Heinemann, BCS ed 1973).
Hastings, Adrian, *A History of English Christianity 1920-2000*, (London: SCM, 2001)
Holmes, J. Derek, *More Roman than Rome*, (London: Burns and Oates, 1978)
Holmes, Richard, *Tommy: The British Soldier on the Western Front 1914-18*, (London: Harper-Collins, 2005)
Holmes, Richard, *Soldiers: Army Lives and Loyalties from Redcoats to Dusty Warriors*, (New York: Harper, 2012)
Horne, John, ed., *Our War: Ireland and the Great War*, (Dublin: Royal Irish Academy Press, 2008)

Howson, Peter, *Muddling Through: The Organisation of British Army Chaplaincy in World War One*, (Solihull: Helion, 2013)
Howson, Peter, *Padre, Prisoner and Pen-Pusher: The World War One Experiences of the Reverend Benjamin O'Rorke*, (Solihull, Helion, 2015)
Jeffery, Keith, *Ireland and the Great War*, (Cambridge: Cambridge University Press, 2000)
Keegan, John, *The First World War*, (London: Pimlico, 1999)
Kenny, Mary, *Goodbye to Catholic Ireland*, (London: Sinclair-Stevenson 1997)
Kinealy, Christine, *This Great Calamity: The Irish Famine 1845-1852*, (Dublin: Gill and Macmillan, 1994)
Klein, Daryl, *With The Chinks: The Chinese Labour Corps*, (Uckfield: Published jointly by the Naval and Military Press, and the IWM, 2009)
Lebon, Jean, *How to Understand the Liturgy*, (London: SCM Press, 1986)
Lee, Joe, *Ireland 1912-1985: Politics and Society*, (Cambridge: Cambridge University Press, 1989)
Leese, Peter, *Shell Shock: Traumatic Neurosis and British Soldiers of the First World War*, (London: Palgrave – Macmillan, 2002)
Littlewood, Joan, *Oh What a Lovely War*, (London: Penguin Classics, 1967)
Lloyd, Nick, *Passchendaele: A New History*. (Penguin: Random House UK, 2017)
Lombard-Fitzgerald, Charles, *English and Welsh Priests 1801-1914*, (Stratton-on-the-Fosse: Downside Abbey Publisher, 1993)
Louden, Stephen, H., *Chaplains in Conflict*, (London: Avon, 1996)
MacGiolla, Choille, B., *Intelligence Notes 1913-1916*, (Dublin: Oifig an tSoláthair, 1966)
Mackenzie, S. P., *Politics and Military Morale – Current Affairs and Citizenship Education in the British Army 1914-1950*, (Oxford: Clarendon, 1992)
Madigan, Edward, *Faith Under Fire: Anglican Army Chaplains and the Great War*, (London: Palgrave – Macmillan, 2011)
Marrin, Albert, *The Last Crusade: The Church of England in the First World War*, (Durham: Duke University Press, 1974)
McCartney, Helen, *Citizen Soldiers: The Liverpool Territorials in the First World War*, (Cambridge: Cambridge University Press, 2011)
McLelland, V. Alan, and Hodgetts, Michael, eds., *Without the Flaminian Gate: 150 years of Roman Catholicism in England and Wales 1850-2000*, (London: Darton, Longman, and Todd, 1999)
McRedmond, Louis, *To the Greater Glory: A History of the Irish Jesuits*, (Dublin: Gill and Macmillan, 1991)
McWilliams, James and Steele, James, *Amiens 1918 – The Last Great Battle*, (History Press 2007).
Milburn, David, *A History of Ushaw College*, (Alnwick: Northumberland Press, 1964)
Middleton-Brumwell, P., *The Army Chaplain: The Duties of Chaplains and Morale*, (London: Adam and Charles Black, 1943)

Morrissey, Thomas, J., *From Easter Week to Flanders Field: The Diaries and Letters of Fr John Delaney SJ 1916-1919*, (Dublin: Messenger, 2015)
Neal, Frank, *Sectarian Violence – The Liverpool Experience 1819-1914: An Aspect of Anglo-Irish History*, (Manchester: Manchester University Press, 1988)
Olusoga, David, *The World's War*, (London: Head of Zeus 3024)
O'Rahilly, Alfred, *Father William Doyle SJ*, 2nd edition, (London: Longmans- Green, 1920)
Orr, Paul, *Field of Bones: An Irish Division in Gallipoli*, (Dublin: Lilliput, 2006)
Peale, John H., *War Jottings*, vols. 1-3, (Calcutta: Catholic Orphan Press, 1916)
Plater, Charles, *Catholic Soldiers*, (London: Longman – Green, 1919)
Plumb, Brian, *Arundel to Zabi: A Biographical Dictionary of The Catholic Bishops of England and Wales (Deceased) 1623-2000*, (Ormskirk: North West Catholic History Society, 2006).
Radcliffe, Timothy, *Why Go To Church?* (London: Continuum, 2008)
Rider, R. J., and Hair, P. E. H., *Reflections on the Battlefield: From Infantryman to Chaplain 1914-1919*, (Liverpool: Liverpool University Press, 2001)
Sheffield, Gary and Todman, Daniel eds., *Command and Control on the Western Front: The British Army's Experience, 1914-1918*, (Staplehurst: Spellmount, 2007)
Smith, Goldwin, *Irish History and the Irish Question*, (Charleston: BiblioLife, 2009)
Snape, Michael, *God and the British Soldier: Religion and the British Soldier in the First and Second World Wars*, (Oxford: Routledge, 2005)
Snape, Michael, *The Royal Army Chaplains Department: Clergy Under Fire*, (Woodbridge: Boydell 2007)
Strachan Hew, *The First World War*, (London: Simon and Schuster, 2014)
Terret, Thierry and Mangan J (eds) – *Sport, Militarism and the Great War – Martial Manliness and Armageddon* – (London Routledge 2017)
Williamson, Benedict, *Happy Days in France and Flanders with the 47th and 49th Divisions*, (London: Harding and More, 1921)
Winter, Jay, *Sites of Memory, Sites of Mourning: The Great War in European Cultural History*, (Cambridge: Cambridge University Press, 1995)
Wolffe, John, *God and Greater Britain: Religion and National Life in Britain and Ireland 1843-1945*, (London: Routledge, 1994)

Journal Articles
Stephen Bellis, 'The Rawlinson Papers', in *The Downside Review*, Downside Abbey, vol. 459, (April 2012) pp. 1-25.
John Davies, 'War is a Scourge: The First Year of the Great War 1914-1915: Catholics and Pastoral Guidance', in *Recusant History*, vol. 30, #3, (March 2011) pp. 485-500.
Frank Neal, 'English-Irish Conflict in the North West of England: Economics, Racism, Anti-Catholicism or Simple Xenophobia?' in *North West Labour History, Journal* of the *North West Labour History Group*, 16, (1991) pp. 14-25.

Oliver Rafferty, 'Catholic Chaplains to the British Forces in the First World War', in *Religion, State and Society*, 39: 1, (2011), pp. 33–62.
A. McLeod, in *Religion, State & Society*, Vol. 39, No. 1, (March 2011).

Unpublished Theses and Conference Papers
Bellis, Stephen, 'Quadragesimo Anno and the Red Threat: Church-State Relationships in Ireland 1931', (unpublished Master's thesis, University of Liverpool, 2006)
Brennan, John Martin, 'Irish Catholic Chaplains in the First World War', (unpublished Master's thesis, University of Birmingham, July 2011)
Brown, A. M., 'Army Chaplains in the First World War', (unpublished Doctoral thesis, University of St. Andrews, January 1996)
Debruyne, E., 'Shadow Fighters but Soldiers of God: The World War One Belgian "Resisters" and their Faith', (unpublished thesis for the Amport, Armed Forces Chaplaincy Conference, 2012)
Finlay, K., 'British Catholic Identity during the First War: The Challenge of Universality and Particularity', (unpublished Master's thesis, University of Oxford, 2004)
Ingram, P., 'Sectarianism in the North West of England, with Special reference to Class Relationships in the City of Liverpool 1846-1914', (unpublished Doctoral thesis, University of Central Lancashire, [formerly Lancashire Polytechnic], December 1987)
Melvin, A., 'Fluid Faith: Religious Rituals and their Emotional Effects', (unpublished Master's thesis Birbeck College, University of London, 2012)
Purdy, Martin, 'Roman Catholic Army Chaplains During the First World War: Roles, Experiences and Dilemmas', (unpublished Master's thesis, University of Central Lancashire, September 2011)

DVD References

Your Old Books and Maps, *World War One British Army Lists*, 1914-1919, (http://youroldbooksandmaps.co.uk/home.php), (2007)

Index

Index of People

Baines, Fr viii, 53, 152, 171-172, 240-241, 244
Benedict XV, Pope 22-23, 25, 33, 203
Bergin, Fr 35-36, 56, 243
Bourne, Cardinal Francis 22-23, 54-55, 142, 172, 180
Brown, Fr Joseph 80, 82
Brown, Fr W J 41, 53
Burdess, Mathew Forster viii, 125-126, 240-241, 244

Cagney, Rev W 76, 157
Carey, Fr Timothy ix, 109, 221
Casartelli, Bishop 29, 35
Clarke, Fr Stephen viii, 137, 141, 240-241, 244
Collins, Fr Herbert John vii, 123-124, 240-241, 244
Crisp, Fr 70-71, 74, 148

Doyle, Fr Denis vii, 45, 102, 240-241, 244
Doyle, Fr William Joseph [Willie] viii, 23, 74, 88, 137-138, 141, 200, 236, 240-241, 244
Drinkwater, Fr Francis 44-46, 48, 67, 85-86, 110, 139, 197, 214
Duggan, Fr Tom 28, 74
Dunn, Bishop Thomas 81-82

Fitzgibbon, Fr John viii, 84, 145, 183, 198, 240-241, 244
Fitzmaurice, Fr 73-74, 199, 213
Foch, General Ferdinand 178, 181, 195

Gill, Fr Henry xv, 26-27, 39, 52-54, 60, 68, 96, 100-101, 103
Gillett, Fr Fred vi-ix, xiii, xv-xvii, xix-xx, 34-37, 39-43, 47, 52, 57, 59-60, 64-65, 67-68, 70-71, 74, 83, 85, 89-100, 102-105, 107, 109-121, 125-134, 136, 138-142, 144, 146, 148-149, 151-163, 165, 168-174, 176-184, 189-193, 195-196, 198, 201-202, 204-206, 208, 210, 214, 216, 218, 224, 226, 229, 232, 234-237, 250-251
Gordon, Fr Michael Patrick viii, 53, 138, 222-223, 240-241, 244
Green, Fr x, 28, 31, 41, 48, 96, 134, 233
Grobel, Fr Peter 39, 94, 96, 99, 103
Guthrie, Fr vii, 107-108, 240-241, 244
Gwynn, Fr John vii, 24, 30-31, 74-75, 99-100, 240-241, 244

Haig, Field Marshal Sir Douglas 50, 90, 117, 178, 181
Hartigan, Fr 35-36
Hegarty, Fr 28-29
Houston, Major 219, 235
Hughes, Fr D 80-81

Keane, Fr Edward 30-31, 46, 192
Keating, Bishop William Frederick xix, 22, 34, 42, 54-56, 62, 65, 73, 75, 77, 82, 103, 127, 135, 180, 197
Keegan, Fr 180, 238-239
Kelly, Fr T 67, 89

Leeson, Fr Jim viii, 65, 126-127, 154, 240-241, 244
Looby, Fr viii, 24, 88, 141-144, 240-241, 244
Ludendorff, General Erich von 150-151, 175, 177

McAuliffe, Fr 56, 88
McDonnell, Fr John J 163, 173, 242
McGrath, Fr 28, 155
McIlvaine, Fr John 55, 69, 88, 154
Monteith, Fr Robert viii, 133, 141, 145-146, 240-241, 244

262

Moran, Fr 28, 86
Myerscough, Fr 89, 144

Nevin, Fr 87, 207
Nolan, Fr 83, 198

O'Connor, Fr 48, 213
O'Herlihy, Fr 53, 61-62
O'Sullivan, Fr Donal Vincent 62, 100, 214
Oddie, Fr Philip 29, 50-51, 66-67

Page, Fr Bernard 36, 59, 73, 200
Phelan, Fr 28-29, 35
Prescott, Fr 64, 110
Prevost, Fr 52, 67

Rawlinson, Principal Chaplain Bernard vii, x, xv, xviii-xix, 23, 27-32, 34-36, 39, 41, 46, 48-59, 61-63, 66-83, 85-89, 94, 103, 118, 126, 135, 143, 145, 154, 163-164, 168-169, 172, 179-181, 184, 197, 200, 213-214, 219, 221-223, 228, 238-239, 248

Richmond, Fr 41, 80-83
Roche, Fr Daniel 36, 83, 221
Rodmore, Colonel 149, 152

Scully, Fr 73, 88
Shine, Fr James viii, 143, 164-165
Staniforth, Fr 49-50
Steuart, Fr Robert v, vii-ix, xiii, xv-xvii, xix-xx, 35-36, 39-40, 43, 48, 57, 59-61, 63-70, 74, 79, 84-85, 89-91, 96, 98-99, 107-117, 119-121, 124-125, 128-136, 138-141, 145-146, 149, 151-164, 168-172, 174, 176-177, 179, 184, 186-187, 189-191, 195, 198-205, 214, 219-221, 223-237, 248-249

Walker, Fr Leslie vii-ix, xiii, 75, 97, 104, 118-119, 121, 123, 140, 142, 170, 186-188, 210, 212-214
Whitefoord, Fr Carl Blaquhoun 169-170
Whiteside, Archbishop 202-203
Wilkin, Fr 158, 168

Index of Places

Abbeville 70, 86, 107, 115
Africa 25, 66, 102, 225, 241
Aisne 54, 151, 160, 192
Albert 42, 47, 65, 69-70, 90, 93, 105-107, 110, 115, 157-162, 168, 171-172, 182, 197, 205, 214-215, 218-219
Alsace 92, 207
Amiens 68-70, 85, 107, 144, 154, 156-157, 160-162, 165, 171-172, 178-179, 181-182, 206, 208, 218
Arras i, vii, xx, 42, 47, 64, 69-70, 98, 103, 112-115, 118-120, 124-125, 128-129, 131, 138-139, 141, 146, 148-149, 152, 154-156, 178, 214
Audruicq ix, 221-222, 240
Australia 25, 87

Baboeuf 154, 156-158
Baizieux 168, 182
Bavelincourt viii, 167-168
Becordel 215-216
Belgium xvii, 35, 55, 214, 234, 243, 250
Bepaume 120, 182, 215
Boulogne vii-viii, 42, 64, 69-71, 76, 90-100, 102-103, 107, 115-116, 128-129, 165, 179, 184, 214, 218, 240-241
Bouzincourt vii, ix, 100-101, 105, 172, 208-209, 214, 240
Buire 159-160, 182

Calais 31, 69-70, 109, 120, 131, 164, 200, 219-222, 234
Cambrai 128, 144-145, 187, 191, 193, 205-206, 208
Chauny 154, 208
China xviii, 41, 115
Cologne 201, 224-225, 229-233
Combles 102, 165, 183, 215-216
Contay viii, 166, 168
Cork 31, 41, 163, 240
Cornwall 69, 134
Courtrai 195, 198

Doullens 85, 110, 168, 170
Dublin viii, x, xviii, 22-23, 26-28, 61-62, 70, 75, 83, 102, 135, 137, 170, 183, 238, 240-241
Dunkirk 219, 223

England ii, x, 21-22, 24-25, 40-41, 46, 53, 65-66, 69, 78, 83, 86, 94, 99, 137, 173, 179, 216, 232, 238, 241, 244, 247, 252-253
Étaples 64, 69, 74

Flanders i, xx, 60, 73
Folkestone 69, 93, 218, 220, 222
France i, xvii, xx, 27-28, 35, 40, 47, 49, 53-56, 60, 62, 65-67, 69, 73, 77, 85-88, 90-92, 94, 96-99, 107, 112, 130, 153, 164, 173, 184, 191, 193, 198, 201-202, 204-205, 208-210, 213-216, 218-219, 222, 224, 229, 240, 250

Galway ii, 25, 87, 99, 240
Germany i, xvii, xx, 73, 151, 174, 191, 195, 201-205, 223-225, 230
Givenchy vii, 75, 118-119, 163-164
Glasgow 24, 51, 53, 56, 79, 138, 154, 223, 235, 240-241
Great Britain xvii, 21-22, 24, 26, 40, 62, 66, 90, 144, 151, 174, 203-204, 225
Guarbecque vii, 70, 115, 120-123, 125
Guillemont 102, 216

Hazebrouck 63, 70

India 25, 231
Ingoyghem 64, 198
Inverness Copse 136-137
Ireland ii, xiv, xvii, 21-22, 24-28, 30, 60-61, 70, 72, 83-84, 203-204, 238, 243-244, 253
Isle of Wight 107, 136, 172, 184

L'Abeele 40, 130, 132
Lancashire ii, vii-viii, x, xiv, xvii, 24-25, 30, 36, 43, 51, 58-59, 63, 105-107, 134, 137, 141, 163-164, 168, 173, 184, 200, 223, 241, 250
Le Cateau 54, 187, 192-193, 195
Ligny 197-198, 205-206
Limerick 23, 36, 56, 88, 221, 243
Liverpool ii, x-xi, xiii-xiv, xvi-xvii, 26-27, 30-31, 41-42, 45, 51, 53, 65, 74, 83, 88-89, 105, 109-110, 126-127, 129, 133, 140, 142, 149, 171, 180, 202, 208-210, 218, 221, 236, 240, 243, 250-251
London vii-viii, x, xiii-xiv, xvii-xviii, 23, 25, 28, 40-41, 46, 48, 55, 67-70, 75, 77, 153, 163, 169-170, 180, 196, 208, 218, 222, 228, 230, 233, 241, 248
Lorraine 92, 207
Lourdes ix, 49, 64, 87, 191, 196, 205-208
Lytham xvii, 110, 206, 250

Mametz 182, 215-216
Marne 54, 178
Méaulte 177, 205, 210, 216, 218
Menin Road 131, 133, 185-186
Middlesex viii, 103, 128-129, 144, 153-154, 164-165, 240-241

Neuve Chapelle viii-ix, 142, 210-211

Paris 64, 75, 90-91, 154, 170, 172, 181, 191, 196, 205-208, 214-216, 218, 240
Passchendaele xix, 24, 36, 56, 131, 137, 141-142, 145, 178
Péronne 120, 157, 190
Perthshire xvii, 69, 85, 129, 136, 154, 172, 184
Picardy i, xx, 60, 220
Poelcapelle viii, 131, 142-143, 240
Poperinge xix, 135, 140, 142, 149, 155, 223, 228
Rhine 204, 223-224, 226, 230, 232
Ribecourt viii, 145, 147, 240
Rome 21-23, 40, 81, 85, 240
Rouen 70, 85, 103, 172, 223, 242
Russia 29, 35-36, 59, 150, 203, 223

Scotland ii, xvii, 21, 24-25, 127, 164, 184, 244, 248
Somme i, vii-viii, xx, 42, 75, 90-91, 94, 96-97, 100, 102-103, 105, 110, 112-115, 118-119, 126-127, 131, 148-149, 157, 162, 178, 185, 190, 215, 219
South Africa 25, 102, 241
Southampton 56, 88, 232
St Omer 70, 137, 200
St Quentin 154, 156, 172, 190-191, 208, 216
Steenvoorde 132-134
Stonyhurst vii, x, 36-38, 109, 141, 145-146, 198, 240, 248

Thiepval 105-106, 117, 120, 162, 215
Tipperary viii, 36, 53, 56, 62, 83, 142-143, 164

Varennes vii, 107-108, 240
Verdun 66, 183
Versailles 75, 151, 191, 215-216

Wales ii, 21, 24, 27, 74-75
Warloy 107, 159-160, 171, 173, 178, 182
Watou 130, 145

Westminster xii, 22, 26, 124, 178, 230

Ypres i, vii-viii, xx, 42, 70, 84, 90, 109, 112-115, 120, 130-134, 138, 141-142, 144-146, 148-149, 152-156, 178, 184-186, 190-191, 199-200, 219, 223

Index of General & Miscellaneous Terms

Australian Army 36, 56

British Army i, iii, v, xvii-xviii, xx, 21-23, 25, 39, 47, 53-55, 60, 83-84, 98, 112, 115, 129, 131, 197, 204, 223, 227-228, 241

Divisions:
  16th Irish 23, 143, 162
  18th Division 117, 152
  36th Ulster Division 58, 137

German Army 174-175, 204
German Spring Offensive i, viii, xx, 46, 72, 74-76, 150-153, 156, 164, 175

Hindenburg Line 113, 119
Home Rule 23, 26

Regiments:
  East Lancashire Regiment 83, 107, 127, 137
  Highland Light Infantry 85, 107, 121, 138, 154, 184, 195
  King's Liverpool Regiment xi, 42, 83, 133, 221
  Northamptonshire Regiment 103, 121, 129, 144, 179
  Northumberland Fusiliers viii, 24, 143
  Royal Dublin Fusiliers viii, 28, 137, 241
  Royal Fusiliers viii, xi, 65, 103, 121, 125-127, 136, 144, 173, 241
  Royal Irish Regiment 54, 135, 199
  Royal Scots xi, 164, 184, 198, 223

Sinn Fein 26-28

War Office xii, 23, 54, 61, 67, 70-72, 76, 85, 142